The Information E-conomy

THE
information
e-conomy

business strategies for competing in the
global age

colin turner

KOGAN
PAGE

First published in 2000

First published in paperback in 2002

Kogan Page Limited
120 Pentonville Road
London
N1 9JN
UK

Kogan Page Limited
22 Broad Street
Milford
CT 06460
USA

British Library Cataloguing in Publication Data

A CIP record for this book is available from the British Library.

ISBN 0 7494 3774 X

Typeset by JS Typesetting, Wellingborough, Northants
Printed and bound by Creative Print and Design, Ebbw Vale (Wales)

Contents

Preface

Since the initial volume of this text was written the experience of the information economy has been tumultuous. All aspects of the information economy have undergone a turbulent period as markets have taken a more sober and realistic assessment of the processes of change associated with them. The large number of 'dot coms' that have gone bankrupt reflects the fact that electronic commerce did not grow as fast as expected and that many of these businesses simply were not viable within a crowded market place of limited size. Increasingly, electronic commerce (especially within the business-to-consumer sector) is seen as just another channel through which businesses seek to generate sales. In the business-to-business sector there is an increasing feeling that many of the models developed did not reflect the practicalities of business. It seems that many of the business models developed to exploit the Internet were based more upon proving the capability of technology than meeting any evident need.

Interlinked with the experience of electronic commerce has been the change in sentiment towards information industries. Many firms within the telecommunications, information technology and content sectors have also been experiencing rapid declines in growth as the perception that the information economy will not evolve as fast as expected becomes more widespread. In the telecommunications sector, enterprises have accumulated large amounts of debt on the basis of a growth in advanced communications that simply has not (as yet) appeared. This has been typified by the experience of third-generation mobile communications firms, where operators have acquired expensive licences to provide services for which there appears little evident demand over the short term.

Despite these experiences there is still evidence to support the growing evolution of the information economy. Many of the world's largest companies are starting to put the Internet at the centre of their business strategy. This has been typified by the experiences of General Electric and Microsoft with their new .Net strategies. Furthermore, there is increasing evidence that viable online business models are emerging. Models such as 'e-auctions' base their success upon utilizing core features of the Internet that give this form of business clear advantages over their traditional rivals. In addition, other business models have exhibited flexibility by adapting their Web sites to support, enhance and complement all channels through which transactions occur.

It is against this background that this text is published. Such developments do not undermine the need for such a text but reinforce its importance. To this author, the information economy was always going to be evolutionary rather than revolutionary. The content and themes engendered within this text are no less relevant for that fact. The issues addressed within the book are still salient for the changing commercial environments of business and still need to be understood by anyone interested in the growth strategies of information industries.

I would like to thank all at Kogan page for their support through the pre- and post-publication stages of this book. I would also like to thank my erstwhile co-author Debra Johnson for the professional support offered during the writing process and to my partner, Karen Wileman, for her companionship and encouragement.

Abbreviations

ADSL   Asymmetrical Digital Subscriber Loop
ATM   Asynchronous Transfer Mode
CATV   Cable Access Television
CMDA   Code Multiple Division Access
CREC   Centre for Research into Electronic Commerce
EDI   Electronic Data Interchange
EU   European Union
FT   Financial Times
FTC   Federal Trade Commission
GDP   Gross Domestic Product
GSM   Global System for Mobile communications
ICTs   Information and Communication Technologies
IPR   Intellectual Property Rights
ISO   International Standards Office
ISP   Internet Service Provider
IT   Information Technology
ITU   International Telecommunications Union
MNCs   Multinational Companies
MP3   Motion Picture group 1/level 3
NPOs   Non-Profit Organizations
OECD   Organization for Economic Co-operation and Development
PCs   Personal Computers
PCS   Personal Communication Systems
PSTN   Public Switched Telecommunications Network
PTOs   Public Telecommunication Operators
R&D   Research and Development
SDH   Synchronous Digital Hierarchy
SDMI   Secure Digital Music Initiative
SET   Secure Electronic Transactions
SMEs   Small and Medium-Sized Enterprises
TRIPS   Trade Related Aspects of Intellectual Property Rights Agreement

UK   United Kingdom
UMTS   Universal Mobile Telecommunications Standard
UN   United Nations
US   United States
VAT   Value Added Tax
WIPO   World Intellectual Property Organization
WTO   World Trade Organization
WWW   World Wide Web

1 The evolving information economy

The information economy is based ultimately upon the increased salience of information as a commercial tool. How information resources are utilized by enterprises is becoming increasingly central to their competitiveness. This highlights the importance of information and communication technologies (ICTs) as key enabling tools in this process of commercial and technological change – something that has its most potent expression in the growth of the Internet. The focus of this chapter is to familiarize the reader with the core trends and developments associated with the emergence of the information economy. The chapter is essentially divided into two sections. The first explores the phenomenon of the information economy, and the second the drivers behind it.

The nature of the information economy

The development of the information economy is closely associated with the process of economic transformation within modern economies. Negroponte (1995) highlights that this economic transformation is about shifting wealth creation from the creation of atoms (eg manufactured goods) towards the creation of goods and services based upon digital bits. Figure 1.1 underlines the core characteristics of this paradigm shift, highlighting how the development of the information economy has the potential to alter substantially all aspects and features of the commercial environment. This figure shows that the information economy, through the increased use of information (and associated technologies) by businesses (and other users), creates new industrial structures, patterns and trends, as well as new services and products. Arguably the most important of these changes is the transition from a market-place (a single place where buyers and sellers meet) to a market space where commercial transactions take place over a broader area without the need for physical contact. This has the potential to alter fundamentally all aspects of the prevailing business model (see Table 2.1). It is likely to push firms towards organizational structures based on networks and away from the traditional form based on hierarchies; it will also require new skills from its work-force (see below) and alter markedly logistical processes. The other notable feature of the enterprise in the information economy is how the resource base is expected to alter as there is a move away from scarcity to excess (driven by the fact that digital bits can be endlessly reproduced).

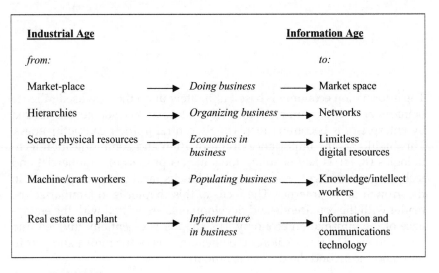

Source: Earl (1999)

Figure 1.1 *The shift from the industrial to the information age*

Paranov and Yakovleva (1998) perceive that the information economy is about four main processes:

1. the growth of Internet technologies and applications;

2. the growth of economic 'settlers' on the Internet (notably through electronic commerce);

3. the emergence of network forms of organizational design;

4. the development of network forms of institutional design (notably for the purposes of trade, finance and labour).

Importantly, Paranov and Yakovleva highlight the pivotal role that the Internet (see the boxed section later in the chapter) will play in the evolution and establishment of the information economy. Indeed, the Internet is gradually evolving towards an open free-market economy of automated agents selling an assortment of tangible and intangible commodities as well as using it as a medium to sell goods and services through more traditional means (see Chapter 3). These changes also extend to logistical processes (for example, to improvements in the distribution and marketing processes) as information and associated technologies become ever more salient.

The key issue is that the evolution of the information economy creates a demand for new products and services to improve and increase the efficiency and effectiveness of commercial processes – a trend that is becoming fairly ubiquitous. Importantly the information economy is not about total digitalization of the business environment; it is more about utilizing information products and services to improve wealth creation through enhancing enterprise competitiveness, highlighting the pragmatic attitude that many businesses take towards its development. This trend has been emphasized in a recent survey by BT, which indicated that over 90 per cent of enterprises see the pace of technological development as one of the main drivers of commercial change, with 88 per cent believing that up-to-date technology usage is essential for sustaining business competitiveness. Additionally, over 82 per cent of businesses surveyed perceived information to be the main strategic weapon of the next decade, with 90 per cent of businesses feeling that telecommunications (and other information and communications technologies) will become ever more important in supporting their relationship with customers and suppliers. The broad strategic impact of the development of the information economy for the commercial environment, derived from Tapscott (1995), includes the following issues:

- the central role played by knowledge in wealth creation;

- the emergence of digital workers;

- the role of digital technology as the key enabler;

- the rise of virtual economic activity, as commercial relationships can be conducted over greater geographical distances (see Chapter 2);

- the rise of molecularization as organizations become disaggregated under the application of ICTs (see Chapter 2);

- the network as increasingly central to economic activity;

- the rise of disintermediation as networks cut out the middleman (see Chapter 3);

- the convergence of technologies within content, IT and telecommunications sectors (see Chapter 4);

- the increased prominence of innovation in business performance;

- a blurring between the respective roles of consumers and producers;

- commercial activity tending to be more immediate;

- global economic activity predominating.

It is important to stress that the information economy is not a synonym for the commercial evolution of the Internet – it is about more than the commercial impact of a single technology. The information economy is also about (amongst other things) the emergence of ICTs in the physical production process, and ancillary services and products (such as outsourcing) that facilitate network usage and value, and give rise to the commercial issues highlighted in the above list. Consequently, the processes involved in the development of the information economy involve firms looking at the current commercial environment and examining how the application of ICTs can improve it. It is important to underline that the information economy is not simply some mass information vision; it is a pragmatic response to the needs of business and economies in an era when knowledge and information are key determinants of commercial success.

   A conceptual model developed by the Centre for Research into Electronic Commerce (CREC) (see www.internetindicators.com) indicates the various layers of commercial activity that will characterize the information economy. At each of these layers, enterprises are emerging or incumbents are altering strategy to reflect the commercial opportunities and challenges posed by the development of the information economy. The establishment of these layers underpins the transition of business towards the information economy and is core to enterprises enjoying its competitive benefits.

Layer 1: The infrastructure layer

This consists of companies that supply products and services that aid the development and establishment of a network infrastructure based upon the Internet protocol (see Chapter 4). The development of this network is essential for the development and spread of electronic commerce. Integral to this stratum are:

- Internet backbone providers;

- Internet service providers;

- networking hardware and software;
- PC and server manufacturers;
- security vendors.

This layer supports the basic components of transmission across space, as well as facilitating the capability of enterprises to process and store information.

Layer 2: The applications layer

Applications are specific uses of the technology usually dedicated to a particular sector, function or usage. These are usually developed through building upon the already developed Internet protocol network. They make it possible to develop online business activities. Categories involved in this stratum include:

- Internet consultants;
- electronic commerce applications;
- multimedia applications;
- Web development software;
- search engine software;
- online training.

The key feature in this layer, as suggested by the name, is the notion of actually applying the technology to real-world commercial situations – thereby enabling the technology to prove its worth. Enterprises involved in this layer are examined in greater detail in Chapter 4.

Layer 3: The intermediary layer

As will be highlighted in Chapter 3, the role of these intermediaries (or 'infomediaries') within online business is to smooth and augment the market/transaction process, largely by facilitating the bringing together of buyers and sellers (who are often geographically dispersed) through the online medium. Thus these enterprises have a largely catalytic function, enabling investments in applications and infrastructure to be translated into business transactions. In this category, the following are included:

- online travel agents;
- online brokerages;
- content aggregators;
- portals/content providers;
- online advertising;
- electronic auctions.

Layer 4: The electronic commerce layer

This involves transactions of goods and services to both businesses and consumers over the Internet (see Chapter 3). In this category are included:

- electronic retailers;
- manufacturers selling online;
- fee/subscription-based enterprises;
- online entertainment and professional services.

Enterprises will tend not to be limited to a particular layer: indeed many will operate across them. This is symptomatic of the convergence process (see Chapter 4). What the above model clearly conceptualizes is the development of an emerging Internet ecosystem designed to stimulate the development of the information economy. The model indicates the evolution of existing systems and business models to meet the requirements of online commerce.

Whilst the model highlights how the information economy is expected to be structured, an enterprise's position within it requires broader transformation if competitive positioning is to be secured. Information is only likely to be of commercial value when it is translated into enterprise-wide knowledge that can be used effectively to secure competitive advantage. Consequently, knowledge and information resources will be the key determining factor of competitive excellence within the information economy. This places new challenges upon the labour market. Without alterations to the form and type of labour utilized, the ability of an economy to synthesize and utilize knowledge and information resources for commercial advantage is ultimately limited.

Human capital has long been recognized as the core determinant of an economy's competitiveness – it is the one core resource that cannot easily be replicated across economies. As suggested above, this is something that is going to be reinforced by the development of the information economy.

In terms of the labour market, the information economy means broadly two things: first, the information economy will generate new types of occupations requiring new types of skills from the labour force; and secondly, traditional forms of employment will also involve higher levels of information intensity. Thus, overall, the information economy means that more workers will be involved in the management, creation and utilization of knowledge and information resources, underlining that economic return will increasingly be based upon knowledge as opposed to physical capacity. This trend is closely interlinked with the broader use and acceptance of information and communication technologies in the workplace.

These trends indicate the anticipated holistic nature of the information economy. Many of its keenest advocates suggest that there should be no part of the global socio-economic spectrum that remains unaffected by its development. Employment, education, professional training, family life, way of life, consumer habits, culture, leisure, health and politics would, if the vision is to be believed, all be affected by the development of the information economy. Clearly the information economy will only achieve maturity when it is able to demonstrate relevance, commercial appeal and meet effective demands right across the socio-economic spectrum.

The Internet

There is perhaps no greater expression of the development of the information economy than the advent of the Internet – a technology that has undergone rapid growth since the mid-1990s (see Figure 1.2). The Internet is essentially a network based upon a series of interlinked computers connected through capacity leased from telephone companies, and is capable of transmitting anything that can be converted into digital format (from voice telephony through to multimedia). Born out of the world of academic research, its spread has been driven more by the needs of users than by corporate marketing and it is the source of much of the innovation and commerce that lies at the heart of the evolving information economy. Its spread has also been aided by a number of key characteristics, namely that it is based upon open as opposed to proprietary standards (which means it is free to users), that the standard agreed is common to all users and that there is no central command controlling its development.

The network emerged from niche academic and public sector groups into the commercial mainstream with the development of the World Wide Web (WWW). The WWW transformed the Internet, allowing it to offer multimedia, as well as facilitating the introduction of 'hypertext' (a tool for the cross-referencing of material, which allows users to move from a word or phrase highlighted upon the screen to related information stored on a computer elsewhere in the world). This was aided by the development of browsers (via portals such as Netscape and Yahoo), which increased the user-friendliness of the Internet by allowing users to search it in an easy and efficient manner.

The rise of the Internet since the mid-1990s has been driven by a number of factors such as:

- reduced cost of telephone calls;

- the spread of the PC;

- the spread of the open standard;

- the development of online services.

This trend ties the growth of the Internet into the liberalization process. The growth of the Internet compared to other media is highlighted in Figure 1.3, which reflects exactly how rapid the growth of the technology has been when compared to other technologies. Despite the evident potential of the Internet, one should not assume ubiquity just yet: there are still evident problems to be addressed before its full commercial potential can be reached. For example, access – in terms of the capabilities of the telephone network – has yet to be upgraded to cope with the demands placed upon it by the Internet. The access concern is heightened by the still relatively poor penetration of PCs – currently the main method through which the network is accessed – within households. There are also quality of service concerns, which may deter users. In addition, competition within the telecommunications sector is only slowly maturing in key information markets (especially the EU and Japan) with the result that the cost of accessing the Internet can often prove prohibitive in these areas of the global information economy. Other concerns are especially evident in areas such as security, privacy and, as mentioned, congestion.

There can be little doubt that the advent of the Internet is going to prove pivotal to the business environment of the 21st century. Its global reach, innovative potential and ability to foster convergence between previously separate industrial sectors (see Chapter 4) all underline this importance.

Drivers of the information economy

The UK Department of Trade and Industry (1999) identified the demands of the market (as expressed in the twin commercial demands of technological change and globalization) as the ultimate core drivers behind the evolution of the information economy. Consequently, the development of the information economy will be mainly driven and signified by the expanding usage of an increasing array of information products and services by users, as well as by the ability of an information industry to deliver such

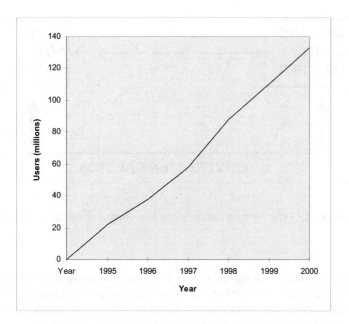

Source: CommerceNet (www.commercenet.com)

Figure 1.2 *The growth of the Internet population*

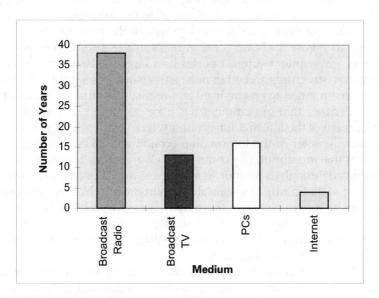

Source: US Department of Commerce (1997)

Figure 1.3 *Time taken to reach 50 million users*

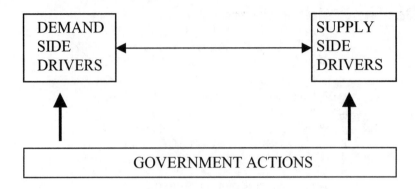

Figure 1.4 *The commercial development of the information economy*

products. In other words, the extent to which the market for information services and products is able to achieve a critical mass, develop a virtuous cycle of development and therefore reach a self-induced maturity is central to the commercial development of the information economy.

In the embryonic stages of the development of the information economy, the ability of the information market to achieve a self-induced maturity cannot be taken for granted, and therefore some policy support (see Chapter 5) may be required to stimulate the commercial drivers. The pattern and expected cycle of development of the information society is reflected in Figure 1.4. Once critical mass in the information market is achieved, government support performs a largely passive role, ensuring competitive structures and other necessities (such as security, privacy and IPR) are maintained to ensure legal and regulatory certainty for business. This underlines that government has a key complementary role in the development of the information economy. Its role as both user of information and promoter of the information economy is a key stimulant to the processes that are stimulating commercial change. This 'promoter' role can be perceived through its position as role model, regulator and, as mentioned, developer of the appropriate legislative environment. Given the importance of competition in the process, this may be a passive role but it is certainly not minor. In addition, governments are supporting more innovative applications through support for market-distant activities such as research and development (see Chapter 5).

The commercial development of the information economy requires that a number of facilitatory measures – on both demand and supply sides – need to be in place before it can hope to reach a degree of commercial maturity.

Demand side drivers

Demand side drivers include the following:

- *Access to advanced infrastructure.* This is seen as essential over the longer term, as the network needs greater capacity to deal not only with increased traffic but also with the advent of bandwidth hungry services. Currently new techniques such as compression are expanding the capacity of the existing infrastructure, which is therefore likely to be able to meet capacity demands over the short to medium term.

- *Ability to consume.* The ability of users to purchase the services offered is a key driver. Generally those states with higher levels of GDP possess the greater propensity to absorb and accept the services and technologies associated with the emerging information economy. A corresponding fear is that such trends could lead to an economy of information 'haves' and 'have nots' on a national, regional and global scale.

- *Competitive pricing.* This is a key driver, as demand for services and technologies will crucially depend upon their affordability. This will influence not only the speed of adoption of necessary technologies but also the roll-out of new services. Price is determined by factors such as market size and intensity of competition. This process is assisted by the gradual encroachment of globalization into more aspects of business functioning.

- *Content.* Content is at the heart of the information economy. Content delivered has to exhibit that it has the capability truly to add value within an economy. Content will generally be driven by user requirements.

- *Convenience.* The easier it is to use a technology and the more easily it can demonstrate usefulness to users, so the more open consumers will be to the technologies associated with the information economy. Correspondingly, the more difficult it is to master a technology, the slower the pace of demand growth.

- *Culture.* The ability of an economy to accept the ICTs will be pivotal in the maturity of the information economy. Factors such as language, willingness to innovate, education and attitude to information will all perform important roles in influencing the absorption of these technologies. Generally the more positive the attitude towards the information economy, the easier it will be for the information market to achieve the necessary critical mass.

Supply side drivers

Supply side drivers include the following:

- *Strong existing supply base.* Having strong telecommunications, IT and content industries is an advantage in the move to the information economy (see Chapter 4). Industries that have a degree of commercial strength are generally well positioned for the emerging information economy through possessing the skills base and proven revenue stream to develop new products.

- *Access to capital.* The ability of the supply side to meet new demands depends upon a pool of risk capital. This supply of funding allows these sectors to be flexible and highly responsive to change. The IT market, especially the software segment, exhibits low barriers to entry, which, with venture capital, leads to rapid evolution. The success of the investment depends upon a financing culture that is open to such risks.

- *Skills.* The supply of skilled IT professionals is pivotal. They are central to market maturity where the existence of such skills stimulates further investment.

These demand and supply side drivers are core to the process of the information economy's development. To turn any vicious cycle of under-development into a virtuous cycle that breeds the full development of the information economy, it is widely believed that the following phenomena need to be stimulated more fully to ensure the aforementioned drivers deliver competitive advantage to enterprises (US Department of Commerce, 1999):

- Building out of the Internet – this is driving dramatic increases in computer, software, services and communication investments.

- Electronic commerce amongst businesses – this is driving productivity improvements for business through the use of electronic networks to buy, sell, distribute and service products and services (see Chapter 3).

- Digital delivery of goods and services – software programmes, newspapers, CDs, etc can now be delivered direct to the home over the Internet. It is highly likely that the electronic sale and transmission of goods and services is likely to be a key factor in the evolution of the information economy.

- Retail sale of tangible goods – the Internet is also being used to order goods that are produced, stored and physically delivered. This is also a market that is growing rapidly in areas such as books and super-markets (groceries).

These trends highlight that the commercial forces expected to stimulate the information economy are ultimately sourced from the expected expansion of electronic commerce (see Chapter 3). They also express how globalization is expected to alter market and trade in information goods and services, and underline the need for business models to change accordingly.

The impact of these drivers upon the information market will be compounded by network effects (a feature especially prominent within this sector). These indicate that the benefits of a particular technology or service to individual users are directly related to the number of other users. Thus rising usage of information and communication technologies stimulates a virtuous cycle of commercial development through encouraging other users to adopt the technology in question. Many of the drivers – notably those related to electronic commerce – rely upon the existence of such phenomena as a means of ensuring the information economy reaches commercial maturity.

These drivers are likely to persist as features within the global economy and will continue to drive the development of the information economy. In turn, these are likely to be complemented by other factors such as the emergence of young entrepreneurs. This is especially important, as the Internet has low entry barriers, low initial capital requirements, and large and growing business opportunities – all of which directly facilitate such developments. These developments are likely to be enhanced by anticipated further falls in communication costs, more ICT-susceptible cultures and more intense levels of competition.

Conclusion

The information economy represents a fundamental sea change in the business environment globally. Its evolution is largely based upon the impact of ICTs (notably the development of the Internet) on commercial activity and has been driven by the twin impacts of globalization and technological change upon the enterprise. The result is a reorganization of economic activity involving the increased utilization of information as a key resource and the wider deployment of ICTs. Central to its development is the commercial maturity of an information market. It is evident that when this market matures the competitive benefits to enterprises and to the economy as a whole will start to be fully realized.

2   *The information economy and competitive advantage*

The shift to the information economy highlighted in Chapter 1 is going to have a profound impact on business strategy as enterprises seek to sustain their competitive position in the face of such changes. According to Michael Porter (1985), the ability of the technological change associated with the development of the information economy to translate itself into competitive advantage is determined by the following factors:

1. *Factor conditions.* It is increasingly pivotal (as highlighted in Chapter 1) that the ability of human resources to assimilate information and turn it into value-creating knowledge is key to enterprise success, as is the wide availability and access to capital (notably hardware and software) that facilities the efficient and effective use of information.

2. *Demand conditions.* The anticipated shift to electronic commerce and corresponding new business models is likely to be driven by the necessity to meet the needs and requirements of consumers. This will be compounded by the desire of users to utilize new technology for the purposes of commercial transactions (see Chapter 3).

3. *Related or supporting industries.* The information economy needs to be supported by an effective and efficient information industry that provides value-adding applications and technologies that constantly innovate to aid competitiveness (see Chapter 4). The products supplied by the information industry need to be accessible to as broad a range of business communities as possible.

4. *Firm strategy, structure and rivalry.* How enterprises use technology within the value chain is key to aiding their competitiveness. The desire to adopt these technologies is a general function of overall strategy and levels of competition faced by enterprises.

This chapter will focus primarily upon the first and last of these factors with the other themes being discussed in the chapters noted. Essentially the purpose and underlying theme behind the diverse range of issues addressed within this chapter is to develop an understanding of how the establishment of the information economy is changing enterprise through stimulating a reassessment of what the business needs to do to sustain its competitive position within such an environment. This should enable the reader to understand fully how and why business models are changing within the information economy and why exactly electronic commerce is becoming such a salient issue (see Chapter 3).

The impact upon enterprise performance and functioning

As this and the following chapter indicate, the application of ICTs is fundamentally altering the manner in which enterprises function. The application of these technologies to business functioning is driven by the compulsion to remain competitive in an era when the intensity of competition is further increasing and when there is correspondingly intensifying pressure upon enterprises to maximize their own efficiency (see below). Importantly these pressures create further strategic issues as lower production costs reduce barriers to entry thereby encouraging new entrants, increasing both the intensity of competition and the pressure upon enterprises to deliver these efficiencies on to the consumer. This pressure upon the cost functions of enterprises is likely to grow as consumers, through electronic commerce, become able to reach an increasing number of potential suppliers.

The maturing market for information is a testament to its growing strategic importance. Increasingly enterprises do not merely need information strategies but a proper assessment and integration of ICTs (as a symptom of the increasing strategic importance of knowledge and information) throughout their organization. This requires the integration of all the information aspects of the business (strategy, people, systems, operations and technology) as a means of ensuring that the value added from the application of these technologies is maximized. Consequently, companies seeking to sustain and enhance their competitive position need to utilize the information they have available at their disposal in a more productive and proactive manner. Information is no longer just stored, analysed and discarded; it is increasingly being used as a strategic resource in its own right to generate sustainable competitive advantage.

There are a number of strategic challenges associated with information, which are as follows:

- understanding and recognizing the forms of information valuable to the enterprise;

- assessing the value of the relevant information in business processes;

- identifying the business processes affected by this information;

- assessing how to integrate the relevant information into business processes;

- identifying necessary core-supporting ICTs;

- understanding core legal and statutory legal obligations in the use of the relevant information;

- understanding the need to assess and monitor the quality, relevance and accuracy of information.

These strategic challenges are core concerns that all businesses will need to assess in addressing the commercial impact of the information economy. They highlight how and where the enterprise will need to develop an information profile to sustain its competitiveness within the information economy. The information that a company possesses will span most aspects of business operation from essential knowledge about suppliers through to specialist customer and product knowledge. All the factors listed above combine to develop a particular identity for the company in terms of how information will shape its corporate position. This highlights how crucial an asset information actually is and how it clearly represents a source of business value. Companies need to develop a clear perspective on what the value of the information available to them actually is and how it can best be used to enhance an enterprise's competitive position. This is leading many enterprises to seek to put a value on information assets within their annual accounts – underlining the key point that information represents business value.

Measuring the value of knowledge in business is important. It helps managers assess the best strategy as well as helping gauge the knowledge assets of competitors. These processes can also assess the cost of knowledge and highlight deficiencies in the information the enterprise possesses in order to achieve its strategic objectives. In this context, three core information resources can be identified:

1.   the human element – the information embodied in the work-force that contributes to strategic objectives;

2.   the structural element – the information regarding specific markets;

3.   the customer element – the information regarding the customer base.

These should enable an enterprise to prioritize information resources and counter the potentially harmful effects of information overload and knowledge deficiency.

From the above, it is evident that there are two critical factors in shaping enterprise operation and functioning in the information economy. The first is how enterprises manage and alter human resources; the second is how the application of ICTs feeds through into enterprise efficiencies (a point more fully explored within the context of value chain analysis in the following sections). Consequently, it is worth while exploring these issues further at this juncture.

Human resources issues

Chattell (1998) underlines that value creation in the information economy depends upon human capital and the ability of organizations to allow the knowledge base of the enterprise to have sufficient freedom to express itself, and to stimulate the necessary invention and innovation to keep the enterprise ahead of its rivals. In truth, because of the complex impact of information upon the value chain (see below), coming to a definitive assessment of the impact of the burgeoning information economy upon human resources and employment is difficult. However, it is already evident that employment will rely less on the distribution of products and more on the transfer of information, with the result that routine, simple tasks will be replaced by increasingly complicated, knowledge-based duties.

Clearly the emphasis for enterprises is upon establishing and accessing a human resource base that has the necessary embedded human capital and flexibility to produce, access, process, assess and apply information in a manner that creates usable and commercially valuable knowledge. Firms (as the emphasis upon knowledge management highlights – see below) need to reconfigure knowledge assets if they are to sustain competitive advantage. This many will do through the medium of ICTs. Human resource functions need to be wired to ensure that available knowledge within staff is maximized and sent to the function where it will be most commercially valuable. In this context, an enterprise's staff is seen as a team of competent people who are more valuable when interacting than when working in isolation. Therefore well-organized team action, where each worker's knowledge is complementary, seems to be central to success, as does the need to manage staff in a cross-functional manner ensuring that the knowledge of each section is shared with all other parts of the organization (see the boxed section, 'Human resources in the information economy: the rise of knowledge management' on p 21).

Firms are likely to be especially keen to protect specific kinds of human capital that are central to strategy and both difficult and costly to replace. Furthermore, firms need to interact with the legal system through intellectual property rights to secure knowledge assets within staff against poaching by other enterprises. These strategies are increasingly underpinned by strategic alliances with other enterprises (notably key suppliers or customers) designed to expand the knowledge resources available to the enterprise. This necessity has to be balanced against the possibility that creating a more knowledge-rich environment leads to a situation of information overload where there is too high a ratio of information to be assimilated to capable staff with the corresponding effect that competitiveness is potentially undermined.

As a result of these and other trends, most developed economies in the late 20th century/early 21st century are experiencing high and rising demand for labour that possesses the necessary information-based skills. This demand is expected to increase as the information economy matures. The onus is therefore upon both policy makers (see Chapter 5) and enterprises to ensure that the pool of available labour resources is able to complement and sustain this growth. It is generally believed that if the wider application of ICTs is to create the desired levels of employment, it needs to be accompanied by moves to stimulate competition within product and service markets as well as by the engendering of higher levels of flexibility into labour markets and work organizations. The latter two imply that there needs to be a concerted effort by economic actors to constantly adjust education and training to reflect the changing requirements of the information economy.

These changes in the labour market are expected to extend right through the enterprise to include the core skills expected of all staff (ie that all staff are IT-literate). These changes could become especially prevalent in an era of electronic commerce, which will require a change in the composition of the work-force as an increased level of sales occur online. Thus levels of retail and sales staff could be trimmed and replaced with the lower levels of specialist employees required to manage an online sales system. This would be especially likely if re-intermediation or disintermediation becomes commonplace (see Chapter 3). Consequently, the emergence of the information economy will lead to a reassessment of the skills businesses require especially if their products and services are now being sold online. In addition, since they no longer need to be near to their market-place they can locate where they can find the right skills at the right price.

This latter point underlines a core concern of many major economies, which fear that the intertwining of the information economy with the process of globalization will stimulate a migration of employment to developing states. There is good reason to believe these fears are overstated especially if the threat stimulates the appropriate policy response. The core challenge for the developed economies is in facilitating the necessary structural adjustment so that the employment costs of the transition from industrial to information economy is minimized. It is already evident that job losses in some sectors are being counterbalanced by the creation of jobs in other areas. The key point is that the information economy – in altering the form and types of job available – should, over the longer term, stimulate higher levels of employment. The universal nature of ICTs, their speed of introduction and the mobility stimulated increases the employment conse- quences of the information economy through its potential to destroy more jobs than other technological changes. Where there are job losses, it is evident that these will be within the low-skilled sectors of the economy, with growth being within those that require a higher level of both education and skill.

There is an emerging demarcation in terms of the impact of ICTs between organizations where information is an input and those where it is an output. In the former (such as traditional retail outlets), the exploitation of the potential of ICTs has been slow and, where they have been applied, they have been linked to the shedding of labour. Redundancies have been linked to facilitating the necessary investment needed to apply these technologies. In the 'information output' organizations (such as dedicated online enterprises), there has been speedier adoption of these technologies. In these enterprises, the focus has been upon providing the existing work- force with the necessary training, and there has been a general avoidance of major lay-offs.

In increasingly competitive markets, businesses can only really flourish by maximizing the potential of their resources, of which human resources and the knowledge embedded therein are proving increasingly important. Knowledge is the information needed to make key business decisions, and most enterprises have to assess the knowledge capital embedded within the organization's human resources and ensure it is utilized effectively to secure the broad corporate objectives of those enterprises. This core concern has seen knowledge management rise up the strategic agenda of enterprises.

Human resources in the information economy: the rise of knowledge management

Knowledge management is concerned with the collection of processes involved in the acquisition, creation, sharing and use of knowledge within organizations. This encompasses a range of activities from learning processes through to management information systems. Generally knowledge management consists of four central elements:

1. valuing knowledge;
2. exploiting intellectual property;
3. capturing project-based learning;
4. managing knowledge workers.

This means finding and capturing the knowledge staff possess, sharing it and exploiting it for commercial benefit. Thus the knowledge of an enterprise is not merely the explicit knowledge held within databases, intellectual property portfolios or the corporate Internet – it is also the knowledge of staff.

Many see the development of knowledge management as a reaction to business process re-engineering where the application of ICTs was almost solely about cost minimization. The key change represented by knowledge management is that it is about networking people as well as ICTs – though this change may come up against a culture clash because of an inertia to change within organizations. People are central to knowledge management, as they possess the knowledge that will improve enterprise functioning. If people are resistant to sharing knowledge, then that asset as a key business resource is lost. The consequence is that information resources are utilized inadequately with the result that the competitiveness of the enterprise is put in jeopardy.

If a company fails to utilize information through a failure to translate human intellectual capital into organizational intellectual capital (as can happen when a key member of staff leaves), it can damage the enterprise by affecting relationships with a key client or supplier or by the loss of knowledge regarding best practice. A survey conducted for KPMG (1998a) by Harris indicated that companies were failing to exploit the technological infrastructure to improve knowledge management, with only 10 per cent of enterprises surveyed making knowledge of competitors available electronically to all who needed it. This is despite the fact that most companies have in place the necessary technology (intranets, extranets, etc) to support this activity.

A recent survey by KPMG (1998b) highlighted that knowledge management is becoming integrated into enterprise strategy, with many believing that they had commercially lost out through failure to address the core issues it poses. This was especially evident in cases where departing staff or poor information-sharing had damaged relations with a key supplier or client or where staff turnover had led to the loss of expertise in a core operative area. Many enterprises are using the advent of new technology to aid competitiveness through the storing of information about customers, markets, own products and services, competitors and employees' skills. The survey also found that, despite having the technology in place, enterprises are still not enabling easy access to mission-critical information, and that they possess relatively immature strategies for knowledge management. Enterprises also feel that knowledge management strategies can ultimately be frustrated through the lack of time individuals have to seek out the information and garner the necessary knowledge, as well as through the aforementioned problems of corporate culture and organizational inertia.

A notable example of a greater degree of competitiveness being sought through knowledge management is Airbus, Europe's largest aerospace enterprise. Airbus recognized that, despite the recent advances in computer-aided design, advanced technologies are still unable to deal with all the knowledge needed to ensure an aircraft design is successful. This is due in no small part to the large body of both written and unwritten rules upon the practicalities of aircraft design, which cannot be captured in computer-aided design. As aircraft design increases in sophistication and as the development time grows, so there is increased competitive advantage in securing this untapped human knowledge to secure first-mover advantage in terms of the latest aircraft models.

Airbus is seeking to develop a new plane to challenge the long-held dominance of the Boeing 747 over long-haul routes. The sooner it can bring the new aircraft to the market, the sooner its strategy for this market niche can become commercial reality. Its new rival to the Boeing 747, the A340-600, is scheduled for initial delivery in 2002, giving it a small window of opportunity over Boeing. The result is that the enterprise is seeking knowledge management techniques to shorten the design cycle to secure or even enhance this first-mover advantage over its key rival.

To aid this, it is using software that links computer-aided design to the body of knowledge within the enterprise, which includes areas such as product rules, performance data, legislative and safety codes, and best practice in terms of manufacturing. Essentially the business has turned to total business modelling where models are developed that integrate everything of concern to the business. The results so far have been promising. For example, the time taken to make the wings was reduced from one man-year to 10 hours using the advanced software.

Impact upon production costs and productivity

The impact of ICTs upon a firm's internal production and transaction costs falls into three broad categories (OECD, 1998a):

1. the costs of executing a sale – there are savings to be had in selling through the Internet rather than through a physical location, by simplifying the process of order placement and execution, easier customer support and after-sales service, and staffing;

2. the costs associated with the procurement of production inputs (see Chapter 3);

3. the costs associated with making and delivering the product (see the boxed section, 'The supply chain and the information economy' on p 35).

Thus within a system where electronic commerce starts to come to the fore, the cost of doing business can be expected to fall. These cost reductions should enable markets to work more efficiently. This trend is likely to continue as the costs of communication continue to fall. Many of these impacts will be upon the costs involved in selling products through third-party agents or brokers. The moves towards disintermediation are already evident as electronic commerce allows the 'middleman' to be removed from the value chain (see Chapter 3). Alternatively there is re-intermediation as the advent of trade over the Internet creates new dependencies upon online intermediaries (so-called infomediaries) such as those providing Internet search services and directories. This should result in lower barriers to entry and create greater incentives to enter the market-place. The cost pressures upon enterprises could be expected to grow as buyer power becomes more evident and as the competition within respective sectors intensifies.

Enterprises should be able to lower inventory costs through adopting just-in-time production methods and improving the ability to forecast demand more accurately. This can be complemented by the aforementioned efficiencies in sales via enhanced online facilities as well as by using these methods to deliver more efficient after-sales service. As the value chain analysis below indicates, the gains from electronic commerce and other aspects of the information economy are dependent upon enterprise 'openness', as firms need to be willing to open up internal systems to trusted customers and suppliers. On an economy-wide level, the OECD (1998b) estimates that the wider use of electronic commerce would lower physical retail and wholesale trade activity by 25 per cent, leading to a 50 per cent decline in the use of buildings and related services. Other cost savings would also be induced by the lower levels of staffing and capital usage.

These impacts upon enterprise production costs from the application of ICTs have been compounded by rapid declines in the price of the technologies themselves. For example the price of computer processing power has fallen by around 30 per cent per annum in real terms over the last couple of decades, a trend that is expected to continue. Never before has business witnessed such a fall in the costs of a key input – a change that has stimulated a virtuous cycle in terms of the adoption of these technologies. These price changes have not only lowered transaction costs but, with the advent of digital technology, have also meant that information can be moved or transacted both within and between enterprises considerably more effectively and efficiently.

Efficiency gains in terms of the application of ICTs should also be realized through improvements in productivity (the output per unit of input). The application of ICTs should enable enterprises to produce more with a given resource base as better information resources and utilization enable it to work 'smarter'. Despite the intuitive logic of this argument, there is a general absence of any evidence to suggest these effects are occurring: the so-called 'productivity paradox'. Rapid investment in ICTs has had, to date, seemingly little impact upon productivity. Indeed initial evidence seems to suggest that productivity increases have been trailing off, with any increases in productivity being driven by the more 'traditional' factors of labour and capital. Consequently some suggest that ICT investment has been wasted. Others are less dismissive, emphasizing that by their nature these technologies will increase productivity less than other resources, and that economies take time to learn and apply technologies in the most efficient and effective manner. This last point is important, for it suggests that once the market for these products reaches maturity their effects upon productivity will become more evident. A final perspective is simply that changes in productivity from ICTs may simply be difficult to measure – a feature that is a common occurrence across the service sector. Within the service sector, there are generally recognized to be two problems in measuring productivity: in measuring, firstly, changes in output and, second, improvements in quality. Given the broad use of ICTs in the service sector, there is a definite case for believing that productivity gains are there; it is simply that they are not captured through statistics. It also needs to be highlighted that investment in ICT is not always designed to boost productivity. For example, there has been a trend towards using this technology for product differentiation and marketing. These activities clearly do not boost productivity directly.

Overall, the greatest benefits from ICTs seem to be derived when investment in this technology is coupled with other complementary investments – new strategies, new business processes and new organizations. This reflects a basic truism that the impact of ICT will vary on a company-by-company basis (see later). In other areas, it may simply be the case that enterprises have to go online out of necessity as a means of preserving or extending market share and therefore do not end up producing that much extra output for the given resources. The true impact of the increased strategic value of information and associated technologies is best expressed within the context of the value chain.

The information economy and competitive advantage of enterprises: a value chain analysis

The framework of the value chain puts the impact of the information economy upon enterprise functioning and performance noted above in a broader context. It suggests that changes in efficiency and human resource requirements occur because of changes within the industry value chain in which the enterprise operates. The essence of the value chain is that an enterprise takes inputs from suppliers to which it adds 'value' (in the context of the information economy, through the application of knowledge and information resources and associated technologies) to create outputs that are eventually consumed by others. The typical, simplified value chain is identified in Figure 2.1.

Source: Tapscott (1995)

Figure 2.1 *The simplified value chain*

The essential theme of the value chain is one of securing competitive advantage through managing suppliers, assessing the requirements of consumers and adjusting internal processes as appropriate. The latter inevitably needs an assessment of the enterprise's core competencies and internal functioning in relation to the themes highlighted above. The value an enterprise creates is measured by the amount buyers are prepared to pay for its product. Thus a business is profitable if the value it creates exceeds the cost of performing these activities. Consequently to gain competitive advantage an enterprise must either perform these activities at lower costs (through using ICTs to improve efficiency) or perform them in an innovative manner (through the utilization of improved knowledge resources).

Porter (1985) divides the value chain internally into five primary activities and four supporting activities. The five core activities are:

1. inbound logistics – all activities linked to receiving, storing and handling inputs into the production process;

2. operations – all activities involved in the transformation of inputs into outputs, such as machinery, assembly, testing and facilities management;

3. outbound logistics – processes involved in moving the output from operation to end user (including movement, ordering, warehousing, etc);

4. marketing and sales – the process of inducing purchase and enabling those who wish to buy to do so (includes activities such as advertising, distribution channels, etc);

5. service – activities involved in the provision of a service to buyers, offered as part of the purchase agreement (includes spare parts supply, repair facilities, etc).

The four support activities (designed to support the primary functions) are:

1. firm infrastructure – includes accounts, finance and quality management;

2. human resource management – includes all functions involved in the process of staffing the enterprise from training through to rights;

3. technology development – the development of technology to support new product development and stimulate new process improvements;

4. procurement – the process of attaining the enterprise's inputs.

It is already evident that, across these primary and support activities, the application of ICTs is having a tangible effect (in addition to the production and human resources concerns noted above) upon enterprise performance – indeed it is difficult to identify an area where business functioning does not now depend to a greater or lesser extent upon information and the application of ICTs. Many of these effects will be discussed in greater depth in Chapter 3, but it is worth noting by way of illustration that there have been impacts upon advertising (for example, through improved knowledge about customers), the nature of shopping (there are anticipated increases in distance shopping) and logistics (via lower distribution costs). In addition, it is felt that the application of these technologies will (as mentioned) lower entry barriers, generate more efficient markets (through the better allocation of resources) and increase the pressure upon intermediaries and agents. It is also already evident that ICTs are having an impact upon operations through the development of computer-aided design and manufacturing, which is having a tangible effect upon the speed of production cycles, improving the quality of output and lowering the time it takes for new products to reach the market-place (see the boxed section above, 'Human resources in the information economy: the rise of knowledge management' on p 21). The impact upon distribution systems is also evident, as the application of ICTs is reducing the time needed to process orders as well as reducing the need for large inventories. In terms of marketing and sales, it is also apparent that a 'digital' shop front is much cheaper to maintain than a physical one, and is able, through Internet technology, to open all hours and reach the global market-place. Finally, the application of these technologies will have an impact upon corporate structure (see below), the nature of human resources (see above) and the location of commercial activities. The support activities (aside from the human resources element mentioned before) are also affected, through the rise of electronic tendering, the need to develop a supporting electronic infrastructure and the application of the correct technology to support the changing information requirements of the enterprise's primary activities.

These reinforce a trend where speed to the market is becoming more important as part of the process of securing competitive advantage, a phenomenon that relies in no small part upon the better use of information. The aim is to lower the unnecessary cost and waste out of the value chain. The savings realized from the improvements in knowledge can be utilized to fund further process enhancement as well as improved products and lower prices. These processes are all core to the enterprise delivering better value added to its customers. These changes, as well as the constant reappraisal of processes and techniques, are necessary in an era of intensifying competition. Strategy therefore constantly has to assess the nature and function of the value chain.

These trends underline the increasingly pivotal role of information in the value chain, which increasingly is not merely about the physical flow of goods and services within and between linked enterprises but is also about the information that flows within and between them. It is evident that branding, customer allegiance and employee loyalty amongst others all depend upon information of various sorts. Supplier relationships are by their very nature based upon channels of communication founded upon the exchange of information. Within these relationships, information can determine the relative bargaining power of the players. Very often one party or the other can gain increased value from the existence of asymmetry of information. In these instances, and where enterprises have better information systems and processes than their rivals, the existence of information can be used as a key determinant of competitive advantage. New advantages will emerge when the value chain, as it is currently developed, deconstructs and is fragmented into multiple businesses, each seeking to define its own competitive advantage. This process is symptomatic of the emergence of a virtual value chain (see the lower segment of Figure 2.2).

The development of a virtual value chain is, as the name suggests, value creation through interactions over the network (via the exchange of information) rather than through direct contact as typified by the traditional value chain. The virtual value chain is essentially the process whereby raw information is transformed into products, delivering value to users through electronic means. It is already evident that information within traditional value chains has had something of a supporting role, acting as a facilitator and often not as a source of value in its own right (for example, in areas such as marketing). Figure 2.2 indicates a number of things. First, it highlights the process of value creation in the production of information-based goods. Clearly the virtual value chain is mirroring the physical value chain as information is collected, processed, packaged and moved to the end user. Second, the growing importance of information means that processes within the virtual value chain can supersede those within the more traditional equivalent. For example, the network can offer alternative means of distribution and can also fundamentally alter aspects of the supply chain (see the boxed section below, 'Intranets and extranets' on p 31). This leads to a third (and final) point, that the virtual value chain is more a complement to the existing value chain than its replacement – there are emerging interlinkages between the two value chains. There are evident interlinkages between the virtual and physical value chains in terms of functional areas such as marketing and sales. Over time, as new markets are created and as more and more aspects of the two value chains become interdependent, it is possible to foresee their integration. Overall, the virtual value chain only applies to information businesses, which rely on these technological methods for their business models. For other enterprises, the virtual value chain is an important source of competitive advantage through using information collected as a complement to existing physical processes – a process also highlighted in Figure 2.2.

Information can evidently be captured at all stages of the virtual value chain and used to enhance the performance of the enterprise. This information need not be used merely to aid existing processes but can also be repackaged and analysed to build content-based products or new lines of business. For example, supermarkets are using their customer information in developing banking or other specialized customer products. This not only enables the enterprise to generate loyalty amongst its customers but can also assist it in reaching out to its competitors' customers. The result

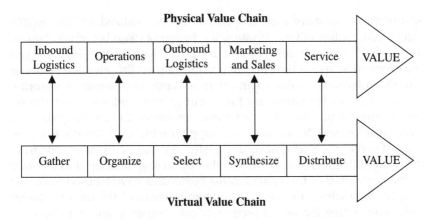

Source: Phillips (1994)

Figure 2.2 *The new value chain*

is to rearrange the value system to create growing interlinkages between various, previously separate, sectors (for example, in the case mentioned above, banking and food retailing) – a variation of the process of convergence most evident in the information industry (see Chapter 4).

The growing use of information and the development of the virtual value chain allow inter-enterprise relationships to expand with added value being generated through alterations to this network to maximize flexibility, speed, innovation and responsiveness (these are evident in terms of the development of virtual enterprises and the impact upon supply chain management noted below). Thus the capabilities of the enterprise to use and share information of common commercial interest create an inter-dependent network of enterprises whose efficiency can work to the advantage of all parties. The development of such networks (within the context of the wider application of ICTs) as the source of value added is, according to Tapscott (1995), creating new dynamics in terms of:

- improving the accessibility of partners;

- establishing new interdependencies between enterprises;

- creating competitive advantage through co-operation;

- value creation through inter-organizational partnerships;

- speeding up inter-organizational transactions.

These trends highlight that the flow of information along the value chain between the enterprise, its suppliers and its customers can be utilized to ensure that efficiencies and competitiveness are realized. On the supply side, sharing information with suppliers brings obvious benefits to both in terms of efficiency of delivery and avoidance of over-stocking, and is a complement to just-in-time production techniques. Bringing the customer into the enterprise's value chain offers advantages in terms of requiring fewer resources for enterprise functioning, increased speed for the re-engineering of products to meet customer needs, the enabling of mass customization and the avoidance of supply problems, as products can be relayed to the customer quickly and easily. The success of these systems to the competitiveness of enterprises relies upon emphasizing the customer as the key driver of the system. Most businesses have focused upon the supply chain within the logistical system in terms of the use of extranet technologies (see the boxed section below, 'Intranets and extranets' on p 31), as this is where they generally exert more influence, but evidently sustaining competitive advantage means integrating consumers.

The above trends indicate that the impact of information upon the value chain (in both its physical and virtual forms) is creating a situation where enterprises are increasingly part of a wider value system. This wider stream of activities, of which the enterprise's value chain is part, consists of the value chains of suppliers through to those of its customers. This system creates interdependence between enterprises and (as noted below) can become a source of competitive advantage in its own right. The external value system is reflected in Figure 2.3.

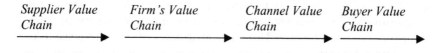

Supplier Value Chain → *Firm's Value Chain* → *Channel Value Chain* → *Buyer Value Chain* →

Source: Porter and Millar (1985)

Figure 2.3 *The external value system*

What this underlines is that the enterprise is part of a network of mutually interdependent value chains, and it highlights how important the virtual chain value can be in allowing information to be utilized effectively to ensure that full competitive advantage is realized from these interdependencies. The virtual value chain should increase the efficiency of these relations through, for example, an enterprise being made aware early of change in the supply of components so that it can then source them elsewhere.

Intranets and extranets

In facilitating the advantages of applying information more completely throughout the value chain, enterprises are utilizing two core Internet-based technologies – intranets and extranets. A brief explanation of each follows, outlining their typical and potential utilization by enterprises.

Intranets

An intranet allows information to be spread around an organization using Internet-compatible standards. Such developments are inevitably interlinked to the emergence of knowledge management as a business issue. By using common Internet protocols in conjunction with their own business applications, enterprises can easily communicate, distribute information and facilitate project collaboration across the business whilst maintaining the necessary security. Use of intranets is growing rapidly. Indeed, it is estimated that internal Web servers are outpacing their external equivalent by a magnitude of five to one. Intranets are fundamentally altering the way companies create and disseminate information, with effects in the following areas:

- Internal e-mail;
- collaborative processing;
- accessing enterprise memory;
- order processing;
- personal pages;
- departmental pages;
- group communications;
- enterprise communications;
- product and company information.

Extranets

A complementary, and arguably more important, technology is the extranet – essentially an intranet connected to trusted customers and suppliers. Developing an extranet initiates the concept of the virtual business by allowing all the organizations in an enterprise's value chain to integrate their systems and operations (value chain). The notion of the extranet is by no means new, as electronic data interchange on private networks has performed similar functions for a number of years. Potentially, extranets offer the prospect of removing many of the problems that have prevented firms from sharing their data with customers and suppliers. The more extensive use of extranet technology is intimately linked to greater development of software offering increased security over data.

Generally, companies are using extranets to:

- exchange large volumes of data;

- share product catalogues with wholesalers and other linked parties;

- collaborate with other companies on joint development efforts;

- develop and use training programmes jointly with other companies;

- provide or access services provided by one company to a group of other companies;

- share news of common interest with partner companies.

As highlighted, these intranet and extranet technologies are being used in a number of ways to complement the development of information (and its dissemination) as a key strategic resource to enterprises. Use of these technologies also highlights the trend towards an enterprise being increasingly perceived, within the context of the development of the information economy, as part of a network of mutually supporting businesses. The enterprise's efficient and effective functioning depends on the internal and external communication networks that aid and enhance its competitive positioning.

Organizational implications

The advent of the information economy and its implications for the value chain are having an impact on enterprise structures (as shown in Figure 1.1 and Table 2.1). It is evident from the analysis throughout this chapter that the source of competitive advantage lies within the organization and how it uses ICTs to alter internal and external processes and structures to secure its strategic objectives. As suggested by the external value system (see Figure 2.3), this is often done within the context of a larger commercial network. The development of electronic links between organizations can alter the concept of the organization, promoting the shift towards virtual organizations. The virtual corporation, in its most basic form, deals with the changes to the internal functioning of the firm in four major areas:

1. decentralization of operational controls as a means of becoming more responsive to commercial pressure;

Table 2.1 *Changing business models*

	Industrial Economy	Information Economy
Companies	inwardly focused	extended/network enterprise
Customers	limited access to manufacturer	direct access to manufacturer
Suppliers	arm's length relationship	electronic relationships
Intermediaries	stand-alone entities/ separate processes	extended enterprise links/shared processes
Employees	hierarchical and functionally managed	empowered and cross-functionally managed

Source: Financial Times (1999a)

2. global enterprises moving into more remote locations;

3. the increased use of electronic links between separate business units;

4. redefining the very nature of the workplace.

Such developments are driven by competitive pressure and by a recognition that it is often cheaper to conduct transactions externally than internally.

The shift towards virtual corporations is altering the concept of the organization, as its boundaries become less readily identifiable and it begins to include elements of other organizations as an alternative to the traditional options of horizontal and/or vertical integration. Such arrangements can work towards securing greater efficiency, flexibility and innovation. At the heart of the concept of the virtual organization is knowledge rather than location as the defining factor in the emerging corporate landscape. In effect, the enterprise can minimize the need for many corporate buildings, outsource many peripheral functions and operate as a virtual company. The existence of such companies is rare today but a survey by Andersen Consulting/*Economist* Intelligence Unit indicates that 40 per cent of executives believe their enterprise will be virtual by 2010, up from a 1998 level of only 3 per cent (BT, 1998).

Within this virtual framework, the enterprise is able to call upon more resources through the development of ICT-induced alliances – many of which may be only temporary – as a short-term means of grasping market opportunities. As suggested, the virtual organization is being applied as a means to aid flows of information within and external to the organization so as to achieve greater efficiency and secure more effective supplier and customer relationships. The enterprise will focus on core activities and outsource those functions that may be better done elsewhere. Outsourcing offers benefits in terms of accessing the skills needed to develop effective online solutions, lowering the risk associated with project development and freeing up existing resources.

In terms of external links, the development of the virtual enterprise is very much based upon stimulating value-added partnerships. These partnerships are based upon a set of organizations that co-operate to manage (information about) the flow of products and services in the value chain. The partnerships can be:

- symbiotic – where different organizations offer complementary services;

- vertical – where parties follow one other in the industry value chain;

- horizontal – where the partners are erstwhile competitors.

The point behind each of these agreements is to establish a competitive advantage over those enterprises that are excluded from the network. When examining this within the context of Porter's Five Forces (see below, p 37), it is clear that these agreements seek to negate the rivalry between the forces – through co-operation between enterprises, suppliers and sellers – thereby improving the competitive positioning of those that participate in the network. For these effects to be felt, enterprises need effective communication systems.

The existence of electronic communication networks between enterprises can improve co-ordination between firms through either: an electronic brokerage, such that the firm is able to lower the cost of searching for and procuring the relevant goods and services; or an electronic integration effect, where there is a lowering of the costs involved in tightly integrating a supplier into the enterprise's functioning (see below, p 37).

The realization of these benefits will depend upon the attributes, the products, the network infrastructure, business environment and network control. These advantages have been employed to great effect by General Electric, which has pioneered the use of devices such as electronic auctions for the purposes of sourcing.

Such enterprises are able to harness the capabilities of many to pursue a strategy of risk sharing. However, it needs to be recognized that virtual firms are likely to face control problems, which may increase with the degree of risk they face. This is important, for the virtual enterprise needs to be a real-time enterprise, responding quickly to changes in business conditions. This relies upon the flexibility and adaptability of staff – underlining that new skills will have to be developed if the enterprise is to succeed with its virtual structure in the information economy. The virtual enterprise will be characterized by flatter hierarchies and a team-based work organization as a means of responding to changes in the business environment and customer demands. The value added is generated through the interworking of these teams.

The supply chain and the information economy

Increasingly the supply chain is being perceived as a key area of competitive advantage for enterprises. Consequently, many enterprises are seeking to achieve efficiency within the supply chain from the innovative use of information and communication technologies. This trend reflects the fact that, for many industries, the use of Internet technology to stimulate supply chain integration is no longer merely a source of competitive advantage but one of competitive imperative. The Internet has aided the integration of supply chains through its reliance on open standards (which allows flexibility in terms of partnerships and avoids lock-in), its relative cheapness (compared to the preceding EDI systems) and its ability to operate securely both inside (intranet) and outside (extranets) the enterprise. Such trends are stimulating a reassessment by many enterprises of their business model, as they realize the application of these technologies can generate extra efficiencies and develop new commercial opportunities (see Chapter 3).

Changes in the supply chain, driven by the application of these technologies, are not merely about cost reduction. They are also a means of revenue creation. The conventional supply chain is built around the assumption that the buyer will come into the traditional 'bricks and mortar' store – with the development of the Internet, this assumption is clearly being challenged. This is in line with the observations regarding disintermediation/re-intermediation within retail markets (see Chapter 3). Internet-based supply chains not only offer businesses a new way to cut costs but also offer forecasting that reflects market conditions more completely. In addition, the sharing of information along the value chain ensures that customers' needs are met more completely, that demands feed through the system and the enterprise's resources meet those demands, and that suppliers are fully aware of market trends and can stock accordingly.

In line with its strategy of offering a greater degree of online sales, Dell (a leading PC manufacturer) is one company that has made progress in terms of using electronic commerce to integrate more completely its supply chain. As its orders are received, information is relayed to its suppliers informing them of its needs in terms of types of components as well as when they are needed and where. This system allows inventories to be kept to a minimum with the newly arrived components emerging as new computers merely hours after they have arrived at the plant. The ability of suppliers to have real-time access to Dell's orders through its corporate extranet allows them to organize their own production and delivery much more efficiently as well as keeping them abreast of changes in demand. This ensures that Dell has just enough parts to keep production running smoothly. The extranet is extended to its customers, allowing them to track their orders. The trend towards the integration of Internet technology into supply chains has been most evident in the most cost-conscious of industries (such as the PC sector) where competition seems to be the most intense. Advances in software have aided this process by enabling enterprises to understand their businesses better and making them more able to identify cost sources. In these sectors, enterprises have been quick to realize, through the more widespread application of Internet-based technologies, that most enterprises paid over-inflated costs for their supplies and operated unnecessarily costly logistical chains. This is reflected in the fact that one of the main sources of efficiencies within the supply chain is the ability to eliminate much of the paper chasing involved in the process.

These trends typify a situation where supply chains are integrated to the extent that they effectively function as a single corporate entity. This integration is driven by the desire to deliver to the end user as efficiently as possible. Thus competition may increasingly occur between supply chains rather than, as traditionally understood, between enterprises. These trends towards integration are already evident in the consumer products sector or where an enterprise has outsourced a great deal of its activity. Highlighting supply chain integration is integral to the virtualization of the enterprise.

These trends indicate how business-to-business electronic commerce is helping to integrate value chains through enabling suppliers and customers to be part of a three-way information partnership. This partnership is based upon treating all partners within the value chain as collaborators in seeking a common goal of increasing efficiency across the value chain. It can overcome the increase in consumer power derived from the Internet by offering a better service and therefore breeding increased consumer loyalty. The true competitive benefit of such an arrangement relies upon long-term commitment by the partners to the system and a continuation of the outsourcing process.

The application of electronic commerce to the supply chain directly indicates the shift towards value chain integration noted above. This process of collaboration allows for the optimization of all internal and external activities. Enterprises have developed data warehouses, which can be accessed by their suppliers to enable them to gauge the sales of their stock. This enables them to predict and plan output. It also allows savings by allowing new as well as current suppliers to service the demands of customers. These trends indicate (as mentioned) that the business is no longer a freestanding entity. The objective is for large enterprises to become electronic business hubs and for smaller enterprises to become spokes vital to the success of the larger enterprise. This implies that the enterprise must let others into its internal functioning and become familiar with the functions of its business partners. This underlines the role of the organization as a network bringing in partners and outsourcing a great deal of its activities.

Despite evident benefits, the process of supply chain integration can be retarded due to the resistance of assorted business partners to open up processes to other enterprises. This reflects a general lack of willingness to share information. There are other fears that this new system could lead to a re-intermediation with the emergence of new – and the removal of existing – intermediaries ('middlemen') (see Chapter 3). These could be natural resisters to change. Finally there are factors that simply reflect that the technology is not fully available to support these changes.

The competitive paradigm within the information economy

By way of a conclusion to the themes addressed within this chapter, it is evident that the form and nature of competition is changing within the information economy. Correspondingly, as businesses respond to the challenges posed by the increased competition associated with the information economy, it is apparent that new sources of competitiveness are emerging. These new sources of competitiveness are reflected throughout this chapter and are broadly indicated in Table 2.1. This table contrasts the business model associated with the information economy with the one that characterized the preceding industrial economy. Within the emerging business model, there is, as discussed in the text, a greater reliance upon using ICTs to develop new commercial arrangements that exhibit the necessary flexibility and to develop the new relationships that are key features of the information economy.

The development of this new business model is derived from changes in the industry structure within which the enterprise is operating, and is needed to secure competitive advantage. According to Porter (1985), industry structure is determined by five competitive forces (the power of buyers, the power of suppliers, the threat of new entrants, the threat of substitutes and rivalry among suppliers). It is evident from the above analysis that all of these competitive forces will be affected by the development of the information economy (as highlighted in Figure 2.4). Many of these changes will be driven by revisions within the value chains of the affected sectors as buyer power and supplier pressures upon the enterprise are intensified. In addition, enterprises are likely to face increasing competitive pressure (both in a potential and actual sense) through the convergence of previously distinct sectors and a lowering of entry barriers.

Such competitive pressures highlight that the development of the information economy extends the enterprise out over ever-widening circles of influence – as witnessed through the external value system (see Figure 2.3). Most immediately affected are its customers and suppliers. To a lesser degree, the suppliers of its suppliers and customers of its customers and so on are also likely to be within the sphere of influence of the enterprise to some extent. Thus as the enterprise extends, there are new requirements to open up the enterprise to customers and suppliers, getting to know customers as individuals, creating mutually successful solutions with suppliers and evaluating alternative sourcing options. These trends will lead to industry transformation. As this happens, so there is a need for the extended enterprise to identify value network roles clearly, develop deep specialization, embrace collaboration and share infrastructure with competitors. Finally, as these industry trends stimulate commercial transformation, so there is pressure upon the enterprise to:

- focus upon customer intentions;
- exploit hybrid markets;
- manage the network of alliances strategically.

Inevitably these changes place pressure upon achieving new forms and sources of competitive advantage in terms of:

- lower costs in a number of areas through the use of the Internet (eg marketing);
- offering greater differentiation through product innovation;
- altering competitive scope through providing increased focus upon customer relations.

These trends highlight that it is especially important that enterprises exploit the full potential of the development of the information economy. In the first case, the cost efficiencies associated with the increased deployment of ICTs become especially important – being a first mover can feasibly deliver market share to the enterprise. The second point stresses the core source of competitive advantage – human resources – and the importance of the enterprise having access to the necessary skills to secure and enhance competitive advantage. The final point stresses, first, the increased importance of information in determining competitive advantage (through, for example, tailored marketing strategies) and, second, that many businesses will seek to compete within the information economy through new or evolved business models based around the increased utilization of online business processes. The generic impact of the information economy within the framework provided by Porter is reflected in Figure 2.4.

Figure 2.4 demonstrates how the forces of competitive advantage are all affected by the development of the information economy. Many of these issues are addressed more in Chapter 3 where the impact of electronic

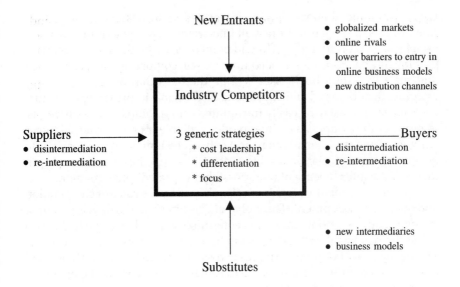

New Entrants

- globalized markets
- online rivals
- lower barriers to entry in online business models
- new distribution channels

Industry Competitors

Suppliers
- disintermediation
- re-intermediation

3 generic strategies
* cost leadership
* differentiation
* focus

Buyers
- disintermediation
- re-intermediation

- new intermediaries
- business models

Substitutes

Source: Adapted from Boch *et al* (1996)

Figure 2.4 *Porter's framework for competitive advantage within the information economy*

commerce is discussed more fully. How competitive advantage is altered depends upon how exposed the industry is to the challenge of online transactions, at least over the short term. As Chapter 3 discusses, those sectors that are especially exposed are developing and implementing new business models to meet head on the challenge and the threat to competitive advantage posed by the information economy. The model is by no means ubiquitous, as the pressure from the development of electronic commerce will be felt asymmetrically across the economy, and is dependent upon the sensitivity of the sector involved.

Clearly strategic goals are influenced and altered by the advent of the information economy. The entire process of competition has the ability to be fundamentally altered by the shift towards the information economy. One of its core features is the creation of new competition by removing barriers between sectors and allowing enterprises from previously distinct sectors to enter one another's – as well as new – markets. This process will be directly affected by the degree of interworking that takes place as a result of the evolution of the information economy. Thus instead of an enterprise carving out a particular niche on a particular value chain, the blurring of demarcations between businesses that results from the information economy will (as mentioned above) lead to integrated value chains across sectors. The result is that organizations will find ways to combine or interwork to establish common strengths. The end point over the medium to longer term is that value chains rather than companies will compete against each other, and the succeeding businesses will be the ones that most successfully integrate their demand and supply chains to enable information of mutual commercial interest to be easily transmitted across companies. Such trends, in terms of the competitive forces model, will integrate the external forces (new entrants, suppliers, buyers and substitutes) much more closely into generic strategy formation. In this context, strategy choice will become an increasingly interdependent (and possibly integrated) phenomenon.

These competitive forces are also shaped by the rules of co-operation and alliance development. The global effects linked to the development of the information economy mean that enterprises will feel pressure to develop value chains that allow them to act in both defensive and offensive ways. The development of these alliances across organizational boundaries will be established through common media such as the Internet. The openness of the system will make both the creation and dissolution of these alliances easier. Competitive forces are clearly changing. The cross-links between virtual and physical value chains and the convergence that is being stimulated are all altering the nature of competition forces within many, and eventually all, sectors.

The development of a new business model (see Table 2.1) and the changing competitive forces that are stimulating it (as formalized within Figure 2.4) are central to understanding the commercial impact of the information economy. They highlight how internal and external processes are responding to the challenges posed by its development. This is especially relevant in terms of the development of electronic commerce explored in Chapter 3. Many of the features of these frameworks – in terms of both the business model and competitive forces – reflect the broad ubiquitous impact of electronic commerce upon the enterprise, both internally and externally. Electronic commerce is the key facilitator behind many of the changes occurring within the value chain (apart, in most cases, from the human resource impact); it is the source of many of the cost efficiencies predicted and allows the organization to 'virtualize' itself. What this suggests is that you cannot really understand deriving competitive advantage from the information economy without comprehending electronic commerce.

3

The strategic implications of electronic commerce

As highlighted in the conclusion of Chapter 2, the evolution of the value chain is increasing the scope for electronic commerce. The emergence of electronic commerce will take place within the context of an evolving business model that reflects the commercial necessities of online trading. This chapter seeks to build upon the analysis of the previous chapter by focusing upon the impact of electronic commerce upon business strategy. Initially the chapter will focus upon the expansion and use of electronic commerce, seeking to stress its growth and strategic impact as well as highlighting those sectors where it is becoming especially prevalent. This is done through an examination of business-to-business and business-to-consumer electronic commerce. After this comes an examination of the impact on business models of the development of the information economy notably in terms of the processes of disintermediation and re-intermediation. The final section of this chapter examines the potential for the integration of SMEs into the information economy via electronic commerce.

The rise and broad strategic impact of electronic commerce

The market for electronic commerce has seemingly come a long way in a relatively short period of time. In 1995, electronic commerce was virtually non-existent. By the formative years of the new millennium, it is expected that sales derived from electronic commerce will be worth over $1 trillion. Despite this apparently recent trend, electronic commerce is by no means a novel phenomenon. It has existed for some time under various guises, notably in terms of the utilization of electronic data interchange (EDI), telephones and videotext systems that stimulate commercial transactions. The Internet has clearly revolutionized this trend, shifting electronic commerce from the margins into the mainstream. The benefits of the Internet in terms of global reach, flexibility and low cost are leading to the migration of these older applications to the new Internet-based format.

Electronic commerce: definition and scope

In broad terms, electronic commerce is defined as the use of electronic networks to facilitate commercial transactions. This underlines that electronic commerce is much more than the online purchasing of tangible and intangible products. In terms of tangible goods, electronic commerce covers online ordering and delivery direct to the customer (thus bypassing traditional retail formats). Electronic commerce also includes the direct sale of intangible, digitized content paid from, and delivered direct to, the home via the PC. These more obvious forms of electronic commerce are complemented by sales that have been stimulated though not actually carried out online. This is especially true for the purchase of tangible goods where the transaction frequently takes place through traditional formats despite the fact that the sale was stimulated through online methods, for example via an examination of the enterprise's online catalogue. Consequently online advertising and marketing to promote the sale of goods and services through traditional means can equally be defined as electronic commerce. Finally the broader definitions of electronic commerce include telecommunications, facilitating hardware and software, and other Internet access services, as these are key catalysts of online transactions.

From the issues addressed in Chapter 2, it is evident that electronic commerce has the potential to impact upon an enterprise's functions in the following areas:

- marketing, sales and promotion;
- pre-sales, subcontracts and supply;
- financing and insurance;
- commercial transactions – ordering, delivery, payment;
- product service and maintenance;
- co-operative product development;
- distributed co-operative working;
- use of public and private services;

- business-to-public administrations (concessions, permissions, etc);

- transport and logistics;

- public procurement;

- automatic trading of digital goods;

- accounting;

- dispute resolution.

The above clearly identifies that electronic commerce has tremendous scope for strategic impact across the enterprise. The extent to which it is adopted across these functions depends upon the form and nature of the enterprise and the commercial environment within which it operates.

Getting exact figures on the level of electronic commerce is notoriously difficult. A recent survey by the OECD (1998b) noted the differences between assorted estimates of the level of electronic commerce with a range of between $23 billion and $1.5 trillion being offered depending upon what group or consultancy house had been asked. The point is that there is little agreement on what actually constitutes electronic commerce (see the boxed section above). Does it just include direct online sales or should instances where consumers use Web sites to be informed about products that they then go and buy in the usual fashion be included? In addition, should electronic commerce just include Internet-generated sales or should all sales generated through electronic means (including EDI, fax and the telephone) be included? Whilst such methodologies do cause disputes, there can be little doubt about the trend reflected in Figure 3.1 (the figures represented are toward the upper end of estimates). These figures are estimates for the level of goods and services that are expected to be traded through electronic commerce, and therefore exclude the value of hardware, software and services that are complementary to the electronic purchasing process. The value of such complementary goods is, likewise, expected to run into hundreds of billions of dollars over this period.

If the most optimistic forecast is to be believed, electronic commerce will account for the equivalent of 15 per cent of retail sales within the major global economies – other forecasts predict less than 5 per cent – by the formative years of the new millennium. This should put the hype surrounding electronic commerce into perspective, as these sales are less than the current sales generated by direct marketing. Though this percentage seems small, it is important to stress that electronic commerce is another channel for conducting business (the other channels being mail, face-to-face contact and telephony). These four channels are all important for the purposes of

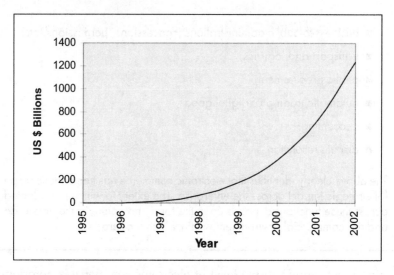

Source: ActivMedia (www.activemedia.com)

Figure 3.1 *Electronic commerce revenue (1995–2002)*

conducting business and any one of them simply cannot be ignored in the pursuit of sales and market share. This is important, for it underlines the fact that, for many businesses, electronic commerce is a complement to other channels for conducting business with the result that few enterprises – at least over the short term – will be dedicated online merchants.

As Table 3.1 indicates, not all Internet users are engaged in electronic commerce – though the numbers are expected to increase markedly. This is due to a number of factors such as security concerns, frustration in the purchasing process and concerns over the credibility of the seller (see Chapter 5). Overall, it is felt that electronic commerce will not be taken seriously until the major players, in both business-to-business and business-to-consumer electronic commerce, start to develop more recognizable and high-profile electronic commerce systems. This process will be complemented by the apparently powerful effect that word of mouth can have on the growth of electronic commerce.

If trends are to be believed (ie that electronic commerce revenue is easily outpacing the number of Internet shoppers), then the revenue growth noted in Figure 3.1 has to be due to existing online shoppers simply buying more. These figures reflect the simple fact that electronic commerce, despite all of its potential and accompanying hype, has yet to reach a marketable critical mass. The predictions may well prove to be widely inaccurate. Much depends upon inspiring consumer confidence and developing the necessary software to complement and breed confidence in its usage. In the meantime,

Table 3.1 *Electronic commerce as a percentage of Internet usage*

Year	Internet Users Engaged in Electronic Commerce (%)
1995	23
1996	26
1997	28
1998	31
1999	33
2000	36
2001	39

Source: ID (derived from www.nua.ie)

it is inevitable that the scope for electronic commerce is going to be limited. It is still very much the case that few Internet sites dedicated to electronic commerce are yet fully profitable. This is reflected by the fact that the vast majority of Internet sites used for electronic commerce are utilized as marketing devices or to assist in consumer support. Only a small minority – less than 10 per cent – offer online transactions.

The core component of electronic commerce lies in its commercial transactions cycle. Surrounding this is the use of electronic methods to advertise and promote products, the facilitation of contracts, market intelligence and sales support (both pre- and post-purchase). The full development of electronic commerce for these purposes requires that users are given certain guarantees (in respect of privacy, security, etc – see Chapter 5). It is also important to highlight differences between the electronic trading of tangibles and intangibles (especially digital content). The former revolve around the utilization of new technology to improve the efficiency of operations (as noted in the preceding chapter). The latter are more revolutionary, and their entire commercial transaction cycle can be conducted through the electronic network. It is also important to highlight that much of the emergence of electronic commerce (around 90 per cent) is represented by sales shifted from existing channels. The remainder is new business that is unique to electronic commerce.

Geographically, the US accounts for nearly 80 per cent of global electronic commerce, with Europe and South-East Asia making up the majority of the remainder. The US also has between 70 and 80 per cent of the top 100 Internet sites in terms of revenue generated from consumer activity. This dominance of global electronic commerce is partly explained by the fact that the US has a more fully developed culture of distance shopping than elsewhere in the global economy.

Electronic commerce in Europe has been curtailed by the limited encroachment of the Internet. This has been directly impeded by the restricted telecommunications competition in Europe, which has kept the costs of Internet access relatively high. This should be overcome as the pace of liberalization takes hold post-1998. Where it *is* taking off, it is the northern European states that are most active, with the UK and Scandinavia being the most prominent participants due in no small part to the maturity of competition in those markets. European use of electronic commerce is also held back because of the less developed culture of distance shopping in Europe as compared with the US, though there is evident potential for electronic commerce in France and Germany where there is a more developed culture of distance shopping online than elsewhere because of a familiarity with the use of videotext systems for transaction purposes within these states. A recent survey by Andersen Consulting (1998) (www.ac.com) suggested that the problems were compounded by a general inertia by management in the desire to implement electronic commerce systems despite an explicit recognition by business that it is important to their competitive advantage. The emergence of electronic commerce in Europe is likely to be driven by user demands rather than technology, as was the case in the US. The inhibitors within Europe have also been features of the lack of take-up of electronic commerce in the Asia/Pacific region. Overall, there is evidently a close link between the use of electronic commerce and the state of liberalization. As global telecommunications liberalization matures, so the electronic commerce arena will develop likewise.

The pace and pattern of diffusion of electronic commerce is likely to continue to be very diverse both across states (as mentioned) and between industrial sectors. In terms of the latter, the take-up of electronic commerce tends to depend upon the type of industry and products involved – though it is evident that the nature of the customer–supplier relationship has also been a key driver. The OECD (1998b) identified that, despite inter-industry and even inter-firm differences, there were a number of common incentives for engaging in electronic commerce:

- *Transaction management.* As highlighted in Chapter 2, the separate steps between customer and supplier can be integrated and fully automated through electronic commerce, thus lowering the transactions costs involved in the buying process. In addition, the use of electronic commerce technology overcomes many of the problems derived from time and distance within market-places. Electronic commerce is also seen as a positive development where the transaction process is complex, especially where the level of transactions is increasing and there is the need to deal with corresponding increases in transaction-related data. In other areas transactions are made easier, as the online store can be kept open 24 hours with considerably lower costs than traditional formats. Price comparisons between rival businesses are also made considerably easier.

- *Business efficiency.* As mentioned in the previous chapter, a major incentive to engage in electronic commerce is derived from the extent to which enterprises use electronic commerce to achieve efficiencies in terms of production and distribution. The effect of electronic commerce upon efficiency depends upon how and where it is employed. Improved efficiency can come right through the value chain from meeting consumer orders more efficiently through to procuring goods from suppliers.

- *New market development.* Firms are moving from a reactive to a pro-active stance in terms of the deployment of technologies to utilize electronic commerce. Many are using the technology to move into new market areas as well as forcing the pace of migration throughout the enterprise's value chain.

- *Reshaping customer relationships.* The gathering of data over the Internet not only allows for improved consumer service but also allows for 'lock in' to occur, through the targeting of products and services. In others areas, there can be a destabilization of relationships, especially in business-to-business markets as new suppliers are given improved access to customers (see below).

- *Reaching new markets and segments.* The oft-mentioned global reach of the Internet allows access to new markets. Enterprises can access the global market-place without the need for a physical presence and will be less hindered (as mentioned above) by time differences between locations.

Research from Andersen Consulting indicates that the aggressive use of electronic commerce has already borne fruit for those businesses utilizing it. These enterprises have seen revenue increases of 10–20 per cent and reductions in costs of 20–45 per cent. In addition, there have been 60 per cent reductions in working capital and physical infrastructure requirements. One of the most high-profile beneficiaries has been Dell Computers, which has increased revenue by 20 per cent and witnessed an 82 per cent increase in profits as a result of an aggressive use of electronic commerce. It has to be remembered that the implementation of electronic commerce systems is an expensive process. The basic Web-based retail solution is likely to cost several thousand dollars, though cheaper alternatives are available for smaller, less sophisticated enterprises. When electronic commerce solutions are developed to include enterprise resource planning, then the cost can range from tens of thousands through to millions of dollars. This has to be coupled to the cost to enterprise margins and the corresponding threat to profitability from the more intense levels of competition anticipated with the advent of electronic commerce.

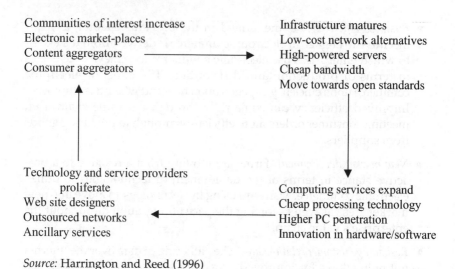

Communities of interest increase
Electronic market-places
Content aggregators
Consumer aggregators

Infrastructure matures
Low-cost network alternatives
High-powered servers
Cheap bandwidth
Move towards open standards

Technology and service providers
    proliferate
Web site designers
Outsourced networks
Ancillary services

Computing services expand
Cheap processing technology
Higher PC penetration
Innovation in hardware/software

Source: Harrington and Reed (1996)

Figure 3.2 *A virtuous cycle of e-commerce growth*

According to Harrington and Reed (1996), the move towards electronic commerce is creating a virtuous cycle of growth, which should secure momentum for the roll-out of this medium (see Figure 3.2). Developments in terms of infrastructure and computer devices are powerful enablers allowing Web designers and hosts as well as ancillary support businesses to supply the overlay technologies that enable the proliferation of electronic market-places. These, in combination, are expanding and enhancing electronic commerce to make it accessible to most sections of the emerging information economy.

Breaking into this cycle is going to be a strategic necessity for most if not all businesses – even if it is merely to complement existing business models. This implies that to varying degrees enterprises have to evolve either fully or partially into electronic businesses. The transformation of enterprises towards electronic commerce is expected by PriceWaterhouse-Coopers (1999) to consist of four distinct stages. These stages reflect the changes to the enterprise's value chain highlighted in Chapter 2. Figure 3.3 shows the practical process of transformation into an electronic business.

The first stage reflects a conventional starting-point where the enterprises will exploit electronic commerce through the integration of the site's buying and selling processes. Many enterprises are currently in the process of undertaking this. The second phase, as mentioned in the boxed section, 'Intranets and extranets', in Chapter 2 (p 31), involves linking key suppliers electronically into the production process. The third stage of alliance development highlights how the introduction and widespread

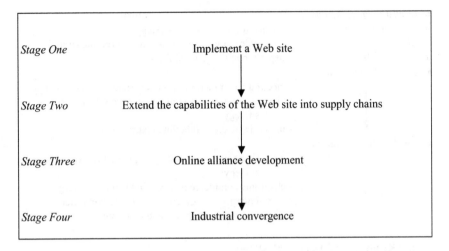

Stage One	Implement a Web site
Stage Two	Extend the capabilities of the Web site into supply chains
Stage Three	Online alliance development
Stage Four	Industrial convergence

Source: PriceWaterhouseCoopers (1999)

Figure 3.3 *The transition to an electronic business*

adoption of electronic commerce as an important commercial tool will alter the way in which the industry operates. The final stage is where there is evident convergence between different sectors to combine expertise and offer innovative products. This final aspect has been most evident in the convergence within the evolving information industry (see Chapter 4).

In terms of these developments, strategies developed within the enterprise tend to go through assorted phases of sophistication. Initially, electronic commerce developments start at the departmental level (for example, in the marketing department). Thereafter their usage spreads throughout the enterprise to represent more completely the overarching business strategy. In this context, electronic commerce strategy is subservient to overall corporate strategy. The final stage is where the impact of electronic commerce becomes all-embracing to the extent that it defines and drives corporate strategy. According to Kittinger and Hackbarth (1999), the growing interaction between corporate strategy and electronic commerce consists of the three phases defined in Figure 3.4.

These provide logical steps towards electronic commerce, though some enterprises may avoid these levels, especially if they are dedicated online businesses. The key phase is between levels two and three where there is intervention from senior management to develop 'breakout strategies' to alter the business model fundamentally. These need an open and aggressive commitment to an electronic commerce strategy.

Such strategies need to recognize a number of specific themes that tend to characterize electronic market-places (Merrill Lynch, 1999):

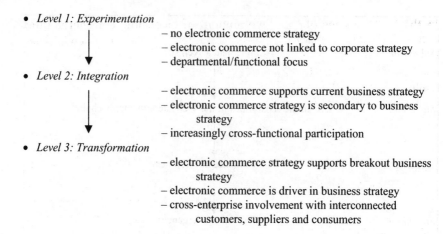

- *Level 1: Experimentation*
  - no electronic commerce strategy
  - electronic commerce not linked to corporate strategy
  - departmental/functional focus
- *Level 2: Integration*
  - electronic commerce supports current business strategy
  - electronic commerce strategy is secondary to business strategy
  - increasingly cross-functional participation
- *Level 3: Transformation*
  - electronic commerce strategy supports breakout business strategy
  - electronic commerce is driver in business strategy
  - cross-enterprise involvement with interconnected customers, suppliers and consumers

Source: Kittinger and Hackbarth (1999)

Figure 3.4 *Electronic commerce and corporate strategy*

- *On the Net, the customer is king.* Consumers are able to gather much more information more easily about rival products than they were before thus enabling them to make the best choice for themselves.

- *Electronic commerce has low barriers to entry.* This is true in the initial stages where Web retailers are small, but as they grow so they need more space for the physical storage of goods to the extent that this becomes an evident barrier to entry. This can be witnessed in areas such as online bookselling where the success of Amazon (the leading online book retailer) has led to expanded capacity and has therefore limited the opportunities of other rival enterprises.

- *Electronic commerce potentially results in disintermediation.* This is an issue that will be addressed in greater depth later in this chapter but it is worth while to note at this juncture that the development of electronic commerce offers the potential for the elimination of the 'middleman' or intermediary in the process. In many cases, this is the distributor. Intermediaries may be replaced by a new group of 'infomediaries' who have the function of finding products for buyers and vice versa (see the boxed section, 'The infomediaries: the new middlemen', later in the chapter on p 82).

- *Scale matters.* As the incremental cost of the incremental transaction is negligible, scale matters. This explains why electronic commerce sellers spend so long acquiring customers – to make the incremental transaction.

In the initial stages of the development of electronic commerce (and accompanying enterprise strategies), it is evident that two commercial rules hold true: first, there is a distinct first-mover advantage; and second, electronic commerce strategy has to be flexible and adaptable to sustain itself. In terms of the former, once one enterprise is established online, all competitors have to define themselves in comparison.

The electronic commerce/corporate strategy integration needs to be reinforced by a number of factors such as an electronic commerce 'champion' in senior management, quick learning and a flexible corporate culture. Such integration has to reflect a basic truism that, for many enterprises, electronic commerce is an evolutionary strategy that alters through experience and corporate change. The box below highlights the interaction between electronic commerce and business strategy in terms of types of business and how they are likely to be affected.

Electronic commerce: classifying businesses and their roles

In terms of the development of electronic commerce, five types of businesses can be identified:

1. *Companies that exist because of the Internet.* These are enterprises that owe their existence to the Internet or would have to alter their business radically if it ceased to exist. They include portal enterprises (such as Yahoo, Infoseek, etc) and the assorted Internet service providers (such as America Online, etc).

2. *New enterprises that exploit certain features of the Internet to employ this technology for business that existed prior to its development.* These are new enterprises in 'old' businesses such as banking or retailing, which have emerged through exploiting this new medium to carve out a novel niche for themselves. They include enterprises such as Amazon (books and CDs) and eBay (auctions). These enterprises have less of the physical infrastructure of their traditional counterparts with correspondingly lower fixed costs.

3. *Old companies transformed by the Internet.* These are enterprises that have had to change their business model as a result of the utilization of this technology. This is evident in the case of enterprises such as Federal Express (see the case study below), which has opened its database to users to enable them to arrange their own pick-up and deliveries.

4. *Other enterprises learning to adapt.* These are enterprises that are using electronic commerce to complement existing business. Many airlines are increasingly using this method to respond more flexibly and completely to the needs of users.

> 5. *Enterprises hurt by electronic commerce.* The enterprises most likely to be adversely affected by the development of electronic commerce are those tending to be heavily dependent upon traditional formats of business and unable to change without a fundamental strategic rethink. Included in this definition are enterprises such as those whose prosperity relies upon the demand for retail space.

Forms of electronic commerce

There are broadly two types of electronic commerce (the public administration-to-business/consumer aspect of electronic commerce is, for the purposes of this chapter, ignored): 1) business-to-business; and 2) business-to-consumer.

As Figure 3.5 indicates, within the US (the leading electronic commerce market) the former is significantly greater than the latter – despite the higher profile of business-to-consumer electronic commerce. Over time it is likely that the two forms of electronic commerce will become blurred as the distinctions between customer-facing and supplier-facing electronic commerce disappear.

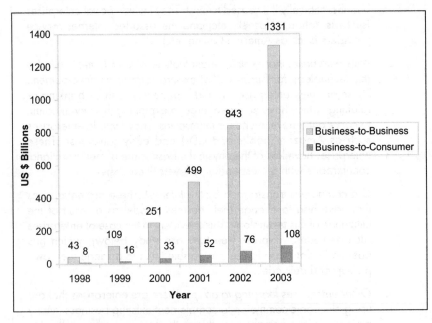

Source: Forrester Research (OECD, 1998b)

Figure 3.5 *US electronic commerce (1998–2003)*

Business-to-business electronic commerce

The fact that this form of electronic commerce has come to be predominant should come as little surprise, for it merely mirrors the physical world where business transactions are worth 10 times consumer sales. Businesses were also quick to exploit the potential of electronic commerce, as many transactions were already taking place electronically through fax, telephony or EDI. The introduction of Internet technologies aided this process by making these transactions cheaper, faster and easier. Businesses are clearly familiar with conducting electronic transactions with one another and will therefore drive electronic commerce, especially within the context of the value chain evolution highlighted in Chapter 2. Increasingly this technology is used for co-ordination between the purchasing operations of a company and its suppliers, that is the logistics planners in a company and the transportation companies that warehouse and move its products, the sales organizations and the wholesalers and retailers that sell its products and the customer services and maintenance operations. The primary classes of electronic commerce applications within the business-to-business sector are noted below:

- *Sell-side.* This focuses upon selling goods or services to business customers where the primary goal is revenue creation. These applications require the capability to integrate inventory and production systems as well as ease of use and access.

- *Buy-side.* This focuses upon helping companies make procurements. These systems are designed for internal staff, and aid the purchasing process enabling those involved to manage spending and acquisition more effectively, as well as facilitating the capability to negotiate more competitive prices. Currently much of the effort is devoted to goods such as office supplies. This method has notably been employed by the National Health Service and Barclays Bank in the UK.

- *Market-place.* In this class of applications an aggregator brings together multiple buyers and sellers thereby providing a community for electronic commerce for its participants. This has traditionally been more prevalent in the business-to-consumer market though it is starting to enter the intra-business market. These communities create secondary markets that make sense for vertical industries such as steel or chemicals. Electronic commerce can also be used for auctions allowing enterprises to get rid of surplus inventories.

Figure 3.6 highlights where the growth of business-to-business electronic commerce is becoming evident and what sectors will exhibit the greatest maturity by the formative years of the new millennium. Many of the sectors, especially travel and computers (including both software and hardware), have developed online capabilities driven largely by business expenditure.

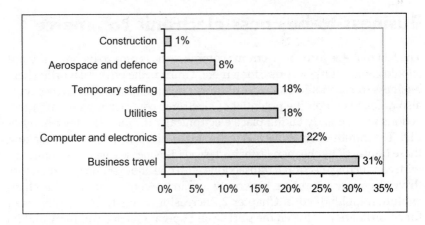

Source: Forrester Research (European Commission, 1999)

Figure 3.6 *US business-to-business electronic commerce (as percentage of total industry revenues (2003 estimates))*

The express delivery sector: the case of Federal Express

The express delivery sector is a key area of business-to-business electronic commerce. Increasingly many of the key players within the sector are utilizing the Internet to support key business processes. The use of the Internet within the sector is a means not merely of facilitating greater efficiencies but also of allowing for the development of more customized services as a way of generating customer loyalty.

Electronic commerce has been utilized within the sector for over a decade with the lead being set by Federal Express, a US-based haulier. Early forms of the system allowed customers to track the status of their order electronically. In the mid-1990s, this was improved with the introduction of a free software program, with the ability to work on any computer, to allow customers greater access to information regarding the status and delivery of their orders. Generally these were limited to the largest customers. Their use was further enhanced by an extension of the capabilities of the Internet in terms of business processes. Through these improved capabilities, customers can request parcel pick-up, find the nearest drop-off point, print label packaging and request invoice adjustments, as well as tracking the status of deliveries. This can all be done without leaving the Web site. In addition, the recipients of deliveries can request an e-mail when the package has been shipped. Thus the enterprise can keep up to date with every package in all parts of the process from the point of pick-up through to final destination via connection to the network. This aids the distribution network and provides better service to customers – something that is especially important when a key part of the logistical process is dependent upon another enterprise.

Federal Express itself can play an important part in the value chain of other enterprises. The information network it possesses allows it to undertake a range of outsourced functions for other businesses. For example, the quality of its network allows it to manage the logistical process of other enterprises through handling the entire process of dispatching goods for the client right across the globe. Thus an enterprise can send its order of what it wants to go and where (in remote locations) and Federal Express performs the process. Given the frequently large distances between an enterprise's headquarters and the place of manufacture and storage, the network's capabilities are important in enabling Federal Express to carry this function out. Thus the development of advanced networks allows Federal Express to operate as a one-stop shop for logistical services, offering the potential for further cost savings for enterprises. It not only offers all back-end logistics for customers, but it also utilizes a vast network of couriers to handle customer service functions such as repairs and returns. For problem goods, a retailer notified by the customer can direct a courier (electronically) to pick up the goods and return them to the original seller.

Federal Express's own network is at the centre of its electronic commerce strategy. The reach of the network has been extended by the expansion of the Internet and allows the electronic interconnection of all its customers. The importance of this network will only be enhanced as more and more enterprises become engaged in electronic commerce, allowing Federal Express to exploit the increased business opportunities that result. It is estimated that the development of its electronic commerce systems has delivered benefits in terms of avoided costs (it negated the need to employ extra staff), lower operating costs (online tracking has replaced extensive use of the freephone service that Federal Express provided) and, as mentioned, better customer service.

The strategy of Federal Express – which gave it an evident competitive advantage – is increasingly becoming the norm across the sector with many more express delivery enterprises developing similar systems. The onus is upon these enterprises to offer better customer service through quicker order processing and faster deliveries. The increasingly close positive link between the speed of delivery – the *raison d'être* of the sector – and the usage of the Internet means that the utilization of ICTs by enterprises within this sector is a competitive imperative.

Despite these trends, most Web sites are not designed for direct selling to other businesses (according to *The Economist* in 1997, business-to-business Web sites that allowed for direct selling accounted for only 3 per cent of the total). Most business-to-business electronic commerce sites are used for customer services, marketing and other enterprise functioning (see below). In this form of electronic commerce, businesses are using the Internet to integrate their value chains from suppliers to final consumer more fully. In 1998, three enterprises – General Electric, CSX and NEC – were conducting over $20 billion in business-to-business electronic commerce. These enterprises, and many like them, benefit from business-to-business electronic commerce through their positions as suppliers of the necessary technology to support it. A notable example is Dell, which uses electronic commerce to sell its PCs to businesses. This trend for hardware is mirrored in terms of software sales, where much is sold via download facilities over the network. This can account for as much as a third of the total quantity of business-to-business electronic commerce. Boeing is using these electronic commerce systems to aid the efficiency of its spare parts business, and has reported immediate benefits in ordering and customer service operations. In addition, two of the world's largest automobile manufacturers, Ford and General Motors (GM), have announced that they are shifting their procurement processes online.

Business-to-business electronic commerce has tended to be driven by the following factors:

- *Lower purchasing costs.* Traditionally purchasing is a complex and protracted multi-tiered process. The use of electronic commerce can lower procurement costs by consolidating purchases and enabling key suppliers to benefit from economies in the purchasing process. The use of Internet technologies also allows these enterprises to seek lower-cost supply sources. It is already evident that the use of EDI has delivered savings of between 5 and 10 per cent in terms of procurement costs. The Internet offers the opportunity for further reductions especially for larger enterprises. This technology also offers benefits to small and medium sized enterprises especially in terms of gaining access to the procurement procedures of larger businesses. The opportunity for enterprises through posting request for bids on the Internet is also evident through the use of business-to-business electronic commerce.

- *Reduced inventory/right products in stock.* Enterprises rely upon the production schedules of their suppliers to know what to hold in stock. The longer these schedules take to develop, the more stock an enterprise needs to hold to account for delays and errors. This renders businesses less responsive to changes in consumer demand. Additionally electronic commerce allows enterprises to hold the right stocks at the right time, as well as allowing for greater scope for reductions in costs and more efficient utilization of manufacturing capacity thereby overcoming the need for extra investment in production infrastructure. In the US, manufacturers, wholesalers and retailers are collaborating to establish standards and guidelines for better forecasting and re-stocking, called 'collaborative planning forecast replenishment'. This allows companies to work together to determine future demand for products and to share information about stock availability. Under this system enterprises across the value chain post forecasts for a list of products where there are differences between supply and demand,

and these are then reconciled through the system. Ernst and Young has estimated that the development of this system could save US enterprises between $250 billion and $350 billion. It is also becoming increasingly common for enterprises to use electronic auction sites to sell surplus stock over the Internet to the highest bidder.

■ *Lower cycle times.* Electronic commerce offers the opportunity for lower cycle times (the time it takes to build a product), allowing more to be produced for the same or lower costs. The establishment of electronic links allows companies to have lower lead times to speed up processes such as product design and development, as well as speedier ordering, shipping notifications, etc. These developments were pioneered by Japanese companies breaking down the organizational barriers between assorted divisions within an enterprise. The benefits were especially evident within the automotive sector where the use of these practices allowed the Japanese to cut production cycles (the time from design to end product) to around three years, compared to the US's four to six years as it was at the time. Many enterprises within the sector are working towards two-year production cycles. The results evident in the automotive sector are being extended to other industries. These are facilitated by the Internet, which accelerates the speed with which businesses communicate. The Internet will offer further advantages by expanding the network of electronically connected businesses as well as facilitating collaboration on projects across work teams and locations.

■ *More efficient and effective customer service.* Enterprises are increasingly finding that providing product designs and descriptions, technical support and online order status also offers opportunities for efficiency gains. These allow for an enterprise's customer service staff to be freed up to offer more complete and satisfactory customer relations. This process of better customer relations is partially aided by the fact that new electronic commerce systems enable enterprises to utilize the information they have always gathered from customers in a more efficient and effective manner. This means spreading information around the enterprise more efficiently. It is already evident that delivery companies are using these technologies to allow customers to track the status of their orders (see the case study, 'The express delivery sector: the case of Federal Express' on p 54). In addition, enterprises have reported savings from order tracking, software downloads and technical support information available online. For example, Cisco has reported a productivity improvement of between 200 and 300 per cent within its customer service department. Dell has reported similar savings – an estimated several million dollars per annum – from having customer service and technical support available online.

■ *Lower sales and marketing costs.* There are evidently savings to be made available within this business function. On an individual level, a salesperson can only sustain as many accounts as he or she can visit. Thus as the number of accounts increases, so there is a corresponding need to increase the sales force. This is also true for direct marketing organizations, which need to increase staff as telephone orders increase. The Internet will allow the establishment of new customers at little or no extra cost. In this instance, the sales function is only limited by the capacity of servers to respond to enquiries and orders, and not by the constraints of physical locations and the location of salespeople. The result is that traditional sales organizations can become more efficient, with automated sales and ordering capabilities freeing up sales representatives to focus more on consumer needs and not on filling in forms for manual orders. In addition, direct online marketing can shorten repurchase cycles and increase the ability to sell extra items.

■ *New sales opportunities.* As the Internet never shuts and has global reach, enterprises can reach markets that they would otherwise be unable to service. This is as true for small businesses as it is for their larger equivalents. Evidence suggests that enterprises using the Internet are able to attract new customers. This has be witnessed by Dell, which has found itself attracting in greater numbers orders from SMEs that were previously not customers of the PC manufacturer. Many of these SMEs have commented that they would not have made these purchases were the online ordering capabilities not available.

Many of the benefits evident from the use of electronic commerce are only likely to grow as usage expands. Despite all the commentary on the possibilities of business-to-business electronic commerce, it still remains some way from achieving a degree of critical mass. A recent report by Shelly Taylor Associates (1999) found that only nine per cent of their sample of global enterprises had implemented online systems to facilitate seamless transactions with other businesses. Frequently where these systems are available they are only accessible to existing customers and unavailable to new clients. This could lead to the more widespread use of electronic commerce via the development of closed communities where existing partnerships are reinforced. It could be the new business model where all partners agree to operate on a closed trading network based upon commonly agreed rules and applications to establish a strong online market. However, this could frustrate the opening up of markets, one of the key benefits of electronic commerce.

The advent of electronic commerce within the supply chain is likely to be an important factor driving the spread of the Internet, allowing the technology to have a rapid multiplier effect throughout the commercial environment. Once large firms move their procurement online, suppliers and commercial partners will have little choice but to do likewise. Consequently it will become progressively harder to avoid using electronic commerce, as it will become increasingly integral to the sustaining of an enterprise's competitive position. This will become increasingly true as more and more large businesses such as Ford, IBM and General Electric move online forcing their suppliers of all sizes to follow suit or else lose their custom.

Business-to-consumer electronic commerce

Figure 3.5 indicated that business-to-consumer electronic commerce was very much secondary to its business-to-business equivalent in terms of volume. Given that household expenditure accounts for over half of domestic demand, there is evident potential for growth in business-to-consumer electronic commerce. As Figure 3.7 indicates, business-to-consumer electronic commerce is growing across a number of tangible and intangible product markets. In terms of product sectors affected by the future development of electronic commerce, it is those that have a high price-to-bulk ratio (such as CDs) and intangibles that are going to be significantly affected; those that have tactile features (eg fashion and expensive items) will be less affected. Some products that may initially have proved unsuitable to electronic commerce (such as cars) are proving adept at the change provoked by the developments, especially where trusted third parties or intermediaries can be established.

The business-to-consumer market is expected to take off when the Internet can be accessed by large numbers of low-cost and ubiquitous devices such as mobile phones and televisions. Over the short term, enterprises will have to compete hard for a limited number of online consumers. Figure 3.7 highlights those areas where business-to-consumer electronic commerce is expected to have an impact. Across more broadly defined commercial sectors, it is already evident that electronic commerce is starting to have a profound effect. The effects across a number of sectors are noted below:

- *Content.* Many newspapers and magazines have developed strategies to offer 'digital' versions of their content. Frequently this is available free of charge to users. In addition, other content providers such as television stations, music enterprises and broadcasters offer content to the consumer over the Internet. This has been driven largely by consumer demand reflecting the fact that the vast majority of users utilize the Internet to garner news and information. To the user, the Internet offers an expanded choice of and access to mainstream – as well as more obscure or niche – journals. The impact of the growth of

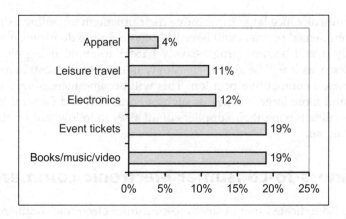

Source: Forrester Research (European Commission, 1999)

Figure 3.7 *US business-to-consumer electronic commerce (as percentage of 2003 revenues – by industry)*

online information gathering is very difficult to discern and, over the short term, has tended to have a minimal impact, as many readers tend to keep to traditional formats. Thus the online content offering – at least over the short term – is a complement to, rather than a replacement for, the traditional physical format. The content providers are less constrained by space on the Internet, and can offer added features and articles unavailable in the physical version. This advantage of offering more content as well as multimedia (newspapers offering online interviews, etc) is compounded by advantages related to lower capital and distribution costs, bringing competitive advantages in terms of content delivered as well as efficiency gains. The success of such a strategy relies on successful marketing and brand awareness – especially important given the choice available. To many enterprises, across all online sectors, access to portals or search engines is important, for these are the most visited sites on the Internet and, for many users, are the logical starting-point for content search. Despite these trends, much online content does not yet offer adequate revenues for its providers and owners. This is due mainly to the fact that content owners do not yet charge for the service, in order to secure a market for their content, and seek to attract revenue through the selling of advertising space. This is likely to change as advertising revenues become more competitive and as online enterprises seek to generate more revenue through subscriptions (see below).

- *Travel.* Many travellers can now find information to arrange their travel plans over the Internet. Across the travel sector, lower sales and marketing costs as well as increased consumer choice and convenience are driving the increased use of the Internet in this domain. The most high-profile of the travel uses of the Internet is in airline tickets where savings have become evident through call centre costs being reduced as online ticketing becomes increasingly common. The Internet is also being used by these enterprises to sell under-utilized capacity quickly and cheaply. Electronic commerce in the travel sector – to both consumers and other businesses – is expected to be worth some $20 billion by 2001. This is fuelled by Internet start-up firms working as intermediaries, leading to increasingly intense competition between hotels, airlines and car rental companies. The market share of each is highlighted in Figure 3.8 – these shares are unlikely to change in the short term.

- *Retail banking.* Despite most banks having their own Web sites, only a few actually offer online banking in the true sense of the word. In the US, of the top 100 banks only around a quarter can be considered true Internet banks. Indeed of the 133 'true' Internet banks, few are big enough to be in the top 100 banks. True Internet banks tend to be smaller banks with less-developed branch networks. Once again the trend towards online banking is driven by the desire for lower operating costs, the offering of new services and the ability to offer one-to-one marketing.

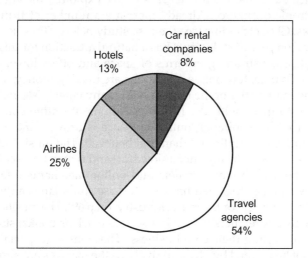

Source: PhoCusWright (1999)

Figure 3.8 *Electronic commerce travel revenues by category (1998)*

- *Insurance.* Like banking, this sector is making the transition towards online services. Many insurance companies are shifting towards online services through the desire for cost savings, as a response to increased competition and because of an increased user acceptance of online insurance. In some areas, the distribution costs for insurance policies can be as much as a third of the total price, so the Internet offers tremendous scope for cost savings. As well as offering new sales opportunities, the changes are expected to lead to further cost savings through cutting agents' commission.

- *Online share trading.* Many brokerages are having a great deal of success exploiting these technologies – a trend that is set to continue with online trading commissions expected to rise to $2.2 billion by 2001. Online share trading was pioneered by E*Trade – a dedicated online service – but increasingly the more traditional brokerages are developing a presence in this sector of the market. There is already evidence of convergence between banking and online share trading with E*Trade's purchase of a small Internet banking offering. The strategy of this enterprise is to spread itself with an Internet presence within most if not all key aspects of the financial services sector. The advent of online brokering is changing the prevailing business model as these enterprises develop a new role based upon providing information but stopping short of all-out advice.

- *Retail.* As is mentioned throughout this chapter, many traditional and dedicated online retail enterprises have exploited the emergence of electronic commerce. Already there are a number of firms offering books, CDs, etc online (see the case study below, 'Toys 'R' Us versus eToys' on p 64). The Internet has a natural attraction for this sector, as it is less constraining in terms of space and offers lower operating costs. To date, few online operations are making money, largely due to the immaturity of the market with many enterprises really failing to get to grips with the full implications of online commerce. In practice, developing an online presence is proving more time-consuming and complicated than first believed. The music industry is a sector that is maturing after a slow start and is now fairly competitive, with both traditional retailers and online merchants offering their wares through this medium (see the case study later in this chapter, 'Online strategy for the music industry' on p 69). This position is likely to evolve as retailers from other sectors (such as books) start to offer CDs alongside their core business. These areas (especially books) cannot be ignored by physical rivals, as the margins are already fairly low within the sector.

- *Cars.* This is not at first glance a sector one would expect to benefit from electronic commerce, but there is increasing evidence to suggest that there are economies for consumers to be made through an online purchase (see the boxed section later in this chapter, 'The info-mediaries: the new middlemen' on p 82). The service is also economical for the dealer who can see a sharp reduction in advertising and marketing costs. It is estimated that by 2001, in the US, some 25 per cent of all cars purchased will be sold through online methods (either directly or indirectly). This trend is being mirrored in the UK where there has been an explosion in the number of online sites selling new cars. Some of Europe's leading car makers have responded to this challenge by threatening to remove the franchise of any operator found engaging in this practice. This could appear to be a pyrrhic victory, for the moves towards these sites are unstoppable and will put the existing dealer network under strain, effectively numbering the days of exclusive dealerships. The use of electronic commerce is not often used for purchase but is more often undertaken as part of the process of garnering information about a potential purchase. According to Forrester (www.forrester.com), by 2003, 8 million will be influenced by the Internet in their purchasing decision with nearly half using this technology to make a direct purchase, generating sales of $12 billion. In the US, nearly two-thirds of car dealers have Web sites, but the success of these sites is limited by the nature of the dealership networks that exist in the US and beyond. The result is that many of the dedicated car buying sites tend to have a high turnover of dealers and, despite the trends, direct online car sales in the US still account for merely 2 per cent of total sales. By late 1999, leading manufacturers, notably GM and Ford, had announced that they were to start direct sales over the Internet in direct competition to dedicated online sellers.

The rates of growth of electronic commerce are expected to vary across these sectors. It is anticipated that the travel sector will evolve quickly, as there are seemingly few constraints. The same basically can be said of financial services as these enterprises explore new business models to secure their existence in the information economy. In other areas, digital delivery has potential (music, software, etc) but is still constrained by concerns over intellectual property rights and the ease with which the material can be copied without sufficient reward going to the copyright owner (see Chapter 5).

Toys"Я"Us versus eToys

Toys"Я"Us, the US's largest toy retailer, started selling online in Christmas 1998 as a response to the growing threat to its traditional business model from a dedicated online retailer, eToys. Founded in March 1997, eToys had a year's start on Toys"Я"Us, and bought out its only dedicated competitor, Toy.com, in 1998. Using heavy advertising spend in traditional media and claiming it held a larger stock of toys than can be held at a traditional store, eToys gained first-mover advantage in the sector. It picked a market segment where the benefits to customers are more than simply the convenience of not having to leave home. Parents would know the item was always in stock and would avoid the inconvenience of dragging a troublesome child round a 'bricks and mortar' store and running the risk of the item not being available. The process is assisted by the fact that eToys tries to make the online shopping experience as easy and enjoyable as possible. This last feature could be especially important in generating the necessary degree of consumer loyalty.

In many senses, the toy sector is typical of others where the small, nimble online retailer with a Web-only store front, seeking to boost brand image via its first-mover advantage, takes on the slower-to-market retail giant slowly evolving from its traditional offline 'bricks and mortar' format. Despite toys only being some 0.1 per cent of the total online market, it is a segment that is expected to grow radically and therefore a segment that cannot be ignored by enterprises within the sector. For many traditional toy retailers, the strategy is not based on whether online sales will be big or not, but on wanting to seek all avenues of sales and defend market share where it is under attack. Despite Toys"Я"Us having instigated an online strategy in February 1997, it was overtaken by eToys, which launched in September of the same year – when the physical retailer was still developing its business plan (the Toys"Я"Us site was finally launched in June 1998).

By August 1998, the Toys"Я"Us site was being visited by 0.5 per cent of all Internet users, compared to 1.2 per cent for eToys. The shift to the Web by Toys"Я"Us came at a time when it could ill afford to lose market share. Securing avenues for new sales was seen as a priority when the physical stores were under such intense competition from lower-price enterprises such as Wal-Mart, though these online sales are perceived as a complement rather than a competitor to the physical stores it operates. This is based upon a belief that the online presence can only benefit from its link to the physical stores. For example, customers who buy goods online can return them to the physical store, and customers can register for items in the stores and purchase them on the Web. Toys"Я"Us also has a tremendous marketing advantage over eToys through its database of over 61 million customers from its physical stores, enabling it to track more easily who is shifting to online purchasing and who is not. Thus the enterprise can only get nimbler and quicker, and potentially outpace its dedicated online rivals.

The core strength of eToys, so it claims, is the breadth of the goods it can carry, yet this would seem to give it only a short-term advantage, as Toys"Я"Us is catching up. It also has the problem of any online enterprise – that of creating awareness, a problem Toys"Я"Us will clearly not have. Ironically, eToys will have to rely upon traditional marketing ploys (magazines, etc) to stimulate its online sales. In addition, it will use portal advertising, but as space in this domain starts to be premium-priced so it could find itself outbid by bigger rivals such as Toys"Я"Us. The importance of marketing is reflected in the fact that the sales effort has consumed the vast majority of the funding raised from venture capitalists to develop the business.

Toys"Я"Us is seeking to strengthen its online positioning by inevitably playing to the well-known brand. It has secured premium position on AOL's and Microsoft's shopping channels and has used its financial muscle to locate and advertise itself on the Web's most visited sites (notably Yahoo!). In addition, it has used the catalogues offered in stores and TV advertisements to notify users of its Web site. Indeed every advertisement issued by Toys"Я"Us in physical formats (TV, newspapers, etc) displays the Web site address.

It is difficult to say how effective the strategy will be, especially as most online shoppers tend to stay loyal. But as the online population grows, you do have to be optimistic that the success Toys"Я"Us has had in its physical format can be translated to the virtual format. In such a scenario, the future for the dedicated online enterprise without an established and recognized brand does not look bright. Despite this (and an admission to its shareholders that it will not make a profit for the foreseeable future), eToys has continued to expand, with the opening of an online book store and baby centre, and a recent move into the potentially lucrative European market. It has seen its product range rise from 1,000 to 10,000 since inception, and a 2,000 per cent increase in sales. However, competition is intensifying with both Amazon (which has opened a toy store) and Wal-Mart going online, and Toys"Я"Us starting to make headway in online selling.

Most online merchants try to make the purchase and search as easy as possible with the use of online catalogues and a plentiful supply of information regarding the product. This may be complemented by third-party reviews to assist the purchasing decision. An effective search engine on the site is also needed to enable consumers to find the product they desire. A user need not go from 'store' to 'store' to buy goods, as many large sites such as the search engines offer explore options across a range of 'stores'. In common with the other areas and forms of electronic commerce, the direct selling of tangible goods is driven by cost savings, the ability to customize marketing and, as mentioned, increased convenience for users – especially those for whom time is at a premium. Evidence is pointing to the fact that inventory management is becoming crucial to the success of online stores. Experience from the US has highlighted that at peak times (notably Christmas) enterprises are often lacking in stock. The fact that these enterprises rely on distributors means that they lack control over their inventory, which can work to the detriment of supplier–client relationships.

As mentioned, many Internet merchants seek to establish a presence on the Web and make themselves known to consumers through partnerships with portal sites – the major gateway to the Internet for the majority of users. The commercial success of these portals has tended to rest upon advertising revenues though many portals are seeking to extend revenues through offering electronic commerce. Enterprises can pay as much as $5 million annually to be featured on the portals and are not eager to see these sites as rivals to their online businesses. This is evidently a worry, given the power of the portals in terms of directing users to particular sites. The strain between the two could alter the strategic landscape of electronic commerce as portal sites are deprived of advertising revenue or as online merchants seek other ways of attracting shoppers. Despite this, it is still widely believed that portal commerce is only likely to represent a small minority of the overall levels of electronic commerce.

Business-to-consumer electronic commerce, in many senses, faces greater impediments to its growth than its business-to-business equivalent. This segment faces barriers, such as concerns that are common to all forms of electronic commerce regarding the security of payment, the potential for fraud, privacy of personal data and the problems in accessing electronic merchants. There also remain other evident problems in the market for business-to-consumer electronic commerce derived from its lack of critical mass. This has been caused by the problems noted below:

- The majority of households within key markets (the EU and the US) still do not have computers in the home.

- Where there are PCs, only a minority of them have online capabilities.

- Where enterprises have no apparent strategy for online sales, this tends to be due to a desire not to conflict with investments in physical stores or simply because of the absence of a technological infrastructure or physical distribution network.

- There is not a culture that breeds familiarity with buying online.

- There is a general lack of corporate resources to develop effective online sites that stimulate consumer purchases over the Internet.

- There is not a corporate culture familiar with the consequences of electronic commerce.

Evidence from the OECD (1998c) for the CD, book and software markets shows prices for these products are not markedly lower when purchased online. This suggests that electronic commerce may not deliver the benefits expected of it. The OECD places the blame not upon intrinsic faults within electronic commerce but upon the market for business-to-consumer transactions still being immature (as mentioned above). Factors such as the wealth of online customers, the premium placed upon goods derived from the convenience offered and the ability of online merchants to segment different online markets are explanations for this apparent anomaly. The evidence suggests that the benefits from the advent of electronic commerce are only going to be realized over the medium to long term. Despite the lack of evidence in terms of price differentials, the ability of the Internet to provide better information about products and services (especially from other consumers) can also be a big draw to consumers to access these sites. Thus price need not be the sole deciding factor driving electronic commerce, especially for the cash-rich, time-poor user. Indeed many consumers are interested in buying quickly and with better information, rather than simply wanting the lowest prices. This is reflected in Figure 3.9, which shows that the more wearisome the purchasing process is in the physical world, the more tempted users may be to find online user-friendly comparisons, especially in areas such as mortgages. The implication for more straight-forward purchases, such as CDs or books, is that the online merchants have to offer something more than a physical music shop if they are to prosper and attract shoppers.

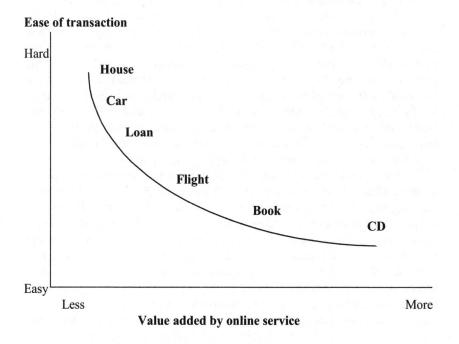

Source: Economist (1997)

Figure 3.9 *Where electronic commerce is likely to be effective*

The future development of business-to-consumer electronic commerce is going to be influenced by any number of factors. Perhaps the most important factor to drive its development will be the maturing of the (currently young) generation who possess a strong familiarity with information and communication technologies, whether it be at home or at work. Its use is also likely to increase as a result of a positive spillover from business-to-business electronic commerce over the short to medium term. This is perhaps natural because, for those businesses that engage in intra-business electronic commerce, many will feel that business-to-consumer electronic commerce is a natural progression.

Overall, those enterprises that seem to be enjoying success from the introduction of electronic commerce seem to be those possessing management structures that regard the Internet as vital to the enterprise's commercial success. This is especially true where the strategic business units operating online sales are given a greater degree of autonomy and where there is a great deal of importance attached to putting the enterprise's brand into cyberspace. The successful enterprises tend to have an Internet-driven business strategy, which stresses the brand within a highly devolved corporate structure. This is coupled with an aggressive stance on the marketing of the online facilities, and generally being user-friendly.

There are serious questions to be raised over the business model for business-to-consumer sites, because despite their relatively high profile few sites break even. Indeed it is estimated that over the short term only 5 per cent of all electronic commerce sites will register a profit. Part of the problem, certainly for the online retailers, is one of trust, as well as the potential risk involved in undertaking online purchases. Building on trust is key to generating a virtuous cycle of growth, and building up the reputation of online retailers is vital over the short to medium term. It is likely that this can only be assisted by established traditional retailers with well-known and established brands developing an online presence.

New models based upon a 'clicks and mortar' scenario (as opposed to the traditional 'bricks and mortar') are emerging as a means to secure the long-run survival of enterprises. These 'clicks and mortar' businesses are based upon an explicit collaboration between online and offline businesses. This is based upon the recognition of the relative strengths and weaknesses of each business model. The offline businesses recognize that they lack the skills to succeed in electronic commerce while the online enterprises are frustrated by a need to have a physical presence to succeed in electronic commerce. This has been especially prevalent, and not surprisingly, in the selling of tangible goods. The reassessment of the dedicated online business model has further to go given research from Boston Consulting (*Economist*, 1999a) showing that, for every dollar spent on the Web, 62 per cent goes to traditional retailers' online sites. This is compounded by the fact that it costs a dedicated electronic commerce enterprise

$42 to attract a customer compared to $22 for the Web site of a traditional retailer. This should narrow, but established brands, distribution systems and better customer support do provide a distinct competitive advantage to online retailers. To exploit this advantage fully, traditional retailers need to employ Internet-competent management – something that in many cases they have failed to do, with many preferring to take a wait-and-see perspective. Thus many of these traditional retailers, despite evident advantages, have failed to understand the full potential of the Internet as they under-exploit revenue from affiliate sites and from advertising and membership fees.

The convergence of online and offline business models appears to be driven by an at least temporary loss of confidence in the purely online business model, a feature evidenced by the intense competition experienced by dedicated online enterprises and by the corresponding losses incurred. High advertising costs – around 80 per cent of revenue for Internet-only enterprises compared to less than 20 per cent for multi-channel (those 'bricks and mortar' enterprises that also sell online) – are a major cause of such problems. Boston Consulting (*Economist*, 1999b) recently reflected on the fact that an online retailer has to spend $26 on advertising and marketing for every order it receives. These marketing costs may subside over time, but are still likely to figure as costs, as they would for any business, virtual or physical. In addition, the new online retailers simply could not compete with brands and the loyalty this gave the traditional enterprises. Traditional retailers can cross between Web site and stores. The integration of the two is not easy given the differing cultures from which each has emerged. It also requires a rethink by traditional retailers as to how exactly they use traditional formats so that online sales do not damage offline sales or vice versa. More enterprises are using the physical sites to create awareness of the online resources as well as employing the more traditional strategy of utilizing the Internet for marketing the wares of the offline store. The trend seems to point out that it will be the multi-channel retailer that succeeds.

Online strategy for the music industry

The digital distribution of music via the Internet represents both an opportunity and a threat to the music industry. The opportunity is based upon enabling record companies to take the retail margin (an average 60 per cent of the final price globally) through cutting out the retail store and selling direct to the consumer. They will need to share a proportion of the margin with the consumer in the form of lower prices, which will eat into their share. The threat, as the case study, 'Protecting intellectual property rights: the case of the music industry', in Chapter 5, p 160 highlights, is in terms of the challenge to intellectual property rights, though the industry has come to recognize that over the longer term the opportunities will heavily outweigh the threats, and that the digital challengers such as MP3 (see the same case study for an explanation) are only able to capture a small percentage of the audience. If the industry acts quickly it can prevent the spread of such captures and gain a share of the growing online market.

The sale of music on the Internet really only started to gain ground in 1997 and was very much restricted to the US. However, 1998 saw a 400 per cent increase in sales, and it is estimated that the market will be worth some $4 billion by 2005. The trend towards online music sales has been cemented by the merger of the two largest dedicated online sellers (CD-Now and N2K) into the new CD-Now, as well as the entry of Amazon (the online bookseller) into the market-place. These enterprises are in effect new intermediaries – so-called infomediaries (see the boxed section later in this chapter, 'Infomediaries: the new middlemen' on p 82). The response of record companies to these challenges will be something different.

Initially, many record companies decided not to go into selling music over the Internet believing that retailers would retaliate. The result was that major online retailers such as CD-Now were able to capture and corner the market. The record companies have come to realize that doing nothing is not an option, especially with the rise of online piracy. The need to respond is compounded by the emergence of cheaper equipment for producing and distributing music (core barriers to entry in the sector), which could cut the record companies out of the process of music production altogether. Digital technology allows users to have more unique tastes, pushing them away from the mainstream acts provided by the large record labels. The audience becomes fragmented, and this makes mass marketing more difficult. The result is that the big five record companies are expected to lose market share – declining to 64 per cent by 2008 from 78 per cent in 1998. At the same time, it is expected that independent record labels will see their market share rise.

In the light of these trends, record retailers are in clear jeopardy of either being disintermediated (by record companies selling direct to customers) or becoming the victims of re-intermediation (where sales are lost to those with a strong online presence). Traditional retailers were initially reluctant to develop an Internet presence, fearing that online sales would hit traditional outlets. As in other sectors, it is evident that the 'bricks and mortar' shops could have a brand-induced advantage if they moved to online sales. It is evident that the enterprises need to act and act soon if they are not to lose out to other developments, notably the direct digital downloading of music. In the UK, the Creation record label – largely for promotional reasons – puts its singles free of charge on the Internet a month before they are released. Not only is Creation pioneering digital download, but it is also selling its music to consumers in traditional formats through online selling. The aim is to eat into record retailers' profits. This trend is compounded by the fact that the largest online retailer, CD-Now, was planning for digital delivery by the end of 1999 – creating yet further pressure upon traditional 'bricks and mortar' retailers.

The proliferation of the Internet and rising PC penetration in the home have made digital delivery of music possible. The technology exists to achieve this and many of the large record companies are following the lead of the smaller independents in utilizing this technology. The big five record labels (BMG, EMI, Universal, Time Warner and Sony) were initially reluctant to get involved due to piracy fears, especially with the rise of the MP3 format. The challenges of the new labels and the possibility that top stars could bypass labels have led to a strategic rethink. The industry's response has been the Secure Digital Music Initiative, which seeks to balance online sales with the protection of intellectual property. In addition, IBM (in co-operation with record companies) has developed a high-security system known as the Madison Project. Initially, many of the large enterprises are moving to selling online and cutting out the retailers. Of the big five, BMG and Universal have established a joint venture to sell their music online; Sony and Time Warner are in talks about developing a similar joint venture; and EMI is developing an independent strategy to sell CDs online, and is developing an innovative strategy of allowing users to compile and customize their own CDs.

Business models in the information economy

It is important to underline that what is driving electronic commerce is the relationship between Internet technology and business models. As Table 2.1 highlighted, business models are being fundamentally altered as the impact of the information economy becomes reality for an increasing number of businesses. The shift to online trading, when combined with user-friendly technology and the Internet, shifts the power within the business model towards the buyer or consumer, who is increasingly armed with better information. Enterprises need to adapt by offering continuity and frequently complementarity between old and new business models. In essence, the precise type of business model chosen (see below) to meet the challenges of the information economy revolves around the core strategic issues of whom the business sells to, what products it sells, how they are sold, how the order is dealt with and who is providing services to the enterprise. The enterprise will then need to assess the extent to which each is impacted upon by or can be improved through electronic commerce.

The choice of business model essentially comes down to a decision as to whether to make the model seller- or buyer-centric. The choice will place the emphasis upon the relevant party in terms of engaging and supporting the transaction. Building upon this theme, Berryman *et al* (1998) highlighted that the strategic model adopted will reflect the market-place within which enterprises are operating. Consequently, models will be based around one of the following frameworks:

- *Seller-controlled market-places.* These are usually established with a single seller seeking many buyers with the purpose of creating or maintaining value as well as market power within the transaction process. In this instance, the Web site can be an online equivalent of the traditional operation or can (as is becoming increasingly common) be a dedicated online service.

- *Buyer-controlled market-places.* These are set either singly or as a result of collaboration between a number of buyers with the purpose of shifting value and market power within the market-place. Some may use an intermediary depending upon the strength of the buyer in question. The rationale is to gain market power through advertising for tenders through online systems to find the most attractive supplier. The intermediary, acting either as an aggregator or an agent, can help smaller enterprises find the most efficient suppliers.

- *Neutral market-places.* These are essentially established to match up many buyers with many sellers. They can work to enable enterprises to lower inventory, as well as enabling buyers access to lower-cost supplies.

It is evident that many of the emerging business models within the information economy are buyer-centric (this is broadly evident in the models noted below). In many instances, it will be buyers who force the change in the business model as their purchasing strategies alter to stress online transactions. In terms of business-to-business electronic commerce, new models based upon automated purchasing and anonymous exchange will shift power towards buyers. In the business-to-consumer sector, consumer information exchange sites will have a similar effect.

The business models that are currently in use or being tested are as follows (Timmins, 1998):

- *E-shop.* This involves the Web marketing of an enterprise. The initial strategy is to stress the promotion of the enterprise's products or services through the medium of the Internet. Over time, the capabilities of the enterprise through this medium are extended to include ordering and payment. These functions are often combined with the more traditional marketing channels. Thus the development of this business model allows for the benefits associated with electronic commerce to be enjoyed in terms of cost reduction and easier access to the global market-place. As the site is used again and again, so the Web site owner is able to use the model to stimulate further demand through means such as one-to-one marketing. The e-shop is the most common expression of the commercial Web site where there is the direct selling of tangible and/or intangible products, and is best thought of as an online equivalent of the traditional 'bricks and mortar' retail store with revenue derived by much the same means.

- *E-procurement.* As the term suggests, this is the online procurement and tendering for goods and services. These systems are increasingly being used by large enterprises and public authorities as a means of securing greater value and efficiency within the purchasing process. The use of this business model allows the purchasers to have a wider choice of suppliers, not only lowering costs but also enhancing both delivery and quality. These processes may also be complemented by electronic negotiation and contracting, and feasibly collaboration between partners over specifications. There are also benefits to tenderers who might otherwise have found themselves excluded from the process. The major sources of revenue within this business model are derived from the savings realized by procurers.

- *E-auction.* This business model offers the online equivalent of the traditional auction, providing for a bidding process where sellers and buyers interact to sell products. Increasingly the bidding function of such systems is being enhanced with payment, contracting and delivery systems. Within this business model, the major sources of revenues are derived from the selling of the technology platform, transaction fees and advertising. For suppliers, the development of online systems offers efficiencies in terms of time savings, lower transaction costs and sourcing efficiencies. There are also benefits to suppliers in terms of the better use of inventories, allowing enterprises to get rid of surplus stock, improve their utilization of productive capacity and, consequently, enjoy lower sales overheads.

- *E-mall.* Like its physical equivalent, this is a collection of e-shops offered together via a single-point-of-access Web site – the e-mall. The stores involved are usually linked together through a common theme such as a brand, industrial sector or even payment method. When the e-mall is focused upon a particular sector, it resembles an industry market-place. Value can be added by the establishment of virtual communities alongside these malls. The development of the business model associated with e-malls varies. In some cases, the rationale for the 'proprietor' is to use the model as a platform for the enhanced sales of supporting technology (such as IBM did with its now defunct World Avenue mall). In other cases, the proprietor may seek to develop the mall to market its own service to those, both sellers and buyers, who operate on the mall. Others who offer the site may seek to generate revenues through advertising or brand reinforcement. There can be benefits expected by the e-shops through traffic spillover, as visitors to sites in the mall also visit the other e-shops, which, it is hoped, generates further sales. The benefits to users of the e-mall arise from convenience, lower costs and, if a brand is used, greater trust. To members of the mall, there are benefits to be had in terms of operating in a more user-friendly environment and gaining greater credibility with users. Revenues to the mall owner, in addition to those noted above, are derived from membership fees and possibly a share of the transactions. Currently many e-malls are commercially immature with some malls opening as others close. Part of this instability is due to the fact that many of the current users do not necessarily need the 'mall' concept to make their shopping easier, as many users are broadly familiar with the Internet and tend not be overwhelmed by the technology. As electronic commerce starts to mature, the need for these malls may become more apparent. Indeed Amazon has announced that it intends to transform itself into the world's biggest mall by opening its site to other retailers.

- *Third-party market-place.* This is still a relatively immature market model developed for those enterprises that may wish to leave the development of their Web strategy to third parties. This could create a common marketing front with transaction support to a number of businesses with a common user interface. This business model could be used in those instances where common marketing is provided to support sales during a one-off event (for example, as a device to aid online Christmas sales). In this business model, revenues would be generated through membership fees and service charges.

- *Virtual communities.* The focus in virtual communities is upon providing members with extra value through the sharing of information. The basic framework is provided by the virtual enterprise, which is able to generate revenues through membership fees as well as advertising. The virtual community can be an extra feature of the online marketing environment as in the case of Amazon and other online retailers where users can offer their own reviews of products to enable others users to possess the necessary information to make a less risky purchase. These communities can also be used to enhance the capabilities of other business models, especially e-malls and third-party market-places.

- *Value chain service providers.* As the name suggests, these specialize within a specific segment of the value chain. This would include aspects such as electronic payments, logistics or security. This business model enables revenue to be generated through fees or extra sales. Typical examples are the uses of this technology offered by Federal Express through its online tracking system (see the case study earlier in this chapter, 'The express delivery sector: the case of Federal Express' on p 54).

- *Value chain integrators.* In contrast to the above, this business model focuses upon integrating different parts of the value chain as a means of aiding the flow of information between its constituent parts. The survival of this business model depends upon consultancy fees or possibly on taking a share of transactions generated.

- *Collaboration platforms.* These are business scenarios that allow for the establishment of collaboration between users. They can focus upon specific functions such as design or engineering. Revenues from this business model can be derived from a number of sources such as managing the platform or selling specialist tools. In many instances, this model exists within research communities.

- *Information brokerage, trust and other services.* This is a new range of services adding value to the large quantities of data generated and available upon the Internet. Included in this domain are information searchers (such as the portals), customer profiling, business opportunities brokerages and investment advice.

Overall, what Timmins offers is an analysis from assorted trials and tests of the form and types of business emerging online. Samuelson (1998) offers a simpler perspective, believing that sites can be categorized according to their core function, which can be either vanity (a mere outlet for self-expression), information (providing users with the knowledge needed for transactions), advertising (using the site to stimulate offline transactions), subscription (content-based sites with a specialist audience) or as a store front (where products are sold direct to the customer). Evidently each of these functions has its own model, and the more commercial forms may simply reflect mature strategies to which enterprises utilizing earlier models gradually adapt as their information strategy matures.

Freeserve: The business model of an Internet service provider

Freeserve, founded by the UK electronic retailer Dixons, is an Internet service provider (ISP) that fundamentally altered the prevailing business model in the sector. Freeserve was conceived in 1997 and since that date has attracted more than 1.3 million users in the UK – some 31 per cent of the market and more than twice the size of its nearest competitor, America On-line (AOL). It is estimated that its user base will grow to 5 million by 2004 – some 24 per cent of the market. One of the core features for successful business models in the information economy is being first to the market, which Freeserve achieved in terms of offering subscription-fee-free Internet access. Its strong position has been enhanced by being founded as a subsidiary of Dixons, the UK's biggest PC retailer, which enabled it to distribute its free software cheaply and easily. The aggressive marketing stance taken by the enterprise has not only allowed it to achieve large market share but also has allowed it to establish a strong online brand. Its timing was also right. It provided user-friendly access at a time when the hype of the Internet was starting to translate itself into mass appeal. Its pre-eminence among UK ISPs is only likely to be challenged if a rival can come up with an innovative business model for delivering online access.

As Freeserve did not charge a subscription fee, it had to generate as much revenue as possible from other sources. Central to this strategy is keeping its customers' attention and ensuring they stay on its site. If it can keep customers on its site and, even better, encourage them to return, then the site will develop loyalty amongst its users – so-called 'stickiness'. The stickier the site, the more it can justify the costs of advertising, etc. Other sources of revenue for the business are derived from a slice of telephone revenues and commission fees from transactions stimulated by its site. Freeserve charges advertisers and electronic commerce groups fees based upon the number of visitors, their length of stay and the amount of shopping they do. Freeserve outsources all of its infrastructure needs; as a result its cut of the telephone revenues is modest – around 10 per cent. Other ISPs with their own infrastructure get the lion's share of this revenue source – an estimated 90 per cent. Despite this, call revenue is currently the biggest earner for Freeserve.

Now that Freeserve has changed the prevailing business model for UK ISPs (there are now over 100 other ISPs), it has to stay ahead (especially as many others are adopting a similar model) and increase the premium attached to developing the stickiness of its site. Without this, advertising and electronic commerce revenues – which are central to the long-term viability of the business model – are under serious question. This is especially important, as increased competition in the telecommunications market is expected to undermine revenues from the cost of telephone calls. Therefore Freeserve is seeking to become more than just an access site through offering a broader range of value-adding services such as financial services, news and travel services with a shift to chat rooms and auctions planned. Currently UK ISPs only sell some 15–17 per cent of advertising space. To attract advertisers, Freeserve clearly has to sustain its dominance, hence its evolution into a hybrid business model: it is seeking to become not just an ISP but also a portal and a focal point for electronic retailing. This latter aspect is especially important to the future of Freeserve. It is putting a lot of faith in the growth of electronic commerce and the revenues it is expecting to earn from that source. However, as an intermediary between retailer and customer, it will only receive a small cut of the revenue generated.

The finances of the enterprise are uncertain. In 1999, it made a loss of £8.8 million though, like other online businesses, it may have to endure losses over the short to medium term while it waits for the Internet market – and especially electronic commerce – to mature. However, concerns over the future of Freeserve have to be expressed, notably whether the business model can survive while the market waits for the Internet market to mature. Can it secure the necessary degree of consumer loyalty? How will it adjust to new forms of Internet access from televisions or mobile phones? These are clearly strategic challenges that Freeserve is facing or has yet to address.

Making money from the Internet is tough, and there are a lot of challenges that the Freeserve business model has to withstand. However, the enterprise has recognized that it needs to evolve constantly if it is to stay ahead of the expanding number of rivals. It clearly needs to offer attention-catching content if it is to prove viable over the longer term. This will be neither cheap nor easy. Other issues are also evident in the free ISP business model of Freeserve, notably that its popularity is derived from its cost to consumers, who are likely to exhibit little loyalty towards it. The model has stimulated copycat enterprises, and users can easily bypass the home page. Indeed it is already evident that Freeserve is starting to suffer as its major rivals (most notably AOL) start to adopt the same business model, with the result that the enterprise will have to place greater emphasis on site content to breed loyalty amongst evidently fickle customers.

To date, the most common business model has been one in which online users pay nothing for content and where advertising underwrites most costs. This model is coming under pressure as the number of users accessing sites through all forms of online advertisements continues to drop. Indeed new software has emerged that allows users to block certain types of advertisement. This, combined with a belief amongst consumers that the content delivered over these free sites is increasingly of little value, means that the traditional online business model begins to look suspect. Therefore many enterprises are moving towards a different transaction model as users shift towards sites that deliver greater value to them, notably in terms of interactivity. Consequently the prevailing business model is shifting towards interactive models based upon subscription or transaction-derived revenue. The model of an Internet driven by advertising is ultimately unsustainable, as enterprises are merely swapping advertising budgets.

Initial evidence in the formative years of the development of electronic commerce does highlight the viability of some business models over others. Initial success seems to be based upon first-mover advantage and establishing a brand that is recognizable, easy to find on the Internet and attractive to users. Aside from the very high profile sites, the most viable business models seem to be those that are able to aggregate thinly spread demand – something the Internet is clearly able to do. In addition, the business models based upon targeting cash-rich, time-poor individuals also seem to have attracted attention. There is still concern over the viability of these business models, despite the high valuations they often receive when they engage in a stock-market flotation. The longer-term viability of these models is as yet unproved, and many sites are earning low returns relative to turnover. Investors are clearly taking a gamble on the belief that business models will achieve viability as and when electronic commerce reaches commercial maturity. When it does, these first starters, so the logic goes, will be in position to dominate their respective market segments.

It is evident that the business models involved with the advent of electronic commerce will alter with the capabilities induced by changes in technology. Initial business models linked to online trading were unsophisticated, based upon operating the physical equivalent, as far as possible, online. This often simply involved utilizing the Web site as a simple marketing function to push users towards the traditional physical outlets. Despite the evident rise in profile of the capabilities of the Internet for electronic commerce, there is still a lot to be done by many enterprises. Many have yet to alter their business models to account for the Internet's interactive capabilities. The result is that many are merely using the new media for simple electronic publishing and the transmission of corporate and product information. A survey in *Information Strategy* (1998) highlighted this lack of alteration in business models. This argued that – for the majority of businesses surveyed – there were only moderate effects in terms of the business model enabling better customer relationships. On the whole, enterprises were poor at offering special promotions or pricing policies through the Web.

The strategy for enterprises that know they need to adopt electronic commerce depends upon their perceptions of what exactly their Web site should seek to achieve. In this context, the adoption of the correct business model is essential. Once this is decided, it needs to be complemented by heavy investment in the enabling infrastructure. Inevitably, the new business model has to be the one that is best suited in terms of the enterprise's response to the challenges posed by electronic commerce. It is evident that greater customization and control of inventories will be integral to the success of the enterprise. Business models are clearly evolving under pressure from the increasingly finite nature of existing revenue streams (ie advertising), from investors who want a return and from software that allows unique services that are more adept at generating revenue from subscriptions, licensing and other similar sources. These trends are resulting in new businesses developing models based upon differentiation rather than competing head on. Consequently business models are evolving from the forms mentioned into ones that stress uniqueness of product or service, competitive pricing, better marketing and smarter technology. These underline the need for flexibility within online business models.

Business models in electronic commerce: the online auction

As highlighted above, electronic auction sites appear to be among the few sites that currently have viable business models in the arena of business-to-consumer electronic commerce. This viability is essentially derived from low entry costs to the Internet and the capability of the model to aggregate a geographically dispersed audience to sell products. Electronic auctions, which started as an alternative to classified advertisements in newspapers, are also seen to work as a business model, as they tend to induce site stickiness, that is they engage users and keep them coming back to the site.

The electronic auction differs from other business models within the information economy, as it works to the advantages of Internet trading rather than simply offering an innovative form of traditional trading. Auctions, based upon soliciting a wide range of bids from many people over the Internet, are possible through the capabilities to offer cheap interconnection to millions of people. Indeed Internet technology makes auctions easier whilst at the same time making them more sophisticated. The leading online auctioneer eBay (which started in September 1995) offers 2.4 million items in over 1,500 categories and attracts over 3.8 million users in this evolving Internet community. Every day, eBay hosts over 1.4 million auctions with a quarter of a million items added to the 'for sale' list and nearly a million bids placed daily. The basis for the success of eBay is collectors, though it is increasingly becoming an online distribution channel for small businesses. In addition, it has successfully established an online community through creating a common interest, which (as mentioned) encourages users to return time and time again. On eBay, there is a great deal of price transparency – all bids and bidders are published.

The attraction of the auction is that it has the capability to generate a great deal of cash for nominal effort. Indeed eBay, the leading online auctioneer, is one of the few online enterprises that is currently exhibiting a viable business model. The costs to the business are minimized, as the customer does much of the work. The seller writes and posts the advertisement and is informed by e-mail who has won the auction when it is over. The buyer and the seller then work out the transaction details. The system is even policed by the users. Thus the role of eBay is merely to maintain the site, offer a minimal level of customer support, and collect fees every time an advertisement is posted and a commission for every item sold. As costs of carriage are borne by the consumer, overheads are kept to a minimum. The result of this business model is that eBay, on a staff base of 138, was able to obtain gross margins of 85 per cent on $19.5 million revenues. One of the other attractions of this business model is that its successes are self-perpetuating in an era of rapid Internet growth – the more people who visit the site and offer goods, the better the choice, the quicker the goods sell and the more people who come back.

The cost level of the enterprise is significantly lower for the online auction when compared to other online trading models. It is estimated that it costs the online auctioneer $12 to get a new customer: for some online brokerages this figure is closer to $400. The success of eBay and other online auctioneers is starting to attract others with new models. For example, Yahoo! is offering its online auction free. This strategy may be undermined if users do not mind paying fees if they know that the pay site has a larger user base and therefore a greater chance of selling the product at a higher sale price.

Currently, many of these sites operate as effective garage sales but the success of the model is leading to others in the retail sector. It can be a more effective device for selling excess inventory than previous strategies of simple discounting. For example, the airline industry is exhibiting this with its yield management techniques, which are sophisticated computer programs to adjust prices with the aim of filling the largest number of seats at the highest possible prices. Lufthansa, the German airline, used this technique when it began auctioning excess tickets. Not only did this get rid of the extra tickets but it also increased markedly the traffic on the site. Hoteliers and car rental firms are trying similar techniques. Enterprises such as Priceline.com have developed on the back of a name-your-price culture on portable consumer commodities such as the aforementioned airline tickets and hotel rooms. Like others, it makes its money on listing fees and commission on sales.

Many of the online auctions occurring are based upon person-to-person selling. Over time this is expected to be dwarfed by business-to-consumer auctions. In addition, the electronic auction is extending to business-to-business electronic commerce. Enterprises such as General Electric are using this method to seek out low-cost suppliers. The notion of consumers buying goods based on what those goods are worth to them and not dictated by the producer is revolutionary. This could be an initial but very tangible expression of the power of consumers in the information economy and offers an environment where online auction houses can only flourish.

The online auction business model is challenged by consumer uncertainties in terms of fraud and the selling of illegal goods – indeed Microsoft and eBay have clashed over the selling of illegal software on the site. This could undermine the viability of the business model, which could come under challenge if these enterprises are forced to monitor every sale. Many enterprises that are losers from fraud or the selling of counterfeit goods are pressing for the online auctioneers to take responsibility for what is sold. The practicalities of this are difficult given the sheer quantity of goods sold (around 250,000 a day) and the fact that the auctioneer never physically has hold of the goods sold and therefore cannot be expected to verify their existence. To help cope with this, many online auctions have set up 'legal buddy' systems where companies can notify the business of the selling of illegal goods, and the illegal auction is then closed. This allows regular sellers to develop a credible reputation through a rating and comment system based upon customer experience. Illegal transactions, so eBay claims, account for a mere 0.01 per cent of all the trade carried out on the site.

Disintermediation and the emergence of infomediaries

With the development of new business models and alterations to existing industry value chains, changes are occurring in the role of intermediaries in the information economy. In traditional retailing, there is a market chain from the creator or manufacturer to the retailer via a distributor. Within this context, the link between the producers and the final consumer has the wholesaler and the retailer acting as intermediaries. The role of the wholesaler is to aggregate products in a central unit and thereafter sell them to retailers. In an environment of electronic commerce, there is the increased possibility of disintermediation, where intermediaries are bypassed with the producer or manufacturer selling direct to the consumer. This trend is potentially evident in areas such as the travel industry and the music sector (see the case study above, 'Online strategy for the music industry' on p 69).

This potential for disintermediation reflects the fact that the Internet can effectively remove bottlenecks (as represented by intermediaries) within many sectors. This process is stimulated by developments such as:

- decreasing search costs – as users start to utilize online search engines to find whatever they want whenever they want it;

- reduced entry barriers – low connection costs provide all online businesses with an electronic distribution channel;

- automation of activity – the development of multimedia also allows for the automation of tasks that were once performed by employees.

The development of electronic commerce has the potential to make a substantial impact across a wide range of functional areas. There is clearly potential for disintermediation in areas such as Web-based sales and marketing services. It is already evident that enterprises are bypassing the need for customer representatives and costly house calls. For example, *Encyclopaedia Britannica* effectively disintermediated its door-to-door sales force when it offered its product free over the Internet. In internal areas, the advent of the Internet facilitates knowledge management by spreading information more easily throughout the enterprise thereby overcoming the need for middle managers and librarians (see Chapter 2). Thus, in sum, the process of disintermediation will allow enterprises to reduce direct costs as well as the time needed to perform certain functions. Consequently adjusting systems to account for the process of disintermediation could prove central to an enterprise sustaining competitive positioning within the information economy and allowing the enterprise to capture extra value through the squeezing out of existing businesses.

Despite the logic of disintermediation, there is increasing evidence to suggest that increases in the level of electronic commerce could actually have the opposite effect and actually increase the reliance upon inter-mediaries through a process of re-intermediation as opposed to disinter-mediation. In terms of re-intermediation, the intermediary function remains though it has been fundamentally altered by the advent of online trading through the emergence of so-called infomediaries (see the boxed section below, 'The infomediaries: the new middlemen'). These infomediaries are often new dedicated online enterprises (such as Amazon or CD-Now). Many traditional intermediaries are altering their business models to take advantage of the Internet to stymie the potential disintermediation and to establish themselves as recognized infomediaries. This has been evident through the strategies of banks and through (as mentioned above) the strategies of traditional 'bricks and mortar' retailers in establishing an online intermediary role. This process is assisted by the relative marketing power of the major incumbents. Indeed an evident threat is posed to travel agents by many of these enterprises establishing online reservation systems and attracting customers through brand loyalty.

The infomediaries: the new middlemen

An infomediary is a Web site that provides specialized information on behalf of producers of goods and services, and potential customers. The development of the Internet has made it possible for users to access online information databases at any time and any place. The advent of information and communications technology has allowed these infomediaries to gather, analyse and redistribute information. In this process, they create new services or add value to existing ones. Bringing these information aggregates together and adding these services to them is a growing business for a number of enterprises. Essentially the function of the infomediaries is to:

- organize buyers;
- organize sellers;
- organize the market through
  - matchmaking,
  - aggregation of needs,
  - a bid/ask engine,
  - hidden inventory,
  - a referral service.

Thus the fundamental role of these infomediaries is to create online markets and stimulate transactions through their ability to synthesize the information available on the Internet in a user-friendly and accessible manner.

Infomediary sites are prevalent in both business-to-business and business-to-consumer electronic commerce. Early experience has highlighted that they are tending to be more common in the former than the latter (as is to be expected given the relative size of business-to-business electronic commerce). The infomediaries have proved especially useful in allowing enterprises to access a broader range of suppliers than would otherwise have been available, offering major sourcing benefits to users. Currently it is estimated that these infomediaries have around 10 per cent of the business-to-business electronic commerce market.

The most successful infomediaries are those that are aggregators and syndicates of electronic content for a particular market niche. In their ability to stimulate transactions and therefore create an environment in which electronic commerce can flourish, these bodies have an important role to play in the development of the information economy. Many of the initial success stories in the early days of electronic commerce have been of infomediaries who exploited general unfamiliarity with the system for their commercial advantage.

In the early stages of the development of electronic commerce, the intermediary function was largely performed by search engines and agents to enable consumers to find the relevant products and services. Increasingly other business models are emerging to perform this intermediary role, notably Internet shopping malls. In addition, assorted payment schemes (such as credit cards) are also performing an intermediary function, as sellers accepted by the major payment cards are seen as possessing the necessary degree of legitimacy.

In terms of business-to-business commerce, it is evident that three business models are emerging for infomediaries:

- *Aggregators.* These assist buyers in fragmented product markets through the provision of information and a single point of contact.

- *Online auctioneers.* These offer a legitimate channel for sellers to dispose of perishable products and surplus goods at the best possible prices as well as allowing buyers to obtain bargain prices.

- *Exchanges.* These create fluidity within fragmented markets by matching bid and ask prices and acting as neutral third parties to enforce market rules and best practice.

These models all have in common the fact that they seek to bring together buyers and sellers in markets that are fragmented due to either geography or to the fact that there are a large number of small operators within the market.

The potential of infomediaries is strengthened by the ability of these sites to exploit the core features of trade on the Internet: they shift power to consumers, lower transactions costs and increase the speed with which information can be distributed and accessed. The strength of infomediaries will also rely upon their ability to be recognized by users within the industry as the key resources for a particular market segment. This will enable them to become the core focus of attention for interested users. If they define themselves too broadly, their focus and impact will be negated. Intermediaries will only prosper if they can be seen to add value. For example, in financial services infomediaries have emerged that not only offer best-buy analysis but also (unlike the newspaper equivalent) offer the ability to purchase there and then. Others use e-mail to keep customers informed of when better products emerge. This can create a problem for traditional financial service players who may wish to cut out the infomediary, but as the latter will effectively own the customer (via its information collection) this will be difficult.

It is predicted that there will be some 100,000 infomediaries by 2001 – up from around 300 in 1999. These infomediaries will not conform to the traditional model of the middleman but will add value by promoting an understanding of the online market-place. These sites exist where there are evident problems that limit market creation and movement, for example in cases such as poor information or high transport costs. Overall, there are clearly assorted intermediary functions needed within the development of the information economy and the acceptance of these players is key to the development of electronic commerce by both buyers and sellers. These intermediary functions are therefore an important facilitator factor in electronic commerce. They stimulate not only competition on the Internet but also competition between intermediaries, which will be just as important in terms of influencing the competitive nature of trade over the Internet.

Re-intermediation in the car retailing sector

This sector provides a good example of the emergence of a new breed of infomediaries. Sites such as Carpoint and AutoWeb.Com have automated much of the process related to the evaluation and processing of bids and loans needed in car purchasing. These sites operate vast databases containing information about thousands of cars, containing all the information needed to make the purchase as easy and risk-free as possible. They allow the customer to have a central reference point of purchase and direct them to the dealer that offers them the best deal. The site can also be used to speed up the obtaining of a loan (through finance partners) to purchase the car as well as enabling all the necessary paperwork to be completed speedily. The key point is that when the customer arrives to pick up the car all the paperwork is completed and the car is ready to the user's specifications.

The by-product of this development is a major change in the role of car dealers and showrooms. Dealerships are moving away from making people buy cars towards customer service. It is estimated that in recognition of the growing importance of the Internet in the car purchasing process nearly two-thirds of dealers have Web sites with even more having staff dedicated to Internet sales. In some cases, there are dealers who estimate that nearly 65 per cent of enquires are derived from online information. Indeed it is now believed that up to a quarter of purchasers of new cars use the Internet at some stage of the process – something that has created a mass of better-informed buyers. The infomediaries have helped solve the problem of asymmetric information between buyer and seller that has always tended to limit car purchases.

Carpoint has a business model based upon a network of over 2,000 dealers, each of which pays a flat monthly fee, has been vetted and has a dedicated Carpoint person on site. The customer e-mails his or her requirements into Carpoint, which directs the customer to local dealerships that can meet these needs. The dealer then contacts the customer. The model is designed to work especially for cash-rich, time-poor people. AutoWeb ensures that all dealers who wish to be referenced on the system are subject to a contract that binds them to offering the lowest prices for their products with an acceptable level of services. Customers of the site are contacted to ensure these guarantees are observed. If they are not, the dealer is dropped from the site.

Many of the infomediaries make their money through online advertising and through user charges. Most of these sites have a high dealer turnover, which means that many of them need to spend substantial revenues upon advertising and reassess the fees charged to dealers constantly. The market leader is AutobyTel, which may not have the largest dealership network but is able to offer most success in terms of sales. In addition, for used car markets, many of the online infomediaries are readjusting business models to facilitate used car auctions. Despite these trends, the infomediaries still account for only some 2 per cent of all sales. This highlights that perhaps the best function of these sites is in the information they provide to users who are thinking about purchasing a car. This information has always been available; it is just that the Internet makes it easier to access. The trends indicate that traditional middlemen are safe for the foreseeable future. However, they do need to be aware that the new middlemen are empowering the consumer.

Small and medium-sized enterprises and electronic commerce

Small and medium-sized enterprises (SMEs) are pivotal to the commercial evolution of the information economy – in most industrialized states they account for over 90 per cent of all businesses. Not only will the utilization of this technology by these enterprises offer them more opportunities to compete more effectively on a global stage with larger-scale enterprises, but also take-up in this segment is key to the information market reaching maturity. The spread of electronic commerce to SMEs is the result of a number of factors, notably a desire by their major customers (especially large enterprises) that these businesses should be more integrated into the industry-wide value chain. Further 'push' is provided by policy measures that directly seek to stimulate awareness of the opportunities of electronic commerce as well as the all-important general market trends. The development of the aforementioned innovative business models should also prove positive, as these are often suited to SMEs (see below). SMEs, through developing first-mover advantages and establishing niches through online sales, have the capability to challenge the larger enterprises seriously. Of course, this does depend on the reciprocated strategies of the larger enterprises resulting in those businesses being slow to adopt the online model.

Evidence does indicate that SMEs involved in electronic commerce tend to be more innovative in terms of their business model. Generally, there are two main kinds of SME in respect of electronic commerce: 1) those SMEs whose existence relies upon the Internet and who therefore generate almost all their sales and customer communications through this medium; and 2) those SMEs that are experimenting with the new distribution channel as a means of complementing their existing capabilities, and that only generate a fraction of their overall sales from this medium as a result.

To date, the majority of SMEs fall into the latter category, though it has to be mentioned that it is very hard to find a dedicated online trader that is not an SME. In many cases, SMEs use electronic commerce as a differentiator to enable them to reach markets that they previously could not reach. In this context, the dedicated Internet enterprise is tending to have greater success.

A survey by Chappell and Feindt (1999) indicated a number of critical success factors for SMEs in electronic commerce (many of which are in fact probably ubiquitous to enterprises of all sizes).

- *Content.* The enterprise offers a unique product or service that is easily deliverable and commercially viable over the Internet – otherwise an electronic commerce strategy may simply drain resources. Ideally the product should be new or innovative, which is important given that many SMEs are customer-facing and need to be seen to be adding value to be attractive to customers.

- *Commitment.* The business model shows a clear set of objectives in the use of the Internet.

- *Community.* The enterprise has the ability to build up a critical mass of customers or business partners for the venture, which enables the objectives of the business model to be realized.

- *Control.* The business is able to integrate external and internal processes to realize cost savings and revenue creation, and also to stimulate innovation and further growth. The integration of electronic commerce into enterprise processes is key to allowing SMEs control of this technology. The integration becomes especially important as the percentage of total sales made online increases.

- *Technology.* Underpinning all these factors is the manner of the usage of technology by SMEs. Clearly if it is not used correctly, it will be difficult to be successful in electronic commerce. Without the technology, a business cannot be built and the enterprise cannot control it. Increasingly the technological competence of an SME will determine how successful that enterprise's electronic commerce strategy will ultimately be.

As mentioned above, over the longer term the take-up of electronic commerce by SMEs is likely to be forced by their position in the supply chains of larger enterprises. There is a risk that if SMEs wait for this to happen they could find themselves disintermediated by larger trading blocks. Alternatively, if they can add value to these large trading blocks they could be re-intermediated. In many cases, SMEs may not be able to enjoy the full benefits of the supply chain integration due to their limited technological know-how. In some cases this can place the emphasis upon larger businesses to educate SMEs and act as overarching catalysts in such matters. Clearly the generic benefits in terms of cost savings, time savings and quality improvements from electronic commerce are available to SMEs. Of these, the latter two seem to be more important than simply utilizing the technology to improve cost positions. However, low rates of adoption will inevitably hinder the benefits. Typically SMEs face large problems in implementing and developing new technological systems and methods. Paramount amongst these have been the inhibitions to uptake of electronic commerce caused by the sheer cost of investment. This is evidently the largest problem for those SMEs that are not dedicated online traders. Other problems likely to be faced include:

- cultural factors (especially for family businesses);

- infrastructure;

- imposition by large enterprises leading to divergence between technology investments and business problems;

- lack of awareness of electronic commerce;

- uncertainty of benefits;

- lack of suitable products to be sold through this medium;

- the lack of maturity of electronic commerce;

- security;

- absence of sound legal framework;

- cost of consumer access;

- lack of adequate human resources and skills base;

- political factors.

Despite these barriers, there are evident successes in SME use of electronic commerce. This is especially true where an enterprise is a dedicated online seller. Small businesses with this technology at the core of their business model have led these enterprises to seek a greater emphasis on making electronic commerce work. Such a strategy allows these SMEs to utilize electronic commerce as a viable distribution channel sooner rather than later. The success of SMEs on the Internet may be due simply to first-mover advantage – the Internet is a new commercial environment and is therefore more likely to be adopted by small low-risk start-ups. Their advantage is coupled with the time bigger businesses take to develop Web sites, the relative youth of the entrepreneurs involved in Internet business and, more importantly, the problem many larger businesses have in reconciling online and traditional business models within corporate strategy.

In the end, SMEs' adoption of electronic commerce depends upon their perception of the opportunities afforded by this technology. In this area, policy makers may play an increasingly important role in terms of spreading best practice, diffusing knowledge and demonstrating the potential of electronic commerce to as broad an audience as possible. Policy makers have been especially keen to include SMEs within the information economy. To assist in this objective, a great deal of effort is directed towards breeding a familiarity within these enterprises of the potential of ICTs for improvements in functioning. Much state support is directed to providing funding for projects relevant to SMEs within particular sectors. Thus programmes have sought to improve online access to information to aid cheap sourcing and marketing. The UK's Information Society Initiative is a good example of how the state is seeking to integrate SMEs into the information economy through the provision of advice and stimulation of awareness.

In addition, there are specialist companies emerging to service the requirements of small businesses through the Internet. Examples include IPrint.com (which offers printing services to small businesses), Eletter.com (offering mailshots from its site) and MyProspects.com (offering commercial mailing lists in small quantities), each of which offers a simplified process for marketing and printing facilities for small businesses. Such enterprises offer the opportunity for the potential savings expected from business-to-business electronic commerce to be realized by all enterprises regardless of size. Enterprises supplying services to small businesses are one of the fastest growing areas of electronic commerce. These enterprises are often able not only to offer lower prices but also to offer a better, more personalized service. It is also evident that enterprises are developing to advise and save SMEs time by finding and recruiting qualified staff. The adoption of electronic commerce by SMEs is likely to be aided by the development of 'server farms' where centrally controlled computer capacity is leased out by large IT businesses (such as Intel) to enterprises unable to afford their own data centres to support their electronic commerce solutions.

Conclusion

Electronic commerce is very much seen as the core driver behind the development of the information economy, and is the source of many of the benefits identified in Chapter 2. This should not be surprising given that it is the most obvious method of transferring activity from the physical to the virtual environment. The emergence of electronic commerce is going to be driven by online transactions between businesses. Although business-to-consumer electronic commerce has a higher profile, it will remain very much the lesser form of online trading. As electronic commerce starts to mature, new business models are expected to emerge and firms will be forced to adapt or flounder. One of the most notable changes in terms of these business models is likely to be felt in the process of re-intermediation, as new online intermediaries emerge to facilitate online trade. It seems that the possibility of disintermediation (where middlemen are removed totally from the distribution process) has been overplayed.

4 The information industry

The technological and commercial convergence of the telecommunications, information technology and content industries is stimulating the development of an information industry. The development of this information industry is key to the development of the information economy, as it is widely recognized that there is a close link between the health of the sector and the ability of ICTs to improve the performance of an economy and the enterprises therein. The commercial impact of the developing information industry is not judged merely upon its impact on other enterprises but also on the ability of these enterprises to be successful in what is an emerging global information market. It is the aforementioned process of convergence that forms the core theme of this chapter. It is deliberately explored at length with the initial and final sections being devoted to the process. The initial section introduces the concept; the final part draws on the experiences of the telecommunications, IT and content sectors (which form the remainder of the chapter) to understand the commercial practicalities of the process. It will be evident throughout the chapter that the process of convergence is having its most visible expression in the growth of the Internet – based as it is upon the interaction of telecommunications, the processing power of computers and online content. Consequently, much of the chapter will analyse developments within this context.

The evolving information industry structure

The information industries (telecommunications, IT and content sectors) are undergoing a process of substantial commercial and technological change. Industry structures are changing and new cross-sectoral relationships emerging, creating a radical restructuring of the information economy's supply side as new players appear and current players establish fresh roles. These changes are spurred by:

- the oft-mentioned convergence of technologies used within the respective sectors;

- the globalization of the markets for information products and services;

- the re-regulation of the information industries (see Chapter 5).

Such changes are creating a situation where existing players across the telecommunications, IT and content sectors are increasingly finding their positions challenged by products and services from outside the traditionally defined domains of their respective sectors. This trend is both enabling and stimulating companies within the information industries to reposition themselves in the integrated value chain that is emerging due to the convergence process (see Figure 4.3).

Convergence in services and distribution technologies is likely to stimulate the integration and transformation of the value chains throughout the information industry. It is likely that enterprises active at particular points in the separate telecommunications, IT or broadcasting industry value chains will have to adjust, develop new strategies and establish new relationships with other enterprises in similar or related fields. As Figure 4.1 reflects, before digitalization, globalization and convergence these sectors were distinctly separate markets, which were often dominated by monopoly suppliers across several layers. In some cases, such as telecommunications and broadcasting, there was a close degree of integration, as the infrastructure owners also controlled the direct relationship with the customer.

The separation and independence of these separate value chains is not going to be sustained, as the process of convergence is likely to affect each in broadly the same way. The integration of the value chains is likely to be driven by the following events or processes (European Commission, 1997):

- *Platform independence of digital material.* The broadcasting and telecommunications sectors are increasingly able to carry the same services, and so the distinction between the two is becoming blurred.

- *Unbundling of services and packaging from infrastructure.* The development of technologies such as the Internet is freeing service providers and content 'packagers' from the dependence upon infrastructure owners, thus facilitating new entry.

- *Direct routes from content originators and packagers to customers.* There are more methods to enable all parts of the value chain to access the end user directly. This has been typified by the use of electronic commerce, which increases markedly the power of content providers.

- *Regrouping for access to new skills.* Convergence requires new skills, which is forcing enterprises to develop new alliances and relationships with both new and existing players across all of the sectors.

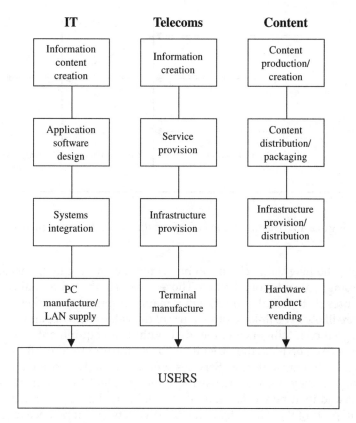

IT	Telecoms	Content
Information content creation	Information creation	Content production/ creation
Application software design	Service provision	Content distribution/ packaging
Systems integration	Infrastructure provision	Infrastructure provision/ distribution
PC manufacture/ LAN supply	Terminal manufacture	Hardware product vending

USERS

Source: Analysys (1998)

Figure 4.1 *The traditional value chain in the information industries*

The trend and process of convergence and its impact over time upon the value chain is represented indicatively in Figure 4.2. This seeks to highlight how the separate value chains shown in Figure 4.1 are moving towards the integrated value chain reflected in Figure 4.3.

Figure 4.3 represents what Analysys (1998) believes the value chain within the integrated information industry will look like. It stresses that players may occupy more than one part of the chain and may indeed develop links with players in different niches to seal strategic objectives. Firms that will survive in this context will be characterized by being multimedia in nature and global in scope, and will focus upon personal rather than institutional markets. Thus public and cable networks will be consolidated into a transport business, and cable TV and broadcast media will be consolidated into an information business. Consumer electronics and personal computer manufacturers will converge into an information devices sector.

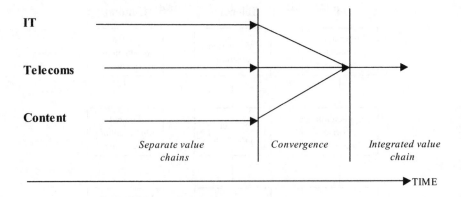

Figure 4.2 *The integration of information industry value chains*

In short, the new value chain can be synthesized as: content, packaging, processing, transmission, devices. Those aspects of the value chain closest to the user (ie terminal market) will remain a commodity market, though there are likely to be links to other parts of the value chain depending upon the degree of intelligence embedded within the equipment. The more intelligence embedded, the easier it will be for the user to access the content through different platforms. Services will increasingly become a distinct category as they become increasingly independent from infrastructure owners and their networks. In total, it is unlikely that one firm will try to span all parts of the value chain due the diversity of competence required. Despite this, firms (as the sections in this chapter indicate) will seek presence in the value chain beyond their traditional market segment. This strategy is especially important given the trend towards platform independence for content and information providers, which enables enterprises to access users through a variety of platforms (as opposed to a single one) – that is they can use telecommunications, the Internet or digital video broadcasting to deliver content or information. This has the effect of limiting the power of information distributors.

The structure of the information industries under the process of convergence will alter markedly from being based upon form to one where function will come to dominate. With the process of digitalization any information can be delivered through any medium with the user deciding what form it takes. Thus competition will be increasingly based upon functions, as the forms will be readily convertible into functional capabilities. The five functional areas across the information industry, as suggested by the aforementioned value chain, are those that:

- create (content);
- store (databases);

Activity   Function

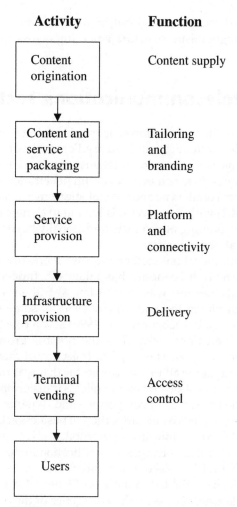

Content origination	Content supply
Content and service packaging	Tailoring and branding
Service provision	Platform and connectivity
Infrastructure provision	Delivery
Terminal vending	Access control
Users	

Source: Analysys (1998)

Figure 4.3 *The integrated value chain*

- display (devices);
- process (applications);
- distribute (transport).

Enterprise strategies within the telecommunications, IT and content sectors will be based upon establishing a presence within and across these functional areas. Sheth and Wallace (1994) suggest that the logical conclusion of these processes, within a multimedia environment, is an industry structure with enterprises specializing in networks, devices or content.

Combined with the trend towards globalization within the sector, this could lead to a global oligopolistic structure emerging across the information industry.

The telecommunications sector

The development of the information economy is having a profound effect upon the global telecommunications industry. For much of the 20th century, telecommunications was a single product business (voice telephony) with the core strategic mission to achieve maximum penetration of this service. Under pressure from commercial and technological environments, the value chain (see Figure 4.1) within the sector is having to change (as mentioned above) to stress the offering of products traditionally beyond the scope of the telecommunications industry.

The telecommunications sector has grown markedly as the progress towards the information economy has taken off. Indeed in 1998, the telecommunications business was worth some $1 trillion. This represents an average growth rate in the mid- to late 1990s of some 5–7 per cent – twice the rate of the global economy. The 1990s saw a constant rise in the number of new fixed lines, as well as the notable growth of mobile telecommunications usage (see below). The trajectory of change within the sector has been evident for all to see. The sector that was once populated solely by staid, government-owned monopolies is transforming into a sector that is arguably the largest, most competitive and dynamic market in the world, underpinning an increasing proportion of business activity (see Table 4.1 for the largest telecommunication operators).

Symptomatic of these changes is modification in the form and type of traffic being carried by telecommunications networks. International traffic, for example, has doubled in the 1990–96 period driven by the rise in data movements associated with the emergence of the Internet. Indeed for many operators, the late 1990s saw data overtake voice telephony as the majority form of traffic. By 2000, Internet traffic was estimated to be some 75 per cent of transatlantic traffic. This trend, as highlighted in Figure 4.4, is expected to be a global phenomenon. The main reason for this shift in traffic is the increased use of digital technology stimulated by the process of convergence, notably through the emergence of the Internet as a communications medium. A further important trend has been the reduction in the cost of telecommunications. This includes not only service provision but also the deployment of new transmission systems. These savings have been evident for over 20 years but have only recently started to feed through to the end user as competition has become more intense across the sector – a trend exacerbated by the fact that many new entrants tend to compete on price.

Table 4.1 *Top 20 telecommunication companies
(by market capitalization: mid-1999)*

Rank	Company	Country
1	MCI WorldCom	US
2	AT&T	US
3	NTT	Japan
4	Deutsche Telekom	Germany
5	British Telecom	UK
6	SBC Communications	US
7	Bellsouth	US
8	France Telecom	France
9	Bell Atlantic	US
10	NTT DoCoMo	Japan
11	Ameritech	US
12	Telstra	Australia
13	GTE	US
14	Vodafone	UK
15	Telecom Italia	Italy
16	Air Touch Communications	US
17	Telefonica	Spain
18	TIM	Italy
19	Cable and Wireless	UK
20	US West	US

Source: Financial Times (1999b)

The development of the information economy is evidently already having a profound effect upon the commercial environment of telecommunication enterprises. The core impact of these changes is felt in terms of changes in the telecommunications market-place, as freer competition, globalization and technological change alter the commercial challenges facing enterprises. Interlinked are the impacts upon enterprises stimulated more directly by new technologies, which are not merely expanding service portfolios but also posing new commercial challenges to telecommunication enterprises as the deployment of these technologies is likely to prove key to sustaining competitiveness in an increasingly competitive environment. The combined effect of these market and technological developments is the convergence of the telecommunication market with the IT and content sectors as enterprises within the sector seeking new alliances to aid their commercial success.

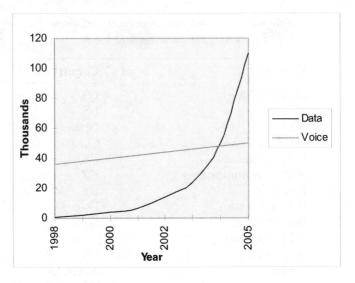

Source: Financial Times (1999b)

Figure 4.4   *Estimated growth of global voice and data traffic (terabytes per month)*

Market developments

The telecommunications market is undergoing change driven by factors such as the growing degree of competition, the growth of mobility and the Internet. These have promoted and complemented broader technological developments to increase the power, capacity and capabilities of the information network. It is already evident that the rise in data networking driven by the rise in Internet usage is altering profoundly the businesses of the traditional telecommunication enterprise with many realizing that any successful enterprise needs to offer Internet and other data services (alongside the traditional voice offerings) as an increasingly prominent part of their portfolio. Others are looking to develop their portfolios even further into areas such as cable access television (CATV). Such developments (as well as those noted below) are all symptomatic of the shift towards the information economy.

Consolidation within the telecommunications sector

The basic and core response to liberalization (see Chapter 5), globalization and the pressures of technological change within the telecommunications market has been a shift towards consolidation right across the sector. This consolidation has been driven by the need to:

- capture customers;

- enhance capacity;

- utilize expanding capacity through new service offerings;

- shape the future of the industry in a manner that is to their liking;

- protect existing business models where only the biggest survive;

- develop complementary regional advantages;

- achieve economies of scale;

- offer lower prices and enhanced functionality;

- create international networks;

- counter the threat of new operators (such as WorldCom and QWest), which are establishing technologically advanced high capacity networks;

- access key regional assets (such as networks).

Overall this consolidation strategy by telecommunications enterprises has been both defensive and offensive as they seek to recover revenues lost from more intense competition in domestic markets with increased revenues from the international market-place as well as enhanced service or product portfolios.

This consolidation has been especially evident in the US where there has been a spate of mergers between local, long-distance and cable suppliers. For example, AT&T acquired the local US operator, TCG, to gain access to the local US communications market. The position of AT&T was improved by TCG's strong position as an ISP. In the US, the activities of AT&T have been replicated within the strategies of both long- and local-distance suppliers, which have sought alliances to further consolidate the market. These trends reflect the fact that it is both difficult and expensive to outflank an entrenched incumbent operator in its core market. The combined effect of competition and technology reflects the fact that operators not only need to defend existing positions but also need to be seen as operating at the leading edge of the deployment of new services. One of the most high-profile features of the consolidation within the sector has been witnessed through the development of global alliances designed to meet the needs of multinational companies (see the case study below, 'Global telecommunication alliances' on p 100). This consolidation has also been evident in both Europe (with the Olivetti take-over of Telecom Italia) and Asia (through, for example, Cable and Wireless's take-over of the Japanese long-distance carrier IDC – despite a counterbid by the incumbent operator, NTT).

This process of consolidation is extending right across the sector. Many equipment manufacturers are developing links with data network equipment manufacturers. This is driven by the desire that these enterprises meet the growing demand for data technology as Internet usage becomes more common. For example, Canada's Northern Telecom became Nortel after its acquisition of Bay Networks. In addition, within mobile telecommunications there is also clearly scope for rationalized market structure. In the UK, there are over 100 operators when clearly the market can only support a fraction of this number. Consolidation is to some extent already evident on a global level with Vodafone's acquisition of Air Touch to create the world's first global mobile operator. The shift towards global players within this sector has been reinforced by a number of other mergers and acquisitions (such as Mannesmann's purchase of the UK operator, Orange). Thus the mobile sector is increasingly coming to resemble its fixed-line equivalent in terms of consolidating market structures.

Global telecommunication alliances

As mentioned within the text, telecommunication alliances have emerged as a direct consequence of globalization and liberalization, based upon meeting the communication needs of large, frequently multinational corporations. This change in strategy and shift into new market segments has emerged as incumbent operators found domestic revenues under attack from new entrants. The perceived need for alliances within this market segment is based upon a belief that only three or four genuinely global telecommunication operators are able to provide multinational businesses with a one-stop shop for their communication needs world-wide. In addition, without a large share of this business it will be difficult for the alliances to attract the ever-growing number of small and medium-sized enterprises, which deal with these multinationals, as clients.

By the beginning of 1999, four major alliances had emerged to meet the requirements of multinational enterprises:

1. Concert – a network of enterprises led by BT to sell branded products to customers.

2. WorldPartners – an AT&T-led alliance that involves a loose confederation of PTOs from Europe and Asia.

3. Unisource – a European-based alliance revolving around a number of small European PTOs. It has more recently formed an alliance with WorldPartners in the WorldSource group, though this has since been purchased by Infonet.

4. Global One – an alliance revolving around France Telecom, Deutsche Telekom and Sprint (of the US).

Around these core alliances a number of approaches have been deployed by PTOs to seek a presence in the global market:

- interconnection agreements for national services and distribution of a common service at an international level (such as WorldPartners);

- creation of a joint venture between different operators for supplying common international services based upon a shared infrastructure – these are sold by a joint company (such as Unisource);

- cross-shareholding between operators and the creation of a joint venture in charge of the operation and distribution of global services (an example is Global One);

- cross-shareholding between operators and the creation of a joint venture for operation of the global services, which are distributed by the respective mother companies (an example is Concert);

- merger of international operators (such as WorldCom and MCI);

- formation of global organizations.

Alliances are merely one strategy that can be deployed. They have been an especially prominent short-term strategic solution to the pressures posed by globalization. There is clearly a strategic logic behind the alliances with enterprises seeking partners in the three core business markets of Europe, Asia and the US. This is coupled with a belief that corporate communications are tending towards an oligopolistic structure, which created a perception that alliances were the only way to gain a share of this lucrative market segment.

The development of these alliances will face a number of core challenges, notably:

- the need to include a US partner given that many MNCs are headquartered in the US;

- the need to integrate different systems to ensure true interconnection and interoperability across the network;

- the alteration of existing alliances to ensure compliance with regulation and the better strategic fit of the partnership with the enterprise's objectives;

- limits to the desire of enterprises to continue outsourcing networks;

- differences in terms of corporate culture – an evident problem as ex-state-owned cultures come into alliance with those developed under more prolonged commercial exposure.

In combination, these have provided impediments to the development of successful global alliances.

One of the core problems encountered by these alliances has been their instability. Enterprises have had problems in remaining committed to these alliances when their strategic conditions altered. Each of the alliances has encountered problems. Concert faced problems when BT's original partner – MCI – was purchased by another party (WorldCom). WorldPartners was dissolved as a response to the decision of AT&T to develop an alliance with BT. Unisource faced similar problems when AT&T left WorldPartners. It also had to leave the Unisource alliance, which left the founding partners adrift and having to consider whether to split the alliance, though Infonet indicated it would participate and replace the departing partner. Global One was hit by a crisis of confidence between partners when Deutsche Telekom bid to merge with Telecom Italia without consulting its major partner, France Telecom. This resulted in the latter suing the former. These problems were compounded when the US partner – Sprint – announced it was leaving the troubled Global One alliance.

To offer a diagnosis of these events is to highlight the changing state of play in the telecommunications market and the failings of these alliances. A key factor is that users were sceptical of the ability of an alliance to deliver what it promised. For example, much-vaunted globality in effect meant concentrating on the three key markets of Europe, Asia and North America, with the consequence that only 15 per cent of the world was covered by the alliances. In addition, instability in the alliances could lead to instability over service. To many users there is simply no substitute for a single company providing a seamless network. This has been especially true for large networks under a single owner such as Equant or Infonet. Consequently, alliances have had to overcome customer cynicism over their stability with the result that consumers have been reluctant to commit themselves to major deals with the alliances. Paradoxically more and more customers are picking and choosing suppliers, recognizing that their competitive strength relies upon exploiting the relative strength of each of the suppliers; thus a one-stop shop for business communications is often simply not desired. This offers opportunities to smaller suppliers.

In addition, enterprises need constantly to reappraise what is in their best interests in terms of cost and services. For example, BT could offer AT&T a better-quality network than many of its other partners. Other enterprises, after flirting with several alliances, decided that it is better to stay partner-free (for example, Telefonica, after flirting with both Unisource and Concert, remains partner-free). Every time an alliance goes through seismic disruptions, questions are inevitably going to be asked by customers over the level of support they are going to get on the ground.

Whilst the market for corporate communications is heading towards an oligopolistic structure, this is seen by many others as the second-best strategy. Many successful and emerging global players are employing different strategies to gain market share. Enterprises such as WorldCom are developing strategies to achieve global presence based upon aggressive acquisitions to develop a true single global entity over which they have a greater degree of control. The alliances are seen to have failed and may need to consider full mergers if they are to operate effectively in global market-places. BT and MCI clearly highlight this. BT could not make Concert work without controlling everything, therefore needed to take over MCI – an objective to which it was ultimately beaten by a smaller, nimbler rival.

Mobility and flexibility

Development work in industrialized states is increasingly controlled by end users' desire for greater freedom of movement and accessibility. There are strong indications that mobile telephony may be the only telephony in common usage in the future, as voice increasingly moves from fixed lines towards the mobile format. This is underlined by the rapid growth rates in mobile telephony – annual increases of 60 per cent have been common – which have exceeded all expectations (see Figure 4.5). Despite this the penetration rates for this technology only remain at 4 per cent (1998), which suggests that there is still considerable scope for growth in what are evidently already fast-growing markets. The take-up rates vary markedly across the globe with some Scandinavian states having penetration rates over 50 per cent. Across all developed states, a penetration rate of 40 per cent is anticipated by 2005. Such demand will be driven by a continued fall in the tariffs charged by operators – rates have already fallen 15 per cent annually since 1995 – and by user awareness as mobile capabilities evolve.

Competition has been a major factor in the rapid market growth within mobile communications, with most states now allowing a number of different operators within their respective markets. As competition intensifies, so it is expected that operators from both fixed and mobile technologies will not only seek to enter one another's market segments but will also seek to offer tailored solutions that combine the best elements of both technologies. Over time the capabilities of the mobile telephone will change, as not only will it take an increasing share of voice traffic but it will also start to exhibit more of the characteristics of portable computers especially when the third-generation mobile technology is rolled out (see the case study in Chapter 5, 'The battle for third-generation mobile standards' on p 155). This trend is important for the mobile telephone is likely to be a key access point to advanced communications for many people and is therefore likely to be a key factor in integrating increasing numbers into the information economy thereby stimulating its commercial maturity.

The Internet

The rapid growth of the Internet is a striking example of the convergence of telecommunications with the other information sectors. The growth in the Internet places heavy demands upon the capacity of telecommunication networks, the pivotal channel for Internet communications. If the mobile is the current driver of the evolving telecommunications sector, then the Internet is the future. The growth of the Internet is both an opportunity and a threat to the telecommunications sector. In particular, a key threat to PTOs is coming from the development of Internet telephony, which is an attack on the core revenue base of the traditional telecommunications

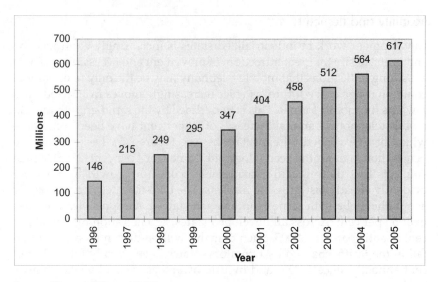

Source: *Financial Times* (1998)

Figure 4.5 *World cellular/PCS subscribers (1996–2005)*

enterprise. Internet networks are faster and cheaper than conventional voice systems. This poses a challenge, for the traditional telecommunication operator's days are numbered as voice starts to be offered over this new channel. Operators will increasingly become information providers, creating the need to develop alliances with other enterprises to secure their future. Thus many operators have been on an aggressive round of acquiring Internet service providers. For example, Deutsche Telekom and MCI have been active in using their positions as large ISPs to offer these services alongside their more traditional forms of voice delivery. This underlines that the strategic impact of the Internet is clearly going to be felt not only in price and cost factors but also in terms of product portfolios.

Many of the leading Internet software enterprises (such as Netscape and Microsoft) have built telephony functions into their browser software – something that is likely to expand its use even further. In its initial phases of development, poor voice quality limited the attractiveness of Internet telephony to customers, but the evolution of new software has rapidly improved the service to the extent that it now represents a credible threat to telecommunication operators' revenue bases. The low tariffs offered by Internet telephony will force a reduction in the levels offered for similar traffic over the PSTN. Price advantage is not the only factor driving Internet telephony, it has also benefited from being able to avoid many of the regulatory constraints imposed upon the supply of voice telephony. There are other drivers such as the perceived technical efficiency of the service. Over the longer term, the core driver may be the fact that service emerged in the world of the Internet - its dispersed development means the potential for greater innovation and deployment more rapidly than would occur under the traditionally centrally controlled PSTN.

Internet telephony has the capability to alter the telecommunications market in a number of fairly profound ways. It will not only alter pricing and cost structures of telecommunications services but it is also likely to alter the nature of the services themselves as more integrated (combining voice and data) solutions become feasible both commercially and technologically. This places the emphasis upon incumbent enterprises to start a cycle of innovation. For example, the recent AT&T/BT alliance seeks to develop a high-capacity Internet network over which a portfolio of services will be offered including Internet telephony. This is part of a trend where many operators are shifting voice service towards packet protocols such as the Internet. Despite this the market for Internet telephony is still dominated by the smaller players such as resellers.

Further convergence between telecommunications and the Internet is going to occur within the forum of mobile technology (as mentioned above). This is an especially important development, not only spreading the use of mobile phones but more importantly also extending the reach of the Internet. This development will make PCs less important (see below) and enable more people to access the Internet on a regular basis. Mobiles will tend to be used by people to check e-mail, and make quick communications and short transactions rather than to spend hours in leisurely browsing as seems to occur in PC-accessed Internet usage.

Technological developments

As has been noted above, the shift towards digital technology has been one of the key drivers of change within the sector: it is enabling improvements in computer technology to be shared by the telecommunications sector. Furthermore there are vast improvements in the cost and performance of satellite technologies, as well as ongoing network enhancements derived largely from the deployment of fibre optic technologies. The result of these continuing changes is that increasingly telecommunication enterprises are able to offer better, more reliable and increasingly 'intelligent' services at lower cost. The Internet is also proving a big factor in facilitating change, as it removes distance as a defining characteristic of telecommunication revenues. These trends are complemented by further technological developments in a number of key areas.

Software

Software is increasingly important as the core source of value creation in the telecommunications sector, and is consequently perceived as the core strategic asset of these enterprises. The success of operators in the future will depend upon the quality of their software applications and their ability to deliver value to enterprises. The rising importance of software in telecommunications enterprises is no better reflected than in the development of intelligent networking. Intelligent networks (where the network itself has some degree of processing capability) have emerged as a response to the desire of users to have greater mobility and flexibility. Thus the growing demand for end-user services will be met through software residing in terminals and servers outside the traditional telecommunications network.

Microelectronics

Underlining the growing links within the IT sector is microelectronics (driven by ever smaller and cheaper circuits as well as greater intelligence and capacity), which makes it possible to create systems offering greater price, performance and quality.

Access technologies

As the traffic over the network increases, and as the array of bandwidth-hungry services expands, so there is the need to expand the capacity of the physical network correspondingly. For this to occur over existing infrastructure, new technologies are increasingly being applied. One such example is the increased use of digital compression techniques (such as ADSL), which allow broadband services to be offered effectively over a narrowband infrastructure. Elsewhere within the network there is the gradual deployment of other technologies designed to support the shift to the wider proliferation of broadband services. Technologies such as ATM and SDH are now being deployed more widely by operators as a competitive response to the changing commercial environment. In addition, the other means of access, namely cable-based TV, is being upgraded, and there is an exploration of the introduction of wireless technology into the local loop to avoid the expense of upgrading and replacing this bit of the network and to negate the need to establish fixed-line infrastructure where it currently does not exist. Thus technology is holding out the prospect of less-expensive deployment of new capacity.

Internet and data communications

As has been a recurrent theme throughout this section, the large growth in the Internet is posing new commercial challenges for operators. New investment in networks and software is driven by the need not only to cope with the extra traffic but also to have the capability to deliver the new multimedia traffic associated with the development of the information economy (see Figure 4.8).

Open standards

Operators are working towards open standards where users can effectively mix and match equipment from different suppliers to enable them to obtain maximum benefit (see Chapter 5). These open standards have been most notably deployed in the development of the Internet – something that has stimulated a great deal of innovation in this medium.

Within this environment the development and deployment of these technologies is going to be driven by effective demand. Investment in technology is important in an increasingly open market for telecommunication services and technologies. If operators are to offer the necessary portfolio of products to enable them to compete effectively, then not only do they need the skills to develop and deploy these products through merger, acquisition and alliance strategies but they also need to invest in the capabilities to actually deliver these products and respond to the technological developments of their rivals. This underpins the close link between the processes of globalization and technological change – the two core themes behind the development of the information economy.

Convergence and telecommunication enterprises

From the above it is evident that there are commercial and technological developments driving interlinkages between the telecommunications, content and IT sectors. Not least amongst these are the challenges posed to current business models from the development of the Internet. It is evident that, in response to these pressures, operators are altering product portfolios. The rationale of strategy in a highly competitive, technologically fluid and global environment has to be based upon accessing as many customers as possible and offering as broad a range of products as possible from basic telecommunications through to more advanced multimedia services.

Initial developments with regard to convergence and the telecommunications sector came as a response to the sharp rise in the levels of data flowing over telecommunications networks. Telecommunication operators themselves have been busy buying up Internet protocol networks and other businesses with a strong expertise in this technology (for example, there has been a spate of mergers between telecommunication equipment suppliers and data network enterprises). This trend reflects a general perception that the future of telecommunications lies in having a strong presence in the data and Internet segments of the market (as noted above). The rise in data traffic has stimulated further convergence in terms of equipment as efforts are made to develop equipment derived from the convergence of the PC and the telephone. This has been typified by the recent alliance between Microsoft and BT to develop hand-held communication devices.

Convergence is also becoming evident as an increasing number of enterprises develop broadcasting capabilities through their ownership of cable television companies. This is a trend that is increasing, notably within the US. Telecommunication operators see the widespread development of digital television as a core turning-point in the process of convergence, because the mass of channels together with embedded software enables users to enjoy greater choice of channels and interactivity, as well as Internet access, through a single point of access. Currently, the telecommunication enterprises offering broadcast services provide content through alliance development with existing broadcasters. Many of these enterprises do not purchase content direct but tend to use existing programming schedules from the broadcasters. The evidence seems to suggest that the strong brand of telecommunication operators when combined with their large networks offers many attractions to users. It is also clear that to survive in the converged environment, size is going to be of prime importance. This is already becoming evident through merger and acquisition activity as well as through alliance formation.

BT is an example of an enterprise that has been especially proactive in evolving its portfolio of services to meet the changing requirement derived from the process of convergence. Increasingly it has reached beyond telecommunications and established partnerships to offer broadcasting services to exploit the potential of digital television through, for example, its stake in the British Interactive Broadcasting partnership. BT hopes that this will prove to be a stepping-stone to further digital outlets and especially more direct broadcasting capabilities. Alongside service provision, BT will still have a key role in network provision and it is therefore testing infrastructure such as compression technology to deliver services such as video-on-demand. However, it has stated that it has no intention of becoming involved in content creation nor in the production of terminals. Thus BT's strategy is to restrict itself to the mid-range of the industry value chain. As mentioned, it will remain in the areas of network and service provision though in sectors beyond the traditional boundaries of telecommunications. Overall BT seems to be adopting what is a typical strategy for many of the traditional incumbent telecommunication operators by taking a pragmatic, if not completely strategic, approach to the process of convergence, and gradually expanding core competencies to take account of technological change and the threat of competition. This strategy is by no means universal, as others, especially US operators, are taking a more aggressive approach, positioning themselves right along the converging value chain.

A daily examination of the media should tell the average reader of the trend and changes in the communications sector and how enterprises are repositioning themselves to exploit and secure their position in an era of convergence. This is clearly a trend that will continue. There is no one strategy being followed. Telecommunication enterprises are following different strategies depending upon their own strategic intent. Some, such as AT&T, are overtly aggressive in developing a presence across the converging value chain. Others, such as BT, are looking at convergence merely as grounds to redefine existing competencies.

The information technology sector

In some senses, the increasing international pressures evident within the telecommunication sector are not as evident within the global market for IT, which has exhibited a greater degree of openness for some time, something that has been enhanced by the WTO's IT agreement (see Chapter 5). The major developments within the IT sector have been more techno-logical, notably the consequences of convergence as expressed through an increasing strategic focus on the development of the Internet. Inevitably the IT sector plays a pivotal role in the establishment of the information economy through the development of a means by which users can access and process the information available through new and evolving media such as the Internet. From Table 4.2 it is evident that the US has come to dominate the IT sector across the global economy. In the US, the IT sector represented some 8.2 per cent of GDP in 1998 (up from 4.9 per cent in 1985).

IT is a large sector, so inevitably this chapter can only offer the reader a glimpse of the changes that are ongoing within the sector related to the development of the information economy. For the purposes of this analysis the sector is divided into two sub-sectors – hardware and software.

Computer hardware sector

The hardware sector includes the makers of mainframe, client-server and personal computers, other computer-based systems, storage devices, networking equipment, peripherals and business equipment (copiers, point-of-sale terminals, etc), as well as wholesalers and retailers of computer equipment. The sector is one that has been in the process of change for some time as new players have emerged and taken over more staid competitors. For example, Compaq Computers was a mere start-up in 1982

Table 4.2 *Top 20 IT companies (mid-1999)*

Rank	Company	Country
1	Microsoft	US
2	Intel	US
3	IBM	US
4	Cisco Systems	US
5	Lucent Technologies	US
6	Dell Computer	US
7	America On-line	US
8	Nokia	Finland
9	Ericsson	Sweden
10	Oracle	US
11	EMC	US
12	Motorola	US
13	Northern Telecom	Canada
14	Sun Microsystems	US
15	Xerox	US
16	Texas Instruments	US
17	Yahoo	US
18	BCE	Canada
19	ADP	US
20	Applied Materials	US

Source: Financial Times (1999c)

when Digital Equipment Corporation was the second-largest player in the computer market. The transition in the industry has been typified by the 1998 take-over by Compaq of its erstwhile larger competitor – a move that made the enterprise the third-largest computer company behind IBM and Hewlett Packard (HP). Figure 4.7 reflects the market share for the leading PC manufacturers in 1999.

The second half of the 20th century witnessed a rapid change in the computer industry, as the product evolved from a large, seemingly monolithic machine (the mainframe) through to the PC. In many ways, the PC was the great kick-start to the sector, with enterprises moving from mainframes to PC-based systems. Thus the major transition within the sector was caused by a shift from centralized, mainframe-based computing to client-server-based computing. This latter approach separates users (clients) and the services (servers) they use. The development of a more distributed computer system offered many benefits to users in terms of costs, flexibility and functionality. Such changes in terms of user needs inevitably had a knock-on effect in terms of the industry, as was witnessed by the highly publicized troubles and consequent turnaround of IBM (see the case study below on p 113). All mainframe manufacturers suffered as a result of this shift towards the PC as the low-cost alternative to expensive proprietary mainframe computers.

The PC market is also one that has undergone a period of rapid change. For many years, the sector was dominated by a David versus Goliath struggle between Apple's computers and the industry standard based upon Intel/Microsoft technology known as 'Wintel'. After years of struggling, Apple seemingly conceded the war as Microsoft's Windows systems became the core operating system upon 80 per cent of the world's PCs, including the top four manufacturers – Compaq, IBM, Dell and Hewlett Packard (see Figure 4.6 for PC market share). The result of this Wintel dominance was the establishment of an alliance between Apple and Microsoft upon developmental issues.

Despite the increased power of PCs, they are still falling far short of meeting computing needs in entirety. It has been notable that the onset of the Internet has led to the reinvigoration of the mainframe market due to their ability to store vast quantities of data. This has in turn fuelled the demand for servers that can handle these data demands. IBM still dominates the mainframe market but Amdahl and Hitachi are eating into its market share. Many of these enterprises have sought to limit their exposure to the mainframe market by shifting into the server market. The ability of servers to distribute applications to hundreds of desktops, as well as sharing other functions such as e-mail, has rendered this market segment one of the fastest-growing segments of the IT market.

The Internet is altering the hardware market as witnessed by the move towards a networking computer environment. Data networking enterprises such as Cisco Systems, 3Com, Bay Networks and Cabletron have risen in prominence. As has been noted above, many hardware producers within the telecommunications sector have been keen to gain a presence in this sector of the computer hardware market for the purposes of accessing the data networking market. This is in addition to the rise in demand for mainframes, which are more able to deal with the large number of hits when compared to other systems such as Unix and Windows NT. It needs to be remembered that hardware within the networking environment is based upon providing the underpinning of business software and solutions, and therefore the rise of networking solutions such as intranets and electronic commerce will increasingly drive the hardware market. This dependence is likely to increase as the networking market (a core feature of the information economy) starts to exhibit a greater degree of maturity, and especially as it starts to become a pivotal strategic resource for enterprises of all sizes.

In the hardware sector, the power of devices will be judged by the network access speed. Furthermore Internet-based languages (such as Java

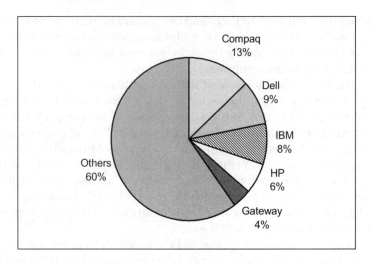

Source: Dataquest (1998) (www.dataquest.com)

Figure 4.6 *PC market share 1998*

– see below) may undermine the importance of the desktop and the dominance of 'Wintel'. With this new language – which all platforms understand – the dominance of the traditional players can be broken and open systems will allow anyone to provide applications.

Increasingly the computer industry has to face the growing power of users who are operating in a freer environment (associated with the emergence of the Internet) and who have been liberated from the dominance of established proprietary brands by open systems. Consequently hardware needs to reflect changes in technology stimulated by the process of convergence. The future of computing is likely to be driven by the need for more complete information appliances that are easier to use and reflect the need for flexibility and portability. Hardware needs to reflect the convergence of technologies by offering telephony alongside Internet solutions. According to analysts, many hardware producers need to change their business models to reflect these changes if they are to be successful. This is driven by a perception that the core value added is going to come from the services added to the network and not from the core hardware platforms. This perception is compounded by a belief that PCs will be replaced by Internet appliances with software written for the Internet and not the desktop. Leading US non-PC computer companies (such as Sun and Oracle) are pushing this perspective and are developing a vision based upon 'thin clients' or very basic computers that rely upon high-speed networks to deliver data and software programmes. These 'thin clients' (for example,

Web phones, smart mobile phones, hand-held computers, TV set-top boxes and network computers) are the new appliances; they should be easy to set up, reliable and devoted to special uses. It is to these that the PC is expected to cede power. These thin-client devices will move the hardware market on to the next phase, which will be heavily interlinked with ubiquitous Internet access. In effect, it will be computing any time anywhere (so-called pervasive computing) with the PC losing its position as the universal computing solution.

The challenge posed to existing business models has been high-lighted by trends in the PC sector where many enterprises are struggling to make money from their products. The industry has over-capacity and endures intense competition. The major cause of these strategic challenges is the Internet, which is taking the steam out of the constant cycle of upgrade that is a core feature of the sector. Indeed some Internet service providers are actually giving away PCs as a means of attracting customers. Increasingly customers are prepared to stick with 'good enough' PCs and are not desiring constant upgrades. The Internet offers little in the way of content that requires upgrades and therefore the spread of the Internet prolongs the life of existing hardware. Web sites are based on attracting as many users as possible and will therefore not seek to limit accessibility through developing sites that can only be accessed by the fastest machines. The result is that spare money is likely to be spent upon better connections and not upon upgrades. This is coupled with the rise of Internet computing, which demands less of PCs – they are required merely to access servers by means of a browser with the result that there is little in effect to differentiate new and old PCs.

The turnaround of IBM

As mentioned in the text, IBM was almost destroyed by the advent of the personal computer revolution – ironically a revolution it helped to start. This revolution undermined IBM's dominant position in the mainframe market – a market that became largely redundant with the advent of personal computing. The anti-trust case that the enterprise faced (over its dominance of the hardware market) took IBM's eye off the market, leading to its failure to spot the rise of the personal computer (a device it invented) and allowed others to reinvent the computing industry. The result was that in the formative years of the 1990s, IBM stacked up losses of nearly $18 billion. This was driven by the fact that IBM decided to go against the market and not with it. Thus it invested heavily in developing new mainframes and believed that the pressure from PCs and cheaper, more flexible UNIX servers could be fought off. IBM believed that hardware was where the profits were and software was dedicated to its own products. What it failed to recognize was that customers wanted cheap PCs.

IBM was simply overtaken by events. It lost core staff and saw products that it had developed turned against it by erstwhile rivals (for example, by Microsoft with the operating system for IBM's PCs). Simply, IBM was not nimble enough to compete with the new enterprises emerging within the sector. This, coupled with IBM's large cost base and sprawling bureaucracy, reinforced its competitive disadvantage in the computing market-place.

Since this nadir of fortune, IBM has managed to turn itself around through a mixture of luck and good strategic guidance. IBM has shifted away from simply providing hardware and software products towards offering 'customized solutions'. This strategic change stresses that service is the key to higher sales and stronger customer loyalty. This point is especially salient in an era when products become increasingly similar. Whilst services were always important to IBM they were often seen as something that was merely a facilitator of hardware sales. Now the tail is wagging the dog, as IBM has transformed itself into essentially a computer services company.

The shift to services has been driven by changes in the sector and led many customers back to IBM. This has been based on its expertise in integration and management of complex systems and the development of powerful reliable servers. This position has been aided by a change in the culture of the enterprise, which makes it more welcoming to open standards, specialization and constant change. The move to solutions was indicative of the corporate culture change. There was a shift away from imposing IBM upon customers toward doing what the customer wanted even if it meant offering third-party solutions, thereby underlining that services are not merely a means of stimulating further sales of IBM products but of giving customers what they want even if it means selling competing products.

The emergence of the Internet was a big plus for IBM. Embracing it before many of its rivals, IBM sought to show customers how the Internet could add value to business. Thus instead of solely promoting its own products, IBM based its strategy around showing companies how they could transform themselves into Internet-based traders, doing trade 24 hours a day. These play to IBM's product strengths of server reliability, large storage capability, massive processing power, expert systems integration and strategic planning. In this way IBM sought to provide the service to pull all aspects of the Internet together as well as the constituent parts of hardware, software, training and security.

IBM's software declined with the mainframe market. This it is also seeking to amend through acquisitions to give it a presence on the desktop (the reason for its 1995 acquisition of Lotus Development, a Boston-based software firm). The combination of IBM's money and distribution has allowed this enterprise to flourish. IBM has proved itself to be the one hardware enterprise that has excelled in software. This software position has been helped by the advent of Java (see text below). IBM is seeking to use this position to create new applications to knit together customers' networks more completely. In addition, IBM is seeking to turn around the mainframe business, which, despite the noted decline, still represents a core part of its business. IBM has gone through a process of strong research in this area to increase power whilst lowering cost. The lesson has been learnt in terms of mainframes, which is that constant renewal and upgrade has to be key.

Despite having star products that are evidently mature (notably hardware), the turnaround strategy has won plaudits. By the end of 1998, the enterprise was growing by 20 per cent per annum. By 2003, the star is likely to be computer services, accounting for 50 per cent of all revenues (it is currently around 25 per cent, with hardware the current leading segment at around 45 per cent – underlining that IBM is still reliant upon this segment for its prosperity). Nevertheless, doubts remain over the longevity of these changes. For example, many believe that IBM is too poorly focused in terms of its solutions business and could therefore, over time, lose out to smaller, better-focused players. There are also concerns that IBM continues to stay in markets (such as PCs) where it is evidently a second-string player. IBM would reply that it needs to be broadly based in order to offer a one-stop shop for solutions, and therefore that the sum of IBM (because of synergies between business units) is greater than the sum of the parts. Thus services could not be successful without IBM's involvement in areas such as PCs, for example. In the future, IBM needs to sell itself as the leader in terms of Internet business solutions – this is central to IBM continuing its rise back to prominence.

Computer software sector

This sector includes companies involved in the design, development and marketing of all types of software; companies that provide both software and services; and those enterprises that provide services such as maintenance and systems integration. The software sector is the key enabling aspect of the information economy and some of the world's highest-profile enterprises stem from this sector of the economy. In terms of the market, 95 per cent of all software sold is within businesses, and the rest is represented by consumer titles. The sector, by the end of 1998, employed some 1 million people with over 50 per cent of these being in the US. The Business Software Alliance expects these figures to more than double by 2005. Despite the large number of small-scale start-ups in the sector, almost half of those employed within the sector are employed by the Top 10 firms (see Table 4.2).

The development of the sector stems from the US Justice Department's decision to force IBM to sell software separately from its then dominant mainframe computers. The result was a proliferation of competition that has multiplied even further with the fuller development of the Internet, though much of the original proliferation was derived from the spread of PCs. These developments offered almost a perfect example of a true competitive market, as the costs were minimal (save the time devoted by an individual developer) and the potential rewards vast. Changes within the sector are being increasingly influenced by the Internet, as software for this market is perceived as the core strategic objective by any enterprise.

Microsoft is the world's largest software enterprise alongside IBM – the latter, through a series of acquisitions of enterprises like Lotus, has also developed a presence in this market. The majority of Microsoft's sales are derived from industry-standard operating systems such as Windows NT and Windows 98, as well as its industry/business software. The result has been that Microsoft has come to enjoy an 80 per cent market share of the operating systems market. In addition, Microsoft is seeking to establish the same form of dominance over Internet software through its browser system. This has brought it into direct conflict with more established Internet enterprises such as Netscape Communications. The high-profile anti-trust trial was based on accusations that Microsoft had abused its dominance of the operating system to ensure that its Internet software became ubiquitous at the expense of Netscape (see the case study in Chapter 5, 'The Microsoft trial' on p 151).

The Linux system (a freeware version of the traditional Windows rival operating system, UNIX) is being lauded as a potential challenger to the dominance of Microsoft's operating system. This system has evolved from the interaction of thousands of computer programs operating across the Internet to develop an open (as opposed to proprietary) system, which users can modify to meet their own needs. Many enterprises are now offering derivatives of this core Linux code to users through the Internet. The growing popularity of the code is witnessed by many of the larger enterprises such as IBM and Oracle starting to offer Linux applications.

Exact figures of the spread of Linux are hard to gauge but an estimate by the *Financial Times* in 1999 (*Financial Times*, 1999d) established a rough estimate of between 7.5 million and 10.5 million copies in use. This represents an increase in market share of some 200 per cent in the 12 months to mid-1999. This is still minuscule beside the dominance of Microsoft, which has some 250 million copies operating. But the rate of growth of Microsoft's Windows and other operating systems is lagging far behind the compound growth rates exhibited by Linux. The advance of Linux has often been by stealth as the computer literate within enterprises 'sneak' in the software to improve the running of the enterprises' IT systems. This infiltration has occurred to the extent that it is estimated that 20 per cent of all enterprises are operating on a Linux system. Linux (as a Unix system) seeks to consolidate the Unix operating system so that the fragmentation of this sector, which allowed Windows to gain its dominance, is in the future impossible. This momentum depends upon the continued support of the large enterprises within the IT sector (such as Intel, IBM, HP, Compaq, Sun and Dell) on both the software and hardware sides. After making initially strong inroads into the Internet server market, the operating system is finally starting to gain a foothold in the desktop market. These trends have started to concern Microsoft, which is now taking Linux seriously as a rival to its own operating systems. The challenger has some way to go before it can be considered a serious rival though the army of dedicated developers who are evolving it could mean that its maturity in terms of marketability may not be too distant.

The shift of emphasis by Microsoft towards the Internet is based upon a market trend that has seen its power over the PC market loosened as this technology becomes more ubiquitous. Microsoft has developed an 'embrace and extend' strategy to the Internet that has put this technology at the heart of many of the company's products and, in an attempt to leapfrog the first movers, ploughed considerable sums into the development of its Internet products. Indeed it has spent considerable sums to develop a more complete rival to Sun's Java programs (see below) through its ActiveX software. This is important if Microsoft is to achieve the same domination over the Internet that it has over the desktop. Microsoft aims to make Windows ubiquitous across all formats. It is advancing into the corporate server market and also, as a result of an agreement between Microsoft and AT&T, into access through televisions via set-top boxes.

Software developed for the Internet is being redesigned to make it directly applicable to this environment. Many leading companies such as Oracle and Sun Microsystems are leading the development of software to extend the capabilities of the Internet through electronic commerce. Sun's Java computer language (see below) has been developed and is able to work on any operating system. Its programs (called 'applets') have the ability to be linked to data on the Internet and deliver it directly to the computer of the end user. Oracle's strength is based upon its leadership of the database software market, with applications to sort, file and access information in a user-friendly and accessible manner.

This shift is likely to result in changes for the software sector (see below), as there will be an evident need for:

- new standards because of the development of new languages such as Java (see below) that enable the unbundling of major languages in applets;

- platform neutrality – interpreters are being developed to run each major platform, thereby enabling Java-like applications to run seamlessly;

- network involvement – the Internet is facilitating network access to information and applets, thereby overcoming the need to store data on the desktop.

Software enterprises and operating systems will lose influence as Java-like interpreters eliminate incompatibilities across platforms. Open software standards are likely to facilitate the entry into the market of smaller, market-specific players.

There can be little doubt that the Internet is going to alter the software industry and will also act as a forum for increased interaction with other sectors. The speed with which it is developing is placing challenges upon software enterprises to develop instantly usable solutions. In response to such challenges, software enterprises are increasingly developing applications using 'components' rather than large, often unwieldy programs. This gives enterprises better flexibility and lower development costs as well as making their applications easier to support – an important feature in an era of rapidly changing user requirements. This enables many enterprises to respond quickly to the demands the Internet places upon their programs, notably for speed and tailor-made solutions. Many of the leading software enterprises are seeking to secure their positions within the evolving Internet market, not only through strong organic growth but also through a series of aggressive acquisitions of smaller rivals.

To many in the industry the Java programming language is seen as the future of the software sector. Sun, which invented Java, hoped to develop a system that would enable any application to run on any platform, thereby breaking the traditional link between the application and the operating system. The result has been a conflict between Sun and Microsoft, which wanted to take the development of Java out of Sun's hands. For Microsoft this was a defensive move to ensure that the spread of Java did not undermine the competitive position of Microsoft's Windows operating system. If Java were successful, it would lower the importance of the operating system in the systems architecture, provide added competitive pressure from rival operating systems such as Unix and undermine the potential of its Internet browser – a key part of its commercial strategy. Java is an open system and is used as the common language for the Internet. Sun's role is effectively to act as a custodian for the language and generally drive its direction, notably in terms of standards development. The central point is that the future of the Internet is based upon heterogeneous networks – Java enables them to interconnect and interwork. This attacks the monopoly of Microsoft and seeks to overcome what many see as the stifling effects of proprietary standards. This attack is strengthened by the alliance between Oracle and Sun to link their technologies to create all-embracing computer systems that compete head on with Microsoft. They seek to develop 'Internet computing' that uses browser software as the interface to all other applications thereby making conventional operating systems (such as Windows) redundant. In late 1998, Microsoft was stopped from shipping its own version of Java, which was incompatible with other versions – therefore violating the 'write once run anywhere' ethos of Java – and which ran only on the Windows system.

Almost all of the leading Internet software providers have agreed to support the Java language. IBM is rapidly seeking to integrate the software into its computer platforms. All of the IT sector will be affected if

Java is fully accepted. For the first time software development can take place independently of the operating system. Software developers are able to develop one version of their program and run it on any operating system. There has been increasing resentment by some software companies, given the rising importance of Java to many enterprises, of the control that Sun has over its development. Many feel that it is inappropriate for a competitor to control a strategic technology that is key to an increasing number of enterprises within the sector. To overcome such problems, Sun has made changes to the licence to enable others to alter the source code to meet their own requirements. There is criticism of the attempts by Sun to limit the ability of developers to develop a platform-specific version of Java. Many enterprises feel that the cross-platform Java is too slow. Microsoft developed a version of Java that worked better on its Windows operating system. The result was the lawsuit from Sun mentioned above. The need to operate across all platforms tended to slow the application markedly. Developing with preference for a single platform tends to overcome this problem. Microsoft for one makes no secret of its attempts to bypass Sun's control over Java.

To complement Java (the universal language for software) Sun has developed Jini – the equivalent for hardware. This enables all devices to act as a community, and could transform computing, enabling the more effective and efficient use of computing resources. This situation is tailor-made for the development of the aforementioned 'thin-client appliances' provided by a range of developers. These should allow diverse ranges of appliances to communicate with one another over the medium of the Internet. In addition, the development of these appliances, in undermining the power of the PC, should also undermine the power of Microsoft.

The software industry has tended to operate under its own fairly unique economic system. Many software developers are increasingly using the Internet to distribute their software free – so-called freeware. The idea is to get users hooked. Once hooked, the developers can sell other software and increase sales to gain a strong market presence on relatively low entry costs. The strategy is based upon securing increasing returns for their product. The industry is characterized by high fixed costs in areas such as R&D and low variable costs. Thus as the units sold increase so the unit cost falls markedly. In addition, there are no inventory and very few raw-material costs. The result is that there is a tendency for monopolies to emerge. The leverage of fixed cost gives the volume producers big price advantages over their rivals. The power of the dominant software is compounded by the existence of network externalities and ongoing incompatibility between rival forms of software as well as the creation of lock-in with some of them.

When Sun announced in late 1999 that it intended to offer its basic office software free through portals as part of its attempt to challenge the dominance of Microsoft Office, it hinted at the opportunities and threats posed by the Internet for the software sector. Microsoft's response to this challenge was more or less to do the same. However, with Microsoft relying upon office software for 40 per cent of its revenue, the losses seem, initially at least, potentially greater for it than for Sun, especially as other pieces of software that it charges for are also offered free over this medium. These revenues may be replaced as users start to rent software over the Internet for a set fee. Consequently, software is moving towards a position of being offered on tap over the Internet and away from loaded technology. This has the potential to be a big fillip to the maturity of the information market.

Sun has also employed this freeware strategy for Java, giving it away free to application developers, though third-party developers (such as IBM and Oracle) that want to embed it in their product have to buy a licence. The strategy means that money will only start to be made on the software when it has achieved a degree of ubiquity. Netscape has also developed a freeware strategy, giving away its server software to users but using this as a platform to sell more intricate or stylized browsers to customers. In the future, the software industry is going to be characterized by alliances, as existing enterprises seek to protect market share and new entrants seek to achieve access to the market-place.

Sun–AOL–Netscape merger

This is a series of agreements with the potential to challenge the increasingly imposing dominance that Microsoft is having over the development of the Internet. America On-line (AOL) is the world's largest online services and Internet access provider and through its merger with Netscape – the pioneer of Internet browser software – provides a powerful counterweight to Microsoft. To AOL, the take-over reinforced its strategy to push its presence on the Internet, allowing it to broaden its global audience, advance its multi-brand strategy, push the growth of electronic commerce and expand the range of products available to the customers of both enterprises. Simultaneously, AOL announced a strategic development and marketing alliance with Sun Micro-systems. This alliance is in effect a joint software company, which seeks to become the leading supplier of electronic commerce systems, placing it in direct competition with IBM and (as mentioned) Microsoft. The aim of the alliance is to develop cheap new Internet access devices using Sun's Java programming language (see above).

The result of these agreements is to establish a single range of products and unified marketing force to push their combined presence in this evolving market-place. As part of the process, AOL is licensing Netscape's electronic commerce software to Sun. The development will centre upon developing end-to-end solutions for those businesses that want to engage in electronic commerce. Thus customers will be offered Sun's servers, Netscape's software tools and support services and a deal for online presence either through AOL or Netscape's Netcenter. In addition, AOL and Sun are collaborating to develop devices for the emergence of pervasive computing – they are already developing a range of cheap and portable Internet devices. Furthermore, the two enterprises are dedicated to challenging Microsoft even further by establishing a presence on the desktop.

The deal seems to make good strategic sense playing as it does the relative strengths of each of the partners. Electronic commerce is set for take-off, and AOL is in prime position possessing as it does the busiest site on the Web, the biggest e-mall in cyberspace and the lion's share of advertising revenue. For Netscape, its value is increasingly in its name, which to many is synonymous with the Internet. Its Netcenter – a portal that functions as a gateway for businesses to access the Internet – is an attraction that should allow Netscape's partners to gain a presence in the business market. In combination, AOL and Netscape can offer a one-stop shop for merchants wanting electronic commerce solutions. With 70 per cent of all users being members of AOL or users of Netscape, the business model looks tempting. Sun is important in facilitating the development of new devices to improve access to these sites by businesses. There are also potential difficulties involved in the agreement, not least of which is derived from the differing types of business each of these partners is from and the culture engendered within each. In addition, the move by these businesses into new fields where they are taking on new rivals may take some selling to potential customers. For example, AOL – a consumer company – is now going to be competing in the selling of services to businesses where it is challenging giants such as IBM. The corporates may be cautious. This underlines the importance of Sun to the profile: it is seen to add credibility to the strategy. However, it is not locked in and, if things go awry, it has the ability to walk away.

In the light of the merger and as a strategic response to the emergence of AOL, Microsoft is fighting back to re-establish a foothold. It is doing this by attacking AOL's dominance of instant messaging, offering free Internet access in the US and pushing for broadband development via its alliance with AT&T (see the case study later in this chapter, 'The AT&T/Microsoft partnership' on p 137). The first attack seeks to undermine the stickiness of customers who use AOL's instant messaging and then go on to use other AOL services; the second seeks to undermine the business model of AOL – the majority of its revenue base comes from subscriber fees; the third is longer term, as broadband technology emerges. Broadband access can weaken AOL with or without Microsoft. AOL needs access to cable to sustain itself even though the CEO believes that broadband is no substitute for dial-up access. It has secured access through local deals. However, the core issue comes down to giving customers what they want and currently AOL seems closer to this than others.

Convergence and IT enterprises

In the IT sector, the process of convergence appears to be generated more through the development of new abilities than through a simple process of acquisitions. For example, Oracle is developing software technology for video servers, HP is involved in PCs, servers and workstations, and Microsoft is involved in multimedia CD ROM and interactive network architecture software. The evident interlinkages between these sectors are most notable in terms of the growing importance of the Internet in business strategies. This is typified by the shift away from client-server computing towards Internet computing. As mentioned above, many of the leading IT enterprises have been keen to expand their reach, notably in terms of their Internet presence. Microsoft has developed its Microsoft Network (MSN) to deliver Internet service provision to users. As a means of securing subscribers to this network, the enterprise is busy putting resources into Web shows as well as commissioning content from third parties. To achieve this it has been busy hiring writers and other content producers to differentiate its Web site and to provide attractive information to users. This reflects the strategy of developing converged products through an extension of competencies.

The IT sector is also likely to be greatly affected by the rise in digital television especially if it translates into an increase in the number of Internet users. The result, when taken with the development of interactive television and a corresponding convergence between this technology and PCs, is the translation of computer technology into a mass-market phenomenon. This is highly dependent upon the state of demand for digital television, which currently seems very uncertain. It also needs to overcome the cultural difference between watching TV and using PCs to stimulate interactivity. Such differences may mean that a single device may be elusive. This could be overcome with the onset of Microsoft's Web TV and other forms of Webcasting. Players from the IT sector will also become increasingly prominent in the telecommunication sector. This will be driven by the need for more advanced services such as security mechanisms and transaction processing.

Microsoft has been especially proactive in seeking to reposition itself. It has established a foothold in the cable market (as a prerequisite for using this medium to deliver its interactive services). This reflects its stance that, after the Internet, television is the next great outlet for its products. In 1997, it purchased WebTV to offer its services through this medium, a central part of its strategy in this domain. WebTV had the products needed to allow access to the Internet through the television. Microsoft has also signed a cross-licensing deal with Sony to converge computer and consumer electronics platforms. Alongside this strategy is the need for the enterprise to engage itself in network build, and hence its growing involvement in cable-access television. In the US, it has invested in the Comcast network and also has extensive holdings in a number of European cable-access companies. In addition, Microsoft, via an alliance with Intel and Compaq Computers, is behind a consortium backing the development of more advanced compression technologies. In all, Microsoft is backing a number of technologies as a means of securing access to the home as a means of being in pole position when the information economy really takes off.

It is increasingly evident that many of the large software enterprises are seeking to develop closer links and even alliances with telecommunications enterprises. To these enterprises, the deployment of broadband technologies (especially with the advent of software on tap) is central to their commercial development. Once again, Microsoft has already made known its intention to develop an alliance with a broadband provider in the near future. However, it is unlikely that it will move completely into this area of the value chain.

Software vendors, as noted above, are seeking to enter the service market, often by applying a 'mass customization' approach to the integrated software platform that they are developing for multimedia and Internet markets. Many software developers such as Microsoft, Netscape and Oracle are including in their packages the capabilities to allow users to self-provide a service, thus bypassing service integration. For example, Microsoft and Netscape are developing software to include Internet telephony capabilities.

Content industries

Content means all forms of information, entertainment, communication and transaction services. Consequently, the content industry comprises all businesses that seek to generate value by the means of creating and delivering analogue or digitized texts and/or sound-based services to readily identifiable user groups. Included in this definition are media companies or studios that focus upon content creation, as well as software suppliers and cable operators that deliver content to end users or provide the hardware needed to access the content provided. This broad definition of the content industry reflects the overlap between content creators and those (notably within the IT sector) that provide the means of access. This not only underpins the notion of convergence but also underlines the characteristics of the content industry value chain (see Figure 4.7 on p 125).

It is widely acknowledged that the creation, management and use of content will be the key driver in the information economy. It is vital in an era when the large quantity of information means that grabbing the attention of the consumer is the key to enterprise success. In entertainment, content has to be appealing. In education, content has to be empowering. In industry, content has to be enriching. Content providers will compete on the value of their content and the cost of distributing it. These trends are increasingly framed within the environment created by the need to provide content for a multimedia market.

Consolidation is occurring within the content sector, driven by the desire of enterprises within the sector to be both creators and distributors of content. This explains why there have been a number of high-profile mergers between content producers (such as Disney and Viacom) and broadcast networks (ABC and CBS respectively). Clearly these broadcast networks are the best way for content producers to reach a mass audience. This may be only a temporary strategy until the Internet becomes more widespread and a more effective distribution channel. Indeed many media enterprises are developing alliances with Internet businesses. This investment by media companies reflects a concern that to survive they must have access to the new distribution channel. Some have developed this strategy through in-house expansion (for example, Time Warner with its Pathfinder site), others through acquisition (for example, Disney's purchase of a slice of Infoseek). This latter point reflects the fact that many of these media enterprises want access to the portal sites (the most popular sites on the Internet) to promote their content. In return, Internet companies can get a higher profile through promotion over existing, older distribution channels.

The application of digital technology is altering the commercial aspects of the content industry. This technology is widely used within the audio-visual sector to develop certain aspects more cheaply (such as special effects in film) but also provides for rapid duplication and dissemination. The development of digital technology has also expanded the capabilities of existing technologies, for example digital television has rapidly expanded the range of channels available. In addition, the digitization of information blurs the boundaries between historically separate industries such as print publishing, music publishing and/or the audio-visual sector. It is evident that the evolution of digital technology is having an impact upon content creation in so far as it is altering how the content sector produces, delivers and shares its products. This reflects the fact that not only are the technologies for production and distribution very similar but also highlights that production itself is increasingly taking place through ongoing communication between content creators, programmers and consumers. These changes in content production are eroding the barriers between assorted media (textual, audio and visual) as well as expanding the possibilities for market development and broadening the range of interests concerned with the value of intellectual content.

The development of the Internet provides new opportunities for content providers, which should see their power in the supply chain increase markedly as well as see them develop new roles and reduce costs. The most immediate benefits will come from being able to distribute products rapidly to consumers on both a national and a global level. Many of the larger enterprises are likely to move down the supply chain to become more closely involved in content packaging and service provision and even moving to deal directly with customers. This should significantly increase cash flow. The Internet allows the smaller content providers to indulge in direct marketing and distribution to end users. If they have little experience in this dimension they will need to develop agreements with others who possess more expertise in this dimension, possibly Internet service providers.

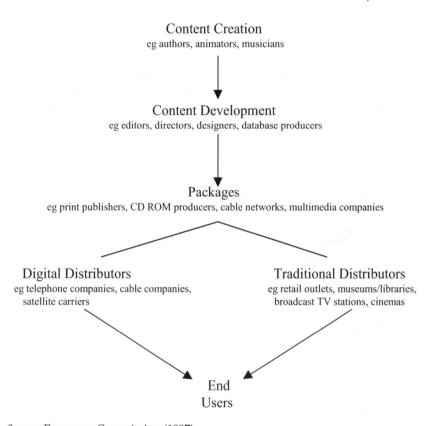

Source: European Commission (1997)

Figure 4.7 *Players in the content industry value chain*

Another important feature of this environment is the advent of platform independence, as content providers have a range of platforms through which they can distribute their work (ie through a telecommunications service provider, an Internet service provider and broadcasting systems). Platform independence will allow providers to deliver their content in a relatively standardized format irrespective of whether the end user has a TV, PC or any other type of terminal. Thus no one type of delivery mechanism will dominate within the multimedia market. The rise of platform independence (through the Internet as well as other forms of distribution) is altering the balance of power within the industry's value chain largely through the fact that content providers are able to exercise greater independence from network operators.

Sony

There is perhaps no stronger brand in the information industry than Sony. However, the emergence of new challengers and new technologies is stimulating a dramatic rethink in corporate strategy as the enterprise seeks to reposition itself within the emerging information economy. In terms of its product portfolio, Sony covers a broad range of areas (audio, video, television, information and communications, and electronic components). In 1999, Sony announced a radical restructuring of its business, seeking to ensure that the enterprise became less dependent upon manufactured products (such as video recorders, television sets and portable stereos) where the margins are declining and shifted towards exploiting Internet opportunities for the business. The strategic vision is essentially to allow customers to download content from Sony's Web site to Sony home audio-visual machines. The plan is to ensure that the hardware made is compatible with providing a capable platform for Internet access. Implicit within the new business model is the view that selling hardware is not where value lies. Value is in providing Internet services. Indeed Playstation II (see below) – via its interactivity – and other hardware will largely generate revenue through the Internet.

The enterprise is being restructured to create greater synergies between different strategic business units to exploit the potential of the network-centred environment. This is being done by investing more in entertainment and services to be provided over its hardware. Its electronic business has been subdivided and given the freedom to create opportunities to exploit technology developments for the network environment. In addition, a separate network business has been established to create a network platform for providing digital content (films, music, etc) to customers.

The impact will be a drastic scaling back of the manufacturing capacity and the bringing back of publicly traded units into the fold. One of these is Sony music, which has co-developed the Playstation with the Sony parent company. The Playstation is Sony's star product, generating 37 per cent of operating profit despite representing only 11 per cent of sales. This move should provide a short-term fillip to the share price, making it easier for the enterprise to raise money to realize its Internet objectives and develop a new range of digital products.

Key to the future is the success of the Playstation's successor, the imaginatively titled Playstation II. This is effectively a 128-bit computer that plays DVS movies, decodes digital TV and allows users to surf the Internet. The device is planned to be priced at a level that should be accessible to most. The aim of Sony is to provide a 'do-it-all' box that allows full multimedia through a single device. The basis of this development is the consumer electronics industry with the games console at its base and extra bits added on. To this end, Sony has announced a joint venture with Microsoft to facilitate the convergence between PCs and consumer audio-visual consoles.

Other bits of Sony's strategy are revealing. Sony set the standard for the content industry's adoption of the belief that there was a direct link between making TV hardware and creating the content. In developing this strategy, Sony bought studios but floundered because, unlike other companies (such as News Corporation – see the case study below, 'News Corporation and the Internet' on p 128), it did not have the cable or broadcast channels it needed. Poor strategy and bureaucracy prevented it from alleviating this problem. Sony's strategy has now altered and it has remedied its strategic error. In contrast to other content creators, it has globalized production of its programming, shifting away from the US-dominated content of its rivals towards local production and marketing. What it is doing is establishing not only its own local TV channel but also local music and film production and distribution. These separate entities use and promote one another's material. There is a core of content that is used and reused across separate media. In addition to this content derived from its film and music channels, it is also seeking to develop content through interactive games (such as the Playstation) and educational software. This change in strategy means that Sony will also have to engage in alliances – a new experience for this enterprise – especially in order to obtain the enabling software for the platforms it is developing.

Content packagers such as online portals and other aggregators of information and content are likely to be pivotal in the information economy by filling an important void in the link between the user and the world of content. Many elsewhere in the communications industry may need to develop agreements with these enterprises if they are not to be marginalized in the information economy. The packagers provide the core value added by promoting the aggregation and accessibility of the key component – content. Indeed over time the content packager could displace the network operators as the key player in the industry value chain. This is reinforced by the trend towards platform independence.

Across the global economy, there tends to be a strong demand for indigenous content with the result that the content industry is often very localized. Through the development of new technologies (such as the Internet) and on the back of more traditional forms of media, notably those from US sources such as the film industry, this is slowly changing. The US is the one state whose content industries have developed international appeal with its content sector (including software as well as films and television programming) being a major export earner. This has helped the English language gain dominance in terms of content, which has stimulated a limited backlash as some states seek to redress the balance through the development of schemes to secure the development of indigenous (often non-English language based) content (see Chapter 5). This still fits in with content generally seeming most attractive when it is local.

The content industry is evidently undergoing change not only through the albeit gradual globalization of content and technological change but also through the radical restructuring of the industry as content production and delivery become increasingly dominated by SMEs. SMEs are increasingly becoming the source of a great deal of innovative content through the use of digital technologies. In addition, SMEs – through the Internet – have a means of delivering their content to a mass audience. In addition, the digitization of the sector is likely to increase competitive pressure further. In areas such as television programming, there is greater scope for diversity and smaller-scale production as well as more intense competition through greater choice for, and interactivity with, end users. This will enable the content industry to target users much more precisely.

News Corporation and the Internet

Initially Rupert Murdoch, the chairman and chief executive of News Corporation, seemed to be bucking a very definite industry trend in being unenthusiastic about the impact of the Internet upon business. Indeed one could argue that Mr Murdoch's attitude bordered upon cynical, stating as he did that the Internet was likely to destroy more businesses than it created. This stance was in stark contrast to other enterprises such as AOL and Bertelsmann. However, it is becoming increasingly clear that News Corporation, as a content creator and distributor, is ensuring that the Internet is moving to the centre of its corporate strategy, believing that over the medium to longer term much of the enterprise's value will be derived from the technology.

The transformation of News Corporation was typified by the alliance the enterprise developed with Softbank (an Internet enterprise). Softbank's alliance with News Corporation's Internet subsidiary E-Partners has enabled the two enterprises to establish a new company, E-Ventures, to promote Internet businesses in European and other non-US markets. The core objective of the new venture will be to assist US-based Internet enterprises establish a presence in non-US markets. The desire is to allow News Corporation to tap into the fast-growing small businesses that are increasingly driving the growth and development of the Internet and also to benefit from the (currently) large valuations these enterprises receive upon flotation. This is based upon a recognition that while News Corporation may be big it is not one of the fastest in terms of technological development. This it needs to secure through the development of E-Partners. Big media enterprises using traditional formats need to be nimble enough to make opportunities from new media investments. This involvement by E-Partners will largely be through taking equity stakes in the small enterprises developing these new forms of media. To kick-start this, News Corporation has provided $300 million equity base.

The E-Ventures alliance is based on the tried-and-tested Softbank model, which it has used to enable 10 US Internet companies to develop overseas offshoots, mainly in Japan. Through the alliance with News Corporation it seeks to spread this to the rest of the global economy to encourage access by existing enterprises as well as new start-ups. To date, it has invested in a number of enterprises that are local equivalents of US enterprises. For example, it has invested in a UK affiliate of the US online mortgage provider, E-Loan, as well as other financial services industries where there is proven online commercial potential. It aims to invest in up to 75 companies by 2001.

Like other broadcasters, News Corporation should have little incentive to embrace the Internet: research has shown that TV watching is the first to suffer from a larger online audience. However, as News Corporation and other broadcast enterprises have shown, ignoring this medium is not an option. Importantly, broadcasters' Internet strategies have to be balanced with a desire not to move so fast that other (current) businesses have their commercial viability undermined. This explains why E-Partners is removed from much of its current businesses – newspapers, publishing and television. However to Mark Booth (the head of E-Partners) the key to success is in combining the best factors of large enterprise (large resources) with the best facts of being small (nimble, fast moving and entrepreneurial).

There is little to be said of what the longer-term objectives of News Corporation are from these investments. Diversification into these areas seems unlikely. What is more likely is that the enterprise will get control of key distribution channels and use this as a method to promote and distribute existing and evolving businesses as well as getting its hands on new technology. What it needs to be convinced of first is that the business models in which it is investing are sustainable and that therefore the presence of News Corporation on the Internet sustains the prominent position of the business within the global media market-place.

Convergence and the content sector

In theory, the process of convergence and the associated rapid expansion of channels that inevitably require filling should spell good times for the content sector. The digital revolution lowers the cost of producing television and printed media to the point where start-ups can occur without a great deal of capital. However, there is the increased threat of competition as telecommunication and IT enterprises start to distribute programming and information directly to their customers. This is clearly something to which content creators and distributors will have to respond.

The impact upon the content sector seems to be, as expected, very much driven by the expansion of channels and the move towards offering Web services through the broadcasting medium – so-called Webcasting. To some, the television is the natural medium to deliver access to more advanced services, as it can negate the need by end consumers to purchase specialized equipment such as PCs. The ability of digital channels to deliver interactive capabilities means that they are a natural medium for such services. To many in the content sector – especially in television – there still seems to be a Rubicon to cross. The broadcasting medium is clearly about entertainment – as opposed to the common conception of the Internet being about information. Thus over the short term, the issues for media enterprises are about developing interactivity to the extent that it meets the requirements of what is entertaining to users – that is, provides value added to the TV experience. In the broadcasting sector, whilst there is a belief that convergence will occur, there is a need to ensure the infrastructure is able to cope with the capacity demanded. This, as mentioned above, is still very much absent. There is a belief that convergence will tend to lag behind developments in digital technology. Familiarity with the TV as a medium will keep it ahead of other forms of delivery.

Many of the large media enterprises have been especially active in moving into other parts of the emerging information industry value chain. Media enterprises such as Canal Plus, News Corporation and Bertelsmann already have their own communications networks. This puts them in prime position to enter the multimedia market at several points in the value chain. However, their lack of knowledge of other parts of the value chain has led to many developing alliances to secure competitive position. This is typified by the alliance between NBC and Microsoft in the US to develop news over the Internet as well as Bertelsmann's link with AOL to develop AOL Europe. This seeks to exploit the core strategic advantages of each in their respective position in the value chain. The lack of knowledge of some parties of the other parts of the value chain has steered them from such an expansive strategy, and they merely seek to consolidate and strengthen their position within their existing niche.

Across the sector there have been a number of alliances signed by content originators with broadcasters in areas such as films and sporting events for pay TV services. These typify strategies where originators use the platforms of content packagers to distribute their material. This group is not interested in the technology, merely in the means to access the maximum potential market. Other smaller enterprises will tend to bypass content packagers and publish material themselves through their own online transaction systems. More still will tend towards renewable contracts with content packagers in order to achieve the best value for content on a regular basis (eg the UK's premiership football).

Content packagers (eg broadcasters and publishers) have become increasingly involved in 'push' media where content is sent direct to the user on a regular basis over an Internet connection. Packagers, because of the need to fill the rapid expansion of channels, will move downstream towards content originators, and will need to provide a variety of open platforms for content providers. This reflects the increased salience of content in an increasingly competitive environment. A move upstream towards service provision and infrastructure incentives may be possible for packagers, so as to limit the access of other rival packagers. This is important in the transitional phase of convergence where telecommunication networks are unable to offer the same degree of functionality as broadcasting networks.

Evidently the development of digital television makes the convergence between that medium and the Internet more likely – this has been increasingly borne out by the experience of sectors such as publishing and broadcasting (see above). It is unlikely that full interactivity will be achieved. What is envisaged is 'lazy interactivity' where only certain aspects are integrated, for example in terms of response to advertisements or games. Across the sector the Internet is not viewed as a competitor or replacement medium but as a complementary one. This is especially evident in the case of portals. These are likely to become the most visited sites on the Internet so obtaining access to this audience is becoming a key objective for media enterprises. In 1998, Disney bought a share in Infoseek (a leading portal), and intends to use the knowledge acquired to develop its own version, GO, and integrate this into its other business operations. A similar approach is reflected in the strategy of Bertelsmann (the German-based publisher) with its take-over of a leading ISP. The knowledge gained was used to enhance rather than replace existing formats. This is notable in other areas as new enterprises seek to use the Internet as an alternative retailing forum. This increased use of the Internet has inevitably led to the potential of alliances with enterprises in other sectors to develop innovative forms of delivery.

The Internet is clearly something that broadcasters need to respond to, as evidence tends to show (as mentioned) that increases in the usage of the Internet are at the expense of television. This is obviously a threat to broadcasters. There are strategies by broadcasters to utilize Internet technology to secure their positioning. Cable enterprises are seeking alliances that provide as wide a range of information and entertainment services as possible through their systems. This strategy has been typified by enterprises such as Time Warner that have moved into interactive services such as video-on-demand. An alliance that typifies the strategies of broadcasters is Fox News Online, which has signed an agreement with the AtHome cable Internet network to provide the news content for its broadband Internet service. In terms of broadcast infrastructure, the links to terminal manufacturers are more important. This is especially important in areas such as the development of the set-top boxes necessary for digital TV, which could prove to be a bottleneck in the system.

Another form of convergence affecting the sector is the gradual increase in the oft-mentioned Webcasting, which is essentially broadcasting using Internet technologies. In this form, information is organized into channels and pushed out to viewers. Essentially Webcasting is based upon the premise that when you sign up for a service you specify the channels you require and how often you want to be updated. Evidently it is more complex than this as software is in action scanning the Internet to provide up-to-date information as and when it is required. Such developments overcome the need for the user to spend an age using search engines seeking to find the relevant information or to have a prolonged wait while the information is being downloaded. This technology is already being utilized by direct marketers who wish to target customers. It is also being used to deliver up-to-date news, sports and weather to customers on a continual basis.

These developments are complemented by more advanced software, such as RealNetworks and Microsoft NetShow, which allows for the transmission of cinema releases over the Internet. So far developments have been limited, with this medium proving to be an outlet for smaller film producers wishing to gain a limited distribution network for their output. The interactivity stimulated by the advent of digital TV is to many the clearest and most evident expression of convergence. Currently businesses such as the BBC, Bertelsmann and BSkyB are developing interactive services with a dual approach, offering both interactive digital broadcast services (such as video-on-demand) and broadband online services (such as high-speed Internet access) with the latter likely to dominate in the short term. The former will be launched only once the new digital television market has reached a degree of maturity. In the light of these developments, many in the software sector are seeking to develop a presence in the broadcasting market to ensure they have access to this burgeoning interactive TV market. Microsoft, NEC and Alcatel have all made moves to gain a stake in this market. Sharp and Mitsubishi are less confident about the market, and stopped production of their 'enhanced TV' models in mid-1998.

The trend towards convergence in the information industries

This chapter started with the viewpoint that the process of technological change and competition is stimulating a process of convergence between the three sectors (IT, telecommunications and content) leading to development of a more fully integrated information industry. It is evident that these processes are only just beginning. It is at this point that I wish to come back to the process of convergence, building on the analysis of the sectors involved offered above, and examine how key players are evolving strategies to meet the challenges it poses. It is important to stress that the changes in industry structure as a result of the process of convergence are not necessarily about conglomeration *per se* – though this has been in many senses the standard industry response – but are more about enterprises responding to their changing technological and commercial environment. The changes in the products and markets arising from the process of convergence, notably in terms of the emergence of multimedia, are reflected in Figure 4.8 on p 134.

According to Oliver, Roos and Bart (*Financial Times*, 1999e), there are two types of convergence. One is driven by demand as customers start to consider products offered by separate industries as interchangeable. The other is supply-driven, when products from separate industries work better in conjunction than they do separately. It is evident in the case of the emerging information industry that both of these forms of convergence are present. In the demand-driven instance, the growing interlinkages across the sectors bears witness to growing interchangeability. In the supply-driven case, convergence is present in various areas, for example the content sector can evidently work better if it has better-developed links to the IT and communications sector giving it more effective delivery platforms and potential interactivity.

In terms of the information industries (see the respective sections of this chapter), convergence could be defined as one or more of the following:

- the delivery of multiple services (eg local, long-distance, international, data, Internet and wireless services) provided from a single service provider within a single integrated package;

- the consolidation of existing networks and systems into a single common service infrastructure;

- (perhaps the most frequent form of convergence) the integration of previously distinct markets and services of carriers, Internet service providers, cable operators, systems integrators and vendors of computer hardware and software.

What these definitions underline is how variable a concept convergence seems to be. The form and importance of each definition does tend to vary within and indeed between the respective value chains. For example, service providers, over the short term at least, are tending to use the first definition in altering their product portfolios though over time it is widely anticipated that this form of convergence will necessitate the other forms noted above.

Research by Andersen Consulting (www.ac.com) suggests that there are three distinct phases to convergence:

1. Convergence takes place between individual sectors, creating new market segments and new entrants into these sectors (eg Internet service provision, Internet telephony, etc). There is, at this stage, still a great deal of uncertainty as to how the industry will evolve.

2. Structural barriers between sectors start to disappear with the result that there is increased competition between dominant players in different parts of the converging value chains. This is driven by the desire of enterprises to position themselves to gain maximum leverage upon the value chain.

3. The success of an enterprise depends upon the development of applications that draw upon all technologies from the communication, IT and content sectors. Vertical integration is common at this stage either through acquisition or through the establishment of a network of partners.

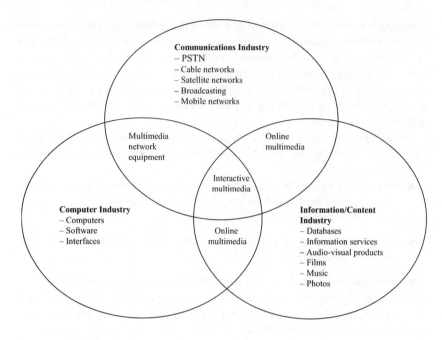

Source: OECD (1995)

Figure 4.8 *The convergence phenomenon*

These stages of convergence and the corresponding development of multimedia offer many attractive prospects for the emerging information industry. It provides opportunities in a number of ways, notably:

■ because of the churn in the markets for business and consumers' terminals, and also for IT and telecommunication equipment, as new applications and services emerge;

■ from the substitution of traditional distribution methods and product formats with less expensive and more accessible network applications, and the diverting of the associated revenues to different points in the value chain;

■ through exploitation of the economies of scale inherent in distributing a broad range of information services across the same infrastructure.

It has been noted above in Figures 4.2 and 4.3, as well as in the preceding analysis, how the process of convergence is altering the value chain within the emerging information industry. In short, the information value chain is changing as new sources of value are detected. This is reflected in Figure

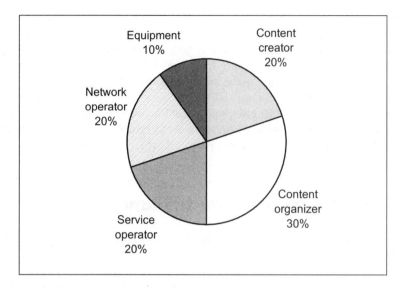

Source: European Commission (1997)

Figure 4.9 *Sources of value in the converging industries value chain (approximate percentages)*

4.9, which indicates how the value chain is being altered through the process of convergence in these sectors. These changes are marked when compared to the traditional telecommunications value chain where 80 per cent of value added was contributed by network and service operators and the remainder by equipment suppliers. These shifts are altering the strategies of enterprises as they seek to reposition themselves to maximize their commercial opportunities in what is an evolving industry. Overall, enterprises are responding to the process of convergence through a mixture of the following strategic options:

- extension of competencies;
- merger or acquisition;
- joint venture or alliance.

As mentioned above, these actions are perceived in terms of enterprises repositioning themselves across the following five functional areas within the emerging value chain: content creation, storage through databases, display via devices, process through applications and distribution through transport. With the advent of multimedia, according to Sheth and Wallace (1994), this will be reduced to three distinct competencies: networks, devices and content. Network providers will not merely transmit but also provide processing capabilities. Alongside this, equipment manufacturers are evolving from simply offering display functions towards offering storage of multimedia information. Content creation is likely to remain a separate function but will evidently be the industry's powerhouse.

In terms of mergers and alliances a recent report by the Analysys consultancy (1998) – commissioned by the European Commission – highlighted the following trends at horizontal and vertical levels in the evolving information industry value chain, many of which have been reflected in the preceding analysis.

Horizontal mergers and alliances

Activity at a specific level of the value chain has generally been prompted by the following factors:

- *Gaining minimum efficient scale.* This has been developed where enterprises need to be of a certain size in order to compete effectively, especially if they are entering new markets. Mergers are used to achieve this objective as witnessed by the consolidation of the UK cable television market.

- *The high cost of digital technologies.* Mergers or alliances allow these costs to be spread and the risks to one individual enterprise correspondingly reduced. This has been evidenced in areas such as the development of terminals to cope with multimedia traffic.

- *The uncertainty of demand for new services.* This has been especially prevalent in the digital satellite sector, though these alliances have tended to be fragile in practice.

- *Internationalization.* As noted above, telecommunications has been a sector where alliance development and mergers have been especially prevalent in response to this pressure.

- *Regulatory change.* Once again telecommunication and cable access television have sought to move towards consolidation as they find new opportunities in other markets and as they find existing subscriber bases under threat from new competitors.

Vertical mergers and alliances

These reflect more completely how many expect the industry to evolve as enterprises seek a presence in other places in the value chain. These vertical activities have generally been stimulated by the factors below:

- *The uncertainty of market demand.* When entering new markets, enterprises are inevitably going to face risks. To overcome such problems, mergers and alliances are clear options. They have been especially evident in the early stages of the development of digital television.

- *Market positioning and access to new skills.* Mergers and alliances have been used to gain the skills needed to succeed in new, strategically important markets. For example, many media and telecommunication companies have been active in alliance formations or mergers with specialist Internet service providers.

- *Control of channels to customers.* This seeks to enhance the power of the enterprise. For example, Disney has sought access via both alliance and merger to a broad number of distribution channels from cable through to the Internet.

- *Moving into higher-value areas of the value chain.* This is evident in telephony where the emergence of competition in the otherwise core voice market has stimulated many PTOs to develop new competitiveness especially in terms of the Internet.

- *Competition from enterprises in other parts of the value chain.* As markets evolve, enterprises need to respond to the actions of their rivals who may have been repositioning themselves.

These trends within the market reflect both offensive and defensive positioning by enterprises. On the offensive side, all of the sectors share a common perception that the emerging multimedia market is an attractive one. The telecommunication operators see it as a lucrative way to use the increasing levels of spare capacity – broadcasters through innovation and new customer relationships, and content industries through less distribution constraints and greater platform independence. It is evident that many enterprises perceive the need to spread themselves across many different functions if they are to survive in the information industry. Indeed many enterprises will need to achieve expertise or obtain access to expertise across a number of functions.

The AT&T/Microsoft partnership

As the text suggests, AT&T and Microsoft are two enterprises that are going to be key players in the development of the information economy. The alliance between the two is part and parcel of the patchwork of alliances that these enterprises have established as part of their strategy for the information economy. The alliance is based upon a series of agreements between the two enterprises to work together to accelerate the deployment of broadband and next-generation Internet services. As part of the agreement, Microsoft has purchased a $5 billion stake in AT&T (to be used to extend the roll-out of its digital boxes) whilst AT&T will increase the use of Microsoft's TV software platform in its advanced set-top boxes (which are essentially small computers). Microsoft will also supply AT&T with 7.5 million to 10 million copies of its Windows CE software – a scaled-down version of its PC equivalent. In addition, the two will work together to showcase new digital cable services, initially in three cities across the US. Whilst each is still investing in other platforms for the delivery of digital services (such as telephony and wireless), this agreement does appear to give cable the edge in terms of becoming the chosen access mechanism to advanced services.

The agreement between the two enterprises seeks to provide extra stimulus to establishing the commercial viability of advanced services, something that has evidently been lacking. These enterprises believe that the market is maturing and that commercial viability is not too distant, as technological developments such as low-cost powerful chips lower the price of access. In addition, through AT&T and its spate of purchases of, and alliances with, US cable TV operators, these new services are capable of reaching 25 million homes throughout the US – approximately a quarter of all US households. It is estimated that Windows CE will be offered to between a third and a half of these. In the short term, the aim is to determine what exactly the consumer wants from the service – a key determinant of the roll-out of broadband technology. It is expected that services such as home banking, video-on-demand, online shopping and local information resources will be offered to drive demand for the service. AT&T does not plan to produce its own content, leaving this up to interested third parties – though this may include Microsoft's own MSN online services.

Despite the evident size of both parties and the controversy surrounding Microsoft, the development is designed to be run in an open environment, thus alleviating any competition concerns that may emerge. The new network should therefore be fully interoperable with technology developed by other enterprises. Despite this, the partnership does seem to give Microsoft a significant advantage over its rivals (notably Sun and Oracle) in adapting cable technology to support Internet and broadband technologies. The fear is that the Windows system, which has proved ubiquitous for PCs, could extend its dominance to interactive TV. The revenue benefits to Microsoft are not great over the short term, as the alliance is best expressed in terms of its long-term objective of establishing and controlling the standard for set-top box software.

As the biggest rival to the alliance, America On-line, is not excluded from the network, rivalry between these enterprises should still be evident. The open environment strategy is central to avoiding the gaze of already wary regulators. To other software developers, the alliance could be a set-back – AT&T already had an agreement (through the TCI merger) with Sun to develop the software for set-top boxes. Sun is assured this agreement is safe. However, it does put pressure upon these enterprises to prove that their software is better than Microsoft's in order to gain the same kind of access that Microsoft now enjoys.

Despite the developments noted above, the process of convergence has been slower to take off than was previously envisaged. This was due to a number of structural barriers derived from:

- the fact that consumer behaviour has proved hard to change;
- the distraction to enterprise strategies caused by the impact of deregulation;
- the continued good performance of traditional businesses;
- the time taken to develop and deploy the technologies associated with a converged environment.

Such barriers should have seemed inevitable. Getting into place the infrastructure as well as the socio-economic culture to support a commercial viable information industry will only occur over the medium to long term. There are likely also to be barriers to convergence stimulated by the lack of a common industry culture, regulation and anti-trust legislation (especially in terms of cross-media ownership) and a number of firm specific barriers related to core competency issues.

What are being witnessed are the birth pangs of an evolving industry. What is happening is, in effect, convergence with a small 'c' and not the grand-vision convergence outlined throughout this chapter. This small 'c' convergence is based on a whole variety of technological changes such as:

- the movement from analogue to digital networks;
- the emergence of satellite radio to compete with broadcast;
- wireless competition with landlines;
- PCs versus TVs.

Thus over the short term, convergence is about the integration of low-level technologies; the new industry value chain is only expected to emerge over the medium to long term.

Conclusion

The development of an information industry is central to the development of the information economy. It is from this sector that the technologies supporting many of the benefits and changes highlighted within previous chapters are sourced. Under the impact of increased competition and technological change the sector is undergoing change as the telecommunications, IT and content sectors start to converge and the technologies used by each and the market each occupies become increasingly intertwined. This is a challenge that many enterprises across all of the sectors are responding to through a mixture of extending competencies, alliances, mergers and acquisition. It is clear that adjusting strategy to reflect the move towards convergence is going to be key to enterprises within the information industry being successful, as well as important in ensuring that the information economy is able to supply what is expected of it.

5 Policy and regulation for the information economy

Throughout its development and commercial maturity, the information economy will require certain forms of assistance in terms of policy actions as well as legal and regulatory guarantees to users and providers of the technologies, services and applications associated with its evolution. Many of the issues involved reflect the broad market-led development of the information economy though others are derived from the changing nature of commercial activity and the challenges it poses for current legal and regulatory frameworks. This chapter seeks to offer a broad overview of these issues. Many of these topics probably require books in their own right, and therefore only a broad outline of the core issues and concerns are addressed within this section. The core theme is to explore why each of these topics increases in salience with the information economy and how industry-led and governmental actions are developing global solutions to what are fundamental issues for the maturing of the information economy. In many instances, the geographical focus of the analysis will be the US and the EU, which as the world's two largest trading blocs are important laboratories for the emergence of the information economy.

Regulating the development of the information economy

The information economy is difficult to regulate for two basic reasons: 1) its scope and technological base evolve rapidly; and 2) it is, by its very nature, transnational.

The latter is especially important, as it calls for a common international legal and regulatory framework. Figure 5.1 highlights the interaction between evolving industry structure (as represented by Eurescom's schematized information value chain) and the regulatory framework required. The regulation of the new economy is based upon the desire that the private sector should ultimately lead its development. In this context, many of the leading industrialized states, often within the framework of the OECD, are generally pushing for a self-regulating framework with industry establishing its own rules and conventions for the operation of the information economy. Within this context, the role of government should be largely complementary, providing a stable, international legal environment to facilitate the commercial maturity of the information economy.

The leading industrial states have recognized and agreed what measures are needed to stimulate the commercial maturity of the information economy. This has not readily been translated into agreed international frameworks due to basic disputes over the manner and form of regulation. There have, for example, been repeated spats between the EU and the US over assorted aspects of the regulation of the Internet. The former tends to possess much less confidence in the ability of the market to regulate itself than the latter. Thus despite states having agreed upon the core issues to be addressed, they differ upon the means of achieving these objectives. The result is a delay in developing the international regulatory framework for the development of the information economy. Many regulators are still uncertain as to the precise impact of the development of the information economy upon their activities and functions and therefore seek to control it more than perhaps they need. Once again this reflects an EU–US culture clash. In developing the Internet, many EU businesses are happy to cede the role of negotiation to government whereas in the US this role is undertaken by industry. These differences are not just over the method of regulation but also about the power of the individual relative to enterprises. The EU wants to protect the individual from the corporation whereas the US wants to protect the individual from government. The OECD recognizes that states have different legal and political traditions, which are inevitably going to be reflected in their perspective on how the information economy evolves. It also underlines that, despite these differences, states need to be flexible due to the common commercial concerns involved in, and the global nature of, the information economy.

Despite differences between states, there is currently little challenge to the influence the US will have in determining the legal and regulatory structures required. In 1999, the US accounted for 80 per cent of all electronic commerce transactions whereas only 39 per cent of EU enterprises had anything remotely approaching an electronic commerce strategy. Thus the US is dealing with issues that for its enterprises are real but for others are merely hypothetical. The US government's *Framework for Digital Global*

Function	Regulatory Issue

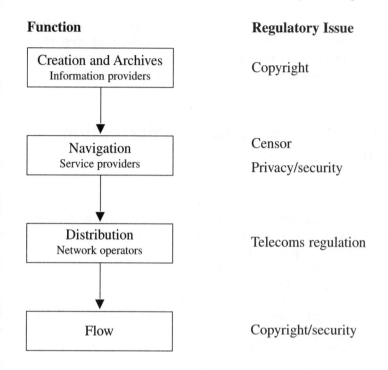

Function	Regulatory Issue
Creation and Archives Information providers	Copyright
Navigation Service providers	Censor Privacy/security
Distribution Network operators	Telecoms regulation
Flow	Copyright/security

Source: Eurescom (1995)

Figure 5.1 *The information value chain framework and regulation*

Electronic Commerce (1997) has helped set the agenda globally not only by promoting self-regulation but also through advocating a commercial code to cover electronic transactions with feasible provisions for governmental recognition of electronic contracts, mutual recognition of electronic signatures, etc. This has been adopted by the UN within its proposed law for regulating electronic commerce. In combination, these should push states towards an agreement upon cross-border dispute resolution based essentially on a US-determined commercial model.

The differences between states over the regulation of the information economy partially reflects the commercial concerns that each has in its development. If the information economy is going to be the new commercial paradigm, providing enterprises with a head start could go a long way to their gaining a secure competitive advantage in the information marketplace. Despite this self-interested perspective, there is a clear recognition that governments need to balance the need for protection (in areas such as fraud) with the need to enjoy the competitive benefits of the information economy. Consequently some minimal level of regulation is clearly going to be needed especially in the formative stages of the information economy's development as a means of securing both consumer and producer confidence. This recognizes that under-regulation could be as detrimental as over-regulation.

Governmental actions in the information economy

Despite disagreements over the manner and form of the regulatory environment for the information economy, all major players are agreed that the private sector through responding to market forces should lead its development. However markets (over the short term at least) are tending to exhibit immaturity leading to a potentially vicious cycle of under-development for the information economy. Consequently many governments have developed strategies, on both the demand and supply sides of the emerging information market, to break this vicious cycle and stimulate a virtuous cycle of growth through which governments aim to kick-start the development of the information economy.

The demand-side actions of governments are partially derived from the simple fact that these bodies will be large users of many of the technologies and products associated with the development of the information economy. This is a role that will be pivotal in establishing a mass market for these technologies. Increasingly states are utilizing information technologies as a means of more efficient and effective delivery of public services. Across many parts of the developed world, there have been trials by states in areas such as transport, healthcare and education where the broader application of ICTs has been integral to service management and, increasingly, delivery. Such activities not only deliver greater efficiency to government services but also breed a greater familiarity with ICTs amongst the mass populace – an essential prerequisite to the fuller development of the information economy. This strategy stresses a more proactive role for the state through the active promotion – and in some cases deployment – of the technologies and capabilities associated with the information economy. It essentially reflects a targeting role by the state upon areas of low-demand intensity that would otherwise be excluded from the processes and benefits of the information economy. Ultimately these actions are also about generating sufficient demand within the economy to negate the need for policy support. Thus these demand-side actions are perceived as largely temporary.

Many states have also been proactive on the supply side. This has been especially notable in terms of research and development activities. In line with the broadly pro-market stance of policy, the majority of research and development activities are in those areas deemed to be fairly market-distant, thus overcoming the potential problem that any investment may disturb the global market forces driving the information economy. This state-sponsored research and development needs to be put into proper perspective, dwarfed as it is by the finance spent by the private sector in terms of its own research and development into information economy technologies. In addition, in areas of low information intensities, many governments have developed schemes to promote the relevant skills to enable otherwise excluded groups to participate in the information economy. This should aid enterprises by providing them with the necessary skilled labour base. It is important that governments should not force the pace of the information society as enterprises may resist and be reluctant to adopt ICTs. These strategies meet an evident need on behalf of both business (which needs the labour) and government (which wishes to avoid socio-economic exclusion) in the evolving information economy.

In sum, government action is best suited to creating the right conditions in which enterprises can adapt to meet the commercial challenges posed by the information economy. Policy has to recognize that the information economy will develop on a piecemeal basis with users integrating themselves as and when the need is there. Policy may add speed to the decision but should not ultimately cause the decision. Action is only valid to the extent that it is able to stimulate the commercial maturity of the information market-place. Once immaturity is overcome any action can arguably be viewed as superfluous. Thus direct government action exists in the background not at the forefront of the information economy. Where action is likely to be most effective is in addressing industry's concerns across a broad range of issues from market access through to intellectual property rights. This is essential in securing commercial confidence in the development of the information economy and is perhaps the most effective and lasting contribution that governments can make to its evolution.

Liberalization

The development of the information economy clearly requires a complementary regulatory structure that allows greater commercial freedom for operators. Such changes are expected to stimulate increased investment across the information industry (notably in terms of network capacity), induce innovation in terms of services and applications, and lead directly to greater value added being available to users. There is inevitably a lag between introducing competition into the market-place and the effects of these changes becoming evident within the sector. Most states across the global economy have moved, albeit reluctantly in some cases, towards a liberalized system, fearing that failure to do so could undermine their competitiveness in the global economy. Most initial efforts have focused upon the gradual liberalization of the telecommunications sector.

The ongoing evolution of the information economy depends upon the re-regulation of the sector across a number of areas:

- *Access.* The key access objective is to ensure that all who require access to telecommunications networks to provide or consume services are able to get it. This does not imply universality, but merely that those controlling the network are prevented from abusing the dominant position they have (initially at least) in the development of the information economy. This is especially important in terms of the local loop (the final link between the supplier and the consumer) and increasingly in terms of the software operated at the consumer's end. Evidently access charges need to be made by the network owner or the proprietor of the software but these should be balanced with the need to sustain effective competition in the sector.

- *Interconnection.* The basis of the information economy is that many of the services provided will be delivered over the network. The 'network' is in fact a virtual network of separate networks that operate seamlessly through being fully integrated. New entrants need therefore to interconnect their network to other networks in order to reach their desired market-place. Rules of interconnection between network operators need to be established especially with regard to the dominant network operator and its relationship with new entrants. Regulation needs to ensure that access is non-discriminatory (for example, connection charges need to be such that competition is fair between new entrants and the rival network owner). It is also clear that these arrangements need to ensure capacity is available to all suppliers who require it. These interconnection issues are heightened through the convergence process where it becomes increasingly important to ensure that technologies from the separate sectors interwork and can be integrated within the networking environment.

- *Interoperability.* Interlinked with interconnection is the need to have all aspects of the network compatible with one another thus enabling them to interwork. Standards (as a later section indicates) are essential to the information economy in terms of determining access and maximizing the reach of services and applications, and enabling their diffusion across the economy. A lack of interoperability can reduce competition and increase dominance with a corresponding reduction in innovation. The Internet provides a good example where open (as opposed to proprietary) standards have led to innovation based upon separate networks that are able to communicate and exchange data.

- *Assistance to new operators.* Given the dominance of the incumbent operators within many markets, many states have developed regulatory structures to encourage the success of new entrants over the short term. In many instances, there is asymmetric regulation to ensure the entrant can become established. Whilst this is not flawless, it does safeguard against the actions of the incumbent in so far as it decides to protect its position. In Europe, this has been enhanced through measures to seek to push telecommunications operators to hive off their cable interests into separate companies, thus allowing much more visible and fairer competition between cable and traditional telephone networks. The hope is that this will stimulate investment in the local loop to increase broadband access.

- *Balancing competition and co-operation.* There is an evident need for competition to feed through into innovation. New commercial pressures may deter investments in technologies that are apparently some way from commercial fruition. In this case, co-operation between the leading market players is required, which will create the paradox of competitors co-operating. State-sponsored R&D programmes are areas where this is already evident. Collaboration may be sanctioned where the market in question is global. Regulatory frameworks also need to be developed outlining where and when collaboration and competition should or should not be allowed.

- *Universal service.* A core concern of the liberalization process is that exposure to competitive forces could undermine the principle of universal access. To ensure that the social aspects of telecommunication are not undermined, there needs to be some agreement either through contract or through operator provision to a collective fund to finance universal service.

International agreements on liberalization are necessary given the global nature of the information economy and the close links that the process perceivably has with the moves towards globalization. Thus there is the need to establish a minimal set of rules within which trade in information products and services can take place. The major measures for the development of a global information market have come through the WTO agreements upon trade in information technology and basic telecommunications services.

The Information Technology Agreement (ITA) sought to eliminate tariffs on IT products by 2000. The scope of the coverage included computers, telecommunications equipment, semi-conductors (and associated manufacturing equipment), software and scientific instruments. There were over 40 signatories to the agreement, covering some 93 per cent of IT trade. There are efforts under way to expand the coverage of the tariff-free products though the WTO is being urged to tackle non-tariff barriers in IT trade (such as out-of-date testing and certification requirements) as an immediate measure. The absence of a one-standard/one-test procedure also has the potential to damage freer trade in ICTs.

The Basic Telecommunications Agreement commits countries to open their telecommunications service markets from 1998. The measures covered include access to public telecommunication networks in a non-discriminatory manner. Around 70 states signed up to this agreement, which varies on a case-by-case basis in terms of commitments but explicitly commits states to a completely liberalized services market. The states covered account for 95 per cent of telecommunications services revenue, with estimated savings to the states involved of $1 trillion over the 13 years from the date the agreement came into effect.

The commercial effects of these agreements depend upon the success with which they are implemented. There have, for example, already been public spats between the US and the EU over the manner in which the former was going to implement these agreements into national law, which would have resulted (according to the latter) in the possibility of explicit discrimination against its operators. It is likely that once the leading industrialized states have implemented these agreements (as many had already done through existing reforms) pressure will grow upon the less developed states to follow suit. Consequently, a full open market for all information economy technologies and services/applications is still distant. Despite these global agreements, the actions by the leading industrial states (notably the US and the EU) to facilitate entry to one another's markets by indigenous enterprises are having a greater effect upon the emerging information economy than these multilateral agreements that do little more than establish a globally minimalist framework.

The impact of liberalization across the major developed economies is already evident with increased investment in all aspects of the network by previously excluded parties. Yet the full gains have still to be realized, reflecting that liberalization is an ongoing process that evolves with technology and is still not fully matured within the context of existing technologies. Consequently, the competitive boost to enterprises from cheaper telecommunications has still not fully filtered through to the bottom line. The eventual competitive effects upon users are expected to be substantial. For example, Ford Europe estimates that it will be able to cut around a third off its $100 million telecommunications bill over the next five years. With EU telecommunication prices still 30–50 per cent more expensive than in the US, it is important that further liberalization occurs to ensure European enterprises are not put at a competitive disadvantage as communications become increasingly central to business functioning. It is also important that many of the benefits from the competitive regime, which have traditionally only really been exploitable by large enterprises, are experienced by SMEs.

The consequences of convergence for regulation

Convergence poses some new regulatory problems, as follows:

- the potential leveraging of dominance in one market to achieve dominance in multiple markets (notably where incumbent PTOs are able to use their extensive networks to dominate new services areas such as interactive television, as witnessed in the EU where the European Commission has insisted upon the separation of CATV and telecommunication services by large PTOs);

- different industries, with their own regulatory structures, bringing with them their own regulatory culture and traditions;

- the desire to 'bundle' services, frequently under regulatory approval (for example, service consumption linked to proprietary terminal equipment), conflicting with the desire for competition;

- the increasing difficulty in distinguishing between, for example, broadcasting services with an interactive component and telecommunications services with a broadcast or video-based component;

- the existence of bottleneck facilities (such as state-owned infrastructure with universal accessibility) causing access concerns for third parties.

Currently there is no uniform method of regulating the diverse sectors integral to the convergence process. For example, some forms of media (notably traditional press and broadcasting) are still subject to close content control; others, such as the Internet and satellite broadcasting, are less easily controlled. Technology knows no legal or regulatory limits and as global competition starts to emerge regulatory segmentation will look ever more archaic. Consequently, it is likely that regulation will not be based upon extending current regulation to new sectors but upon the convergence of separate regulations under a single 'super-regulator' covering all the relevant sectors.

Telecommunications and audio-visual convergence is the broadest, and potentially most lucrative, case, where the previously separate common carrier (telecommunications) services and content-based broadcasting (primarily television) market segments converge. The prospect is one of telephone companies offering broadcasting services and of cable TV operators and the like providing telecommunications. This implies telecommunications enterprises need to be increasingly aware of content and the audio-visual sector aware of the need to manage both customers' interface to the service and the wider choice of distribution methods.

Inevitably the traditional modes of regulation of these sectors will need to be reassessed. Telecommunications regulation will need to be altered, notably with regard to defining universal service within an era of convergence. Audio-visual regulation was traditionally split between the film and broadcasting industries with both regulated on the content provided to ensure broad public interest objectives were met. Now that a plethora of services can be delivered via assorted segmented broadcasting formats (such as closed-user, pay-per-view methods), the traditional rationale for regulation (broadcasting as a scarce good in the public interest) is increasingly less valid.

In line with its pro-market outlook, the ITU (International Telecommunications Union) (1997) argues that certain regulatory actions should be followed in order to realize convergence in a broadly pluralist manner, notably that:

- dominant PTOs should be restricted as to which 'converged' services they offer, or even prohibited from offering services, to avoid a re-monopolization of the market (this is the approach that has been taken in the EU – see above);

- telephone companies should be regulated as broadcasters when they seek to offer video services, and this control should be separated from the regulation applied to telephony;

- entry by PTOs into the audio-visual sector should be delayed until competition in that sector has reached some degree of maturity;

- the regulation of transport should be separated from that of content to ensure that all are treated equally.

As the reach of the Internet extends, what users expect from it and what service providers are enabling it to achieve are growing. In terms of convergence, the Internet poses regulatory problems due to the emergence of interactivity and the increased levels of audio and video capabilities being built into applications. The challenges posed by the Internet upon regulation can be expected to grow, as hardware, software and information companies expand the range of 'converged' services offered and, more importantly, as Internet penetration expands. Regulatory challenges from Internet-based services are also likely to be posed by its convergence with broadcasting. Technological upgrades are likely to develop, involving interactive home pages with three-dimensional features and home pages that increasingly resemble 'broadcasting stations', as converging technologies are offered via a single access point. Such developments further highlight how regulations are being left behind by the pace of technological development. Broadcasting over the Internet highlights how digital technology is drawing together previously separate markets. To date, such services have tended to be closer to electronic publishing than the traditional conception of broadcasting. For this reason, regulators have tended to regard broadcasting regulation as inappropriate. This is despite the fact that these services should count as broadcasting in many developed states.

The US is taking a hands-off approach to the regulation of convergence, generally pursuing a pragmatic approach to these developments. The EU has started to address these issues with some states considering a merging of the telecommunications and broadcasting regulators. A more pressing concern is the consequence for the ownership issues presented by cross-ownership between sectors, for reasons of ensuring plurality within the media and preventing dominance in 'old' services being transferred into dominance in 'new' and 'innovative' services. Thus regulators have placed constraints over the activities of the incumbent public telecommunication operators (which possess the significant advantage of a large customer base and brand loyalty) in new sectors such as cable-access television. Such regulation needs to be seen as temporary, as competition becomes embedded and matures within the converging sectors. Consequently, many are calling for the adjustment of existing competition rules to attack and address such dominance rather than the development of a new set of regulations to cover the process of convergence, thereby possibly stymieing the development of the information economy. Others are taking the opposite position, arguing (as mentioned above) for a 'super-regulator' to cover all of the information industry. Indeed the EU was recently arguing for a European equivalent of the US Federal Communications Commission (FCC) to overcome the patchwork of rules that currently cover the EU.

The Microsoft trial

In late 1998, the federal government of the US and 19 US states brought a case against Microsoft, the result of which is likely to prove pivotal in establishing the competitive rules of engagement for the development of the information economy. The trial, given the stakes, was a protracted affair with no final decision likely until the end of 2000 at the earliest. The dominance that Microsoft has had, in conjunction with Intel (through the Wintel system), over the PC operating systems market and the very aggressive strategy the enterprise takes to any potential or actual rivals in this market have long raised issues for competition authorities both in the US and elsewhere. The core concern is that the dominance Microsoft has over operating systems is virtually unassailable given its sheer size (its profits are bigger than those for the next 49 biggest software companies together).

Traditionally, the authorities have used persuasion and compromise rather than the courts to tackle Microsoft's market power. However, a full anti-trust hearing was eventually viewed as inevitable, as new concerns emerged about Microsoft's strategies to protect the dominant position of its Windows operating system from the threat of Java (see Chapter 4) and its challenge to the position of Netscape's Internet Navigator browser (which provides user-friendly access to the Internet). These two developments were seen to threaten the dominance of Microsoft by creating an alternative interface to Windows and through the development of Web browsers that could provide an alternative access point for applications (many written in Java), with the result that the importance of the operating system is reduced.

The accusation is that Microsoft used its dominant Windows program to 'pollute' Java, thereby limiting its potential for many types of machine. This Microsoft tried to achieve through creating a Java interpreter or 'virtual machine' best suited to Windows. Therefore Java developers would have had to write programs for Window-specific applications. This was in effect a breach of its Java licence. Microsoft also developed a habit of holding back crucial details of the Windows system to any enterprise suspected of developing a rival platform – this applied whether they were rivals or partners. The actions against Netscape were manifold. First, it gave away its own browser. After this failed to achieve the desired objective of undermining Netscape, it sought to achieve guarantees that enterprises would use its browser as part of its Windows licence. In addition, it sought to use its resources and dominance of the PC desktop market to recruit ISPs and content providers as exclusive dealers in its browser software. Finally it sought to use the latest version of Windows 98 to ensure that the operating system and browser were interdependent. These strategies were designed to sustain the dominance of Microsoft – something ultimately achieved. Many in the industry doubted whether this was entirely fair or ethical.

Microsoft's chief rivals made a series of anti-competitive accusations against it:

- Netscape accused Microsoft of making an offer to carve up the Internet market between them. When Netscape refused, Microsoft (as mentioned) merged the browser and operating system and, via a series of exclusive deals with other suppliers to use the Microsoft browser, cut off Netscape's ability to compete effectively.

- America On-line (AOL) accused Microsoft of sacrificing its own online service in order to stop AOL choosing Netscape's software. This would have handed AOL a dominant position on computer screens and was therefore an abuse of Microsoft's monopoly.

- Intel accused Microsoft of bullying it into stopping the development of its own software.

- Sun Microsystems accused Microsoft of trying to hijack Java technology and replace it with a version in contravention of its licensing agreement.

- IBM accused Microsoft of raising the price of Windows to IBM because it supported and developed rival products.

Naturally, Microsoft has rejected these accusations, arguing that what it was doing was in the competitive interests of the economy. Netscape was merely beaten by a better system, and Sun was out to kill Windows so therefore its actions were fully legitimate. Thus most of the actions were done out of vigorous competition rather than any deliberate attempt to undermine the opposition. Microsoft insists it must have the right to improve, and integrate new features into its products. More recently Microsoft has highlighted that the development of the alliance between AOL, Sun and Netscape (see the case study in Chapter 4, 'Sun–AOL–Netscape merger' on p 120) shows that competition is alive and well within the Internet sector and therefore proves that it cannot have crushed Netscape as the government claims. In addition, software developers, it claims, will increasingly write products to run over the Internet encouraged by the AOL–Netscape–Sun deal.

The strategy of Microsoft towards Sun (and its Java technology) was reversed in 1999 when a US district court upheld a complaint from Sun that Microsoft had infringed the terms of its licence. Microsoft must now adjust its programs. Microsoft did have a success when the court of appeal ruled that the bundling of Windows and the browser was legitimate. This does not excuse the strategy of taking no prisoners, which has won Microsoft few friends. Evidence in the trial has suggested that Microsoft bullied not only rivals but also partners (such as Intel and PC makers). It is alleged that if they failed to do as Microsoft wanted then it threatened to remove their Windows licence. Authorities are clearly worried about the ability of enterprises (whether Microsoft or any other) to co-opt the technologies of others to reinforce their position.

In late 1999, the judge in the case ruled against Microsoft, finding that not only was the enterprise a monopoly but that it had abused this power. The decision as to whether these actions had contravened US competition law is still pending. Though Microsoft will appeal, it is clear that if it loses then its dominance is in jeopardy. Indeed some are suggesting that the company should be broken up and the licensing of the Windows source code be open to competitors. The trial highlights the delicate path needed between the requirement to protect intellectual property rights and the need to sustain competition and innovation. Most favour direct efforts to modify behaviour. This could include the end of the preclusive or prohibitive contracts Microsoft has signed with PC makers, surrendering the space on the desktop to allow other services and content, an undertaking on predatory pricing and greater openness on Windows to other software enterprises that could then develop it and sell their own version. Others suggest that Microsoft be split into a Windows operating system company and an applications business, and others still that it be split even further into as many as four or six different companies that would then compete with one another. Some are less aggressive, merely stating that what is needed is a process of constant scrutiny of activity in the same way as applied to IBM when it faced similar controls. The one thing that is clear is that there will be no quick and easy solution to the dilemma Microsoft poses for regulators.

Standards and interoperability

The process of standardization is central to the development of the information economy. In functional terms, it allows all parts of the emerging information network to integrate and interoperate – two crucial building blocks of the information economy. Commercially, standards offer a number of benefits such as:

- a larger market for complementary products as a result of the freely available interface specifications;

- more widely available economies of scale for manufacturers;

- increased connectivity;

- the ability to mix and match technologies to meet more completely the exact functional requirements of users;

- allowing for a larger network, which increases functionality to all users (so-called network externalities);

- allowing innovators to find a ready market for their products;

- increased competition between manufacturers of core products.

Generally the realization of these benefits requires that standards be user-led and deliver the functionality users expect of them (such as security and privacy protection). This implies a market-determined process. Within such a process, as the above suggests, the role of government will vary: in technical issues, the private sector will take the lead with the government merely seeking to establish the minimum level of regulation for public interest; and in policy issues (such as IPR), the role of government is to provide legal and regulatory certainty by the establishment of a framework that has both consistency and credibility, and sustains the commercial development of the information economy.

A core issue for the development of standards for the information economy is whether they emerge via open or proprietary standards. The former is public property (as is the case with the Internet protocol) and available freely; the latter is corporate property and under the control of its owner (such as the Windows operating system). A fear is that the latter type will dominate the former and thereby limit access to the technologies associated with the development of the information economy. Policy makers seek to develop the system within the context of open standards to enable exact consumer requirements to be met and to facilitate the expansion (through integration) of the scope of the information market. The forms and types of standard adopted depend ultimately upon the forum for their development. Traditionally there are three approaches to standardization: market-driven, government-imposed and technology-driven. Which approach is taken tends to be very specific to the industry or sector concerned. To many (notably the strong US ICT sector) voluntary, industry-led codes are best. Others feel that this may simply impose US dominance upon the emerging global information economy and that consequently a stronger governmental role is needed to ensure that this control does not move against the desire to have active competition in the sector as proprietary standards emerge to limit the scope for effective rivalry.

In an era of converging technologies, the priorities and goals of standardization are shifting. As standards for network-to-network interfaces (ie the point of contact between a user and a system) are pretty well defined, the key issue is increasingly to develop standards for appliance-to-appliance and application-to-application interfaces. These are the areas of multimedia, and are those where market growth is expected to be strongest. Furthermore, standardization activities will need to include authentication of content, addressing, security, quality of service and content control.

The battle for third-generation mobile standards

Previous sections have highlighted the importance of mobile communications in the future development of the information economy. Third-generation mobile telephones differ from the current generation in terms of the technology and the services they will offer. They will use packet connections that will enable them to be the intersection between voice and data. The killer application they will offer is portable Internet access and other multimedia services. The development of this technology has been dogged by disagreement between the leading players in Europe and the US over the standards that will dominate this technological development.

Clearly what is at stake in this development are clear industrial policy issues over which enterprises will dominate the development of this technology. Two industry groupings have emerged, each developing its standard for third-generation mobiles. The first, European-based grouping is centred around Ericsson and Nokia, and includes all other GSM (global system for mobile) manufacturers and operators. These enterprises wish to build upon the success of GSM – the core standard for second-generation mobiles through its UMTS (universal mobile telecommunications standard). This standard was backed by the leading Japanese players, which were willing to sacrifice their own proprietary standards, which was a huge boost to this grouping. The second, US-based group revolves around Motorola and Qualcomm, as well as Lucent and Nortel – with the implicit support of the US government. It wants to get recognition for the w-cdmaone (wideband code multiple division access) technology pioneered by Qualcomm. Controlling the global standard for this technology equates to billions of dollars of revenue for those companies that back the winning standard. Both standards use a variation of a common technique that allows many users to use a piece of the spectrum at the same time. The core conflict is not so much one of technology as of vested interests.

The stalemate over standards is seen by some as an attempt by the US to wrest the standards process back from Europe, which dominated the second-generation technologies. To the US, this dominance (especially since it was reinforced by a memorandum of understanding by European operators) of the standards process was akin to an exclusive industrial policy to protect European manufacturers. The US is accusing the Europeans of trying a similar strategy with the third-generation technology and avoiding attempts to establish a global consensus through the ITU. Part of the problem is that the Europeans believe that, over the short term, third-generation technology is not profitable and therefore has to coexist with second-generation technologies. International standards, according to the US, have to be based upon fair competition between technologies and not the preferences driven by industrial policy. The belief that the EU was planning to mandate its agreed standard was typical of this active industrial policy stance. These trade issues are compounded by inevitable interoperability problems but the biggest issues have tended to surround IPRs.

The Europeans' need to license technology off Qualcomm if they are to develop their standard has created a great deal of the friction between the parties. Qualcomm refused to grant them a licence to use its technology on the grounds that the Europeans were being unfair and discriminatory in the development of their standards. In addition, Qualcomm wanted to make sure that the European system was backwards compatible with its own standard. To the Europeans, such a change would lead to a dramatic drop in the performance of third-generation technology – the US standard requires lower chip rates. Europe disputed any charges of being discriminatory and believes that Qualcomm cannot claim ownership for all of the technologies it has been involved in developing. The Europeans believed that CMDA patents were not Qualcomm's to distribute and control. The Europeans also believed that Qualcomm was using the IPR it holds to hold other enterprises hostage for its own commercial advantage. There are clear US interests in ensuring backwards compatibility, as many of the US partners have considerable investment in this technology. As a retaliatory measure Ericsson also withheld key IPR. It is clear that a global system is needed if economies of scale are to be enjoyed and the costs of accessing the third-generation system are not to be prohibitive.

The dispute between the two parties ran the risk of undermining the credibility of the ITU. The commercial stakes brought an entrenchment in both positions and the ITU seemingly could do little to move either party. Thus the planned introduction date of third-generation technology was looking increasingly doubtful. Indeed by the beginning of July 1998, the ITU had received 15 separate proposals for standards for third-generation mobile phones. By the end of 1998, pressure was being brought to bear by both the ITU and leading global players upon the two main protagonists (Ericsson and Qualcomm) to end the dispute.

The deadlock in the development of a third-generation standard was eventually broken as Ericsson agreed to harmonize the standards and lower the chip rate as required by the US standard. The enterprises have agreed to cross-license technology and support the development of a single CMDA standard. The new common standard has three 'modes', each of which conforms to the requirements of the respective parties (Europe, Japan and the US). That the handsets will be able to handle all three modes is merely the start for common standards. Elsewhere the standards battle continues as agreement on technologies for base stations and software still needs to be sorted out as well as technology for transmitting pictures over the system. There is clearly still a long way to go in the standards process.

The actual winners are hard to discern. Some claim the Europeans are the winners, as the prospects for their standard to be adopted as the global norm have increased markedly. The effect is seemingly to prolong the life of second-generation mobile technology and, given that most US users are still with the first-generation technology, this enhances the position of the Europeans with their better GSM system to capture the benefits of the migration. Thus, paradoxically, the battle for third-generation standards may result in a victory for the Europeans in second-generation standards, which should prove to be a good platform to secure dominance over third-generation technology. Achieving a foothold in the US for second-generation technology will enable the Europeans to use this as a base to push their own version of third-generation technology. This position is enhanced by technological developments associated with the GSM standard, which enable second-generation services to offer third-generation technology. This is important, for it is perhaps the first time in the evolving information economy where the US has begun to share its pre-eminence in standard setting.

International standards bodies

International standards bodies – such as the ITU and the ISO (International Standards Office) – working alongside national and regional standardization bodies (such as European Telecommunications Standards Institute) and new industry-led standards bodies (such as the Asynchronous Transfer Mode (ATM) forum) highlight the increasing complexity of standards formation in the information economy. The mushrooming of a large number of industry bodies indicates that industry has a better ability to recognize its needs than the more traditional bodies. The ITU (the body traditionally charged with developing telecommunications standards) has found itself under increasing criticism due to the slowness of its standards-making process. Industry bodies are putting the ITU under increasing pressure, feeling that their proximity to the market-place renders them better standard-setters. As a short-term reform, industry bodies exasperated with the speed at which the ITU conducts its affairs are seeking to refine and achieve more influence over the process. EU bodies are especially concerned by this development, as a decline in the power of the ITU could see the resulting power vacuum filled by US-based standards bodies.

This complexity of the standards process has been further complicated by the process of convergence and technological change. These processes have expanded the range of standards bodies that have a direct commercial interest in standards development. Increasingly standards development for the information economy stretches across telecommunications to include IT and software concerns. Many of the standards bodies are broadly independent of the formal – frequently governmental – standards bodies. Notable examples include the ATM and Frame Relay Fora, which are dominated by manufacturers of these technologies, though there are other standards consortia that represent users and other interested parties. This broad cross-market involvement reflects the priority that new standards should reflect pressures within the commercial environment.

Problems may emerge from the fact that the new bodies have developed to aid the commercial realization of a particular technology associated with the information economy and therefore have different motives from the more traditional formal standards bodies (such as the ITU). If the concerns of marketing and pushing the commercial realization of these technologies take precedence over the need to be interoperable and interconnected, then these bodies can be counterproductive. In practice, the bodies are closely regulated (both formally and informally) to ensure co-operation in standards development does not extend into more explicitly commercial activities.

Despite the readily identifiable benefits from standardization this does not preclude conflict in the standard-setting process. There is evidently a lot at stake in getting the standard chosen to reflect as closely as possible an enterprise's (or state's) particular interests. Powerful industrial lobbies emerge to stress one standard over another and increasingly political pressures become involved in the standardization process. In short, as the information economy matures greater industrial policy concerns will inevitably enter the standard-setting process, while competitive advantage and standardization become increasingly intertwined. Such developments can delay standard setting and ultimately retard the maturity of the information economy. Such trends underline the need to achieve consensus on standards and therefore avoid standards wars (see the case study above, 'The battle for third-generation mobile standards' on p 155). Competition in standards development may prevent one standard achieving the necessary critical mass, thereby limiting the deployment of these technologies. Alternatively, there is the opposite danger of the premature setting of standards that are inflexible in dealing with the rapidly changing nature of technology. This reflects the danger that co-operation between operators may seek to prolong the life of existing technology, thereby limiting the scope for new variants to emerge, or to protect the owners of the established standard from new competition.

The US has been the pre-eminent force in the development of standards. Many of the informal standards bodies noted above are sourced in the US and have predominantly US membership. In international efforts, the US has gone along with co-operative actions but this has often been misleading, for US standards have in many instances come to be international ones. Thus in some cases all the formal bodies have done is ratify the leading US standard. In some instances this is good, as the US has a record of strong innovation, but the competitive process (through which the leading standard usually emerges) does not always produce the best results. Increasingly, developments in mobile telephony and Internet governance indicate that this traditional dominance of the US over information economy standardization is coming under challenge from EU and Asian enterprises.

Intellectual property rights

Intellectual property rights (IPR) are the rights given to persons over their own 'creations' and apply to all aspects of the information industry (hardware, software, content, etc). These rights usually give the creator exclusivity over the use of the creation for a specified period of time. Within the era of electronic communications, IPR law faces two core challenges: that intellectual property can be cheaply and easily distributed and, more importantly, that it can be reproduced without the permission of those who own the rights to such property. For example, industry (through the Business Software Alliance) has estimated that some 40 per cent of software in usage is derived from pirated sources – amounting to some $1 billion per annum. In addition, the information economy will stimulate the value of intellectual property through global marketing tools to make users aware of this property, rendering national protection systems inadequate.

IPR are traditionally divided into two main areas: copyright and rights related to copyright; and industrial property. The rights of authors of creations are protected for a minimum of 50 years after the death of the creator. These protections cross a very broad range of media from literature through to broadcasting. The main purpose of such rules is to encourage and reward creative work. Industrial property can be subdivided into the protection of distinctive signs (such as trade marks) and geographical indications (such as those identifying place of origin) and the protection of property to stimulate innovation, design and creation of technology.

These rights act as a basic market protection mechanism. In terms of the information economy, clarity is needed over the management and acquisition of rights in the digital environment. It is evident that the digital environment, through the electronic transmission of documents, challenges existing copyright law in a number of ways:

- Copyright law has traditionally protected the intellectual property of a book or other copyrighted material by protecting the reproduction and distribution of copies of the work. With electronic transmission, there are no physical copies.

■ Copyright law offers different results depending upon whether the work is in published or unpublished form and whether it is used for non-commercial purposes. With the development of the information economy, these distinctions are blurred and difficult to draw.

■ Copyright laws are territorial; the information economy is a global phenomenon where copyrighted material is available anywhere and everywhere.

■ The PC allows the user to access information networks, clone copies of the copyrighted work and transmit these documents electronically to any number of other users.

Without protection of these rights copyright owners will have precious little incentive to innovate and offer for sale core information-economy products. The knock-on effect of this will be to limit the commercial evolution of the information economy.

Protecting intellectual property rights: the case of the music industry

An earlier case study (see Chapter 3, 'Online strategy for the music industry' on p 69) has highlighted the quandary the music industry is in regarding stimulating electronic commerce within this sector. The Internet clearly offers them an opportunity to increase revenues but it also increases the potential for piracy and other infringements of their intellectual property rights. Piracy within the music sector has always been a problem but the development of the Internet is much more difficult for business. The traditional techniques of tracking piracy (employing investigators) cannot readily be used on the Internet due to the logistical difficulty of tracking down the potentially thousands of Web sites globally that may contravene copyright. The current strategy of enterprises to tackle this problem is through digital detection units to surf the Internet and track down these sites. This is currently the only effective method they have in engaging the pirates. This process is evidently time-consuming, costly and very difficult, as shutting one site down does not prevent others emerging elsewhere. Though both US- and EU-based record labels have established 'digital detection units', these are seen as a temporary measure while the industry finds its own solutions to the problem.

The music industry places much of the blame for its copyright problems at the door of a compression technology called Motion Picture Expert Group-1/Level 3 or, as it is more commonly known, MP3. MP3 was derived from an attempt by governments to create standards for interactive television but has ended up being adopted widely on the Internet by music Web sites through to recording artists. Its popularity has been pretty universal except amongst the record industry, which dislikes the fact the MP3 files can be easily copied and distributed. It is estimated that there are over 200,000 songs available on the Internet that can be downloaded illegally, that is without paying royalties to the copyright owner.

Attempts by the record industry to limit the spread of MP3 have failed miserably. Indeed MP3 is one of the most common terms now searched for on the Internet. In late 1998, the problem was compounded when Rio, a portable device on which MP3 files can be downloaded (up to 60 minutes of music can be stored), was put on sale – despite attempted injunctions by record enterprises. Since Rio, a number of other similar devices have found their way on to the market. However, (as the case study in Chapter 3 highlighted) MP3 is not merely about piracy, but is also about the ability of bands and smaller record labels to side-step the dominance of the large record companies in terms of distribution and access to customers. That is, MP3 is also a means of increasing competition in the music industry. In fact, these effects – as opposed to the piracy problem – represent a greater threat to the incumbent enterprises within the sector.

The five largest record enterprises (BMG, EMI, Time-Warner, Universal and Sony) have launched the Secure Digital Music Initiative (SDMI) along with 150 content, hardware and software enterprises. This is essentially an industry standards group dedicated to IPR protection. The purpose of SDMI is to offer a secure digital delivery system for music (to protect copyright holders and limit potential piracy) and encourage its use by largely overcoming the core weaknesses of the MP3 system (especially in terms of the quality of the download). This latter objective is especially important, because the SDMI has to persuade customers to pay for a download that they could otherwise get for nothing. This stresses not only quality but also convenience.

SDMI seeks to develop an open interoperable architecture and specification for digital music security. The trials began in June 1999 with the industry developing an active strategy to roll out the technology by the end of the year. In addition, this model for secure delivery is expected to be copied across other forms of media. Initial actions within the SDMI are working towards developing specifications for portable devices. Thereafter security issues are on the agenda. Increasingly the SDMI seems to be moving towards digital watermarking – the hiding of information within an audio signal to identify ownership or origin of material – for its system of Internet music players. Watermarking is seen as a complement to the planned encryption to be used by the SDMI. The industry believes that encryption (it has chosen a content scrambling system) will eventually be broken – watermarking of the machine allows them to know who did it and provide a mechanism to limit additional copies. In addition, many plan to offer certificates of authentication with downloaded music. This provides information about where and by whom the music was purchased.

Alongside the SDMI has been the development of another secure system – the so-called Madison Project. This is a project between IBM and the record companies to develop a secure system where music can be downloaded and effectively 'burnt' on to CDs, which can then be played on a regular stereo. The music will be encrypted to prevent unauthorized copying. In addition, the development of the Madison Project inhibits the attempts of MP3 to enter the legitimate market.

The industry has tried to protect its copyright for years from what it sees as home copying. In the analogue era, many pushed for a levy on cassette tapes to make up for lost revenue. In the digital era, some sections of the industry are pushing for an equivalent upon blank CDs and the like to make up for any corresponding shortfall. In this case, it is seen as especially important because the home copying that can be made is of a higher quality and is therefore a more direct substitute. However taping for personal use and taping for public consumption are hard to differentiate between and even harder to police.

The industry has developed a number of intermediate methods for seeking to overcome the problem of piracy. It has developed software to identify copyright owners whenever music is played and, as mentioned, it has established digital detection units. Clearly these enterprises will never eliminate all piracy (as they never could for CDs or cassettes), but what they need to do is prevent this new format from eroding revenue bases. The only way to achieve this effectively is to control the distribution channels, that is to reimpose the dominance over the traditional format on to the new online format. This is the only way it can be sure of ensuring piracy has no great effect upon revenues.

International agreements upon IPR

The increasingly global nature of communication flows and the result that material can be copied, altered or manipulated anywhere or by anyone highlights the need for global harmonization of IPR as a prerequisite for the successful development of the information economy. This does not mean that all systems need to be uniform, but merely that they need to be compatible and able to interlink. International agreements have been established to lay down minimum standards of protection a signatory may offer and a promise not to discriminate against foreigners. International action towards such harmonization occurs through two bodies: the WTO (via the Trade Related Aspects of Intellectual Property Rights Agreement (TRIPs)) and the World Intellectual Property Organization (WIPO):

- *The WTO Agreement on Trade Related Aspects of Intellectual Property Rights.* The TRIPS Agreement, which came into force in 1995, is the most comprehensive multilateral agreement upon IPR. The agreement itself covers three main features. It offers a minimum standard of protection for each of the areas covered by the agreement to be provided by each signatory, establishes a set of common principles and procedures for the enforcement of IPR and offers a dispute settlement mechanism. The basic premise is to offer equality of treatment between member states over IPR through establishing a common, if rather minimalist, framework to ensure that national or regional rules do not impede trade in or flows of information. With direct reference to the information economy, TRIPS covers areas such as computer programs and databases.

■ *The World Intellectual Property Organization.* The WIPO is a UN organization responsible for the promotion and protection of intellectual property on a global basis whose work is complementary to that of the WTO. It seeks to establish a co-operative agenda to alleviate such problems and is involved in, and ultimately responsible for, the assorted multilateral treaties (such as the Berne Convention) dealing with intellectual property. As of 1997, 161 states were members of the WIPO. In late 1996, the outcome of a special conference led to two key developments in IPR – the WIPO Copyright Treaty (which updated existing legislation to include digital technology, especially the Internet) and the WIPO Performances and Phonograms Treaty (which applied the rights of performers and their performances to the digital technology).

Of these bodies, the WIPO has been especially active in developing and seizing the initiative in the development of an IPR framework for the information economy. The WIPO has been active in the field of trade marks and Internet domain names where it is seeking to establish a role for itself in dispute resolution and the harmonization of Internet domain name policies. For example, the WIPO has sought to overcome the problem of 'cybersquatting' – where users register Internet names and addresses that are registered trade marks in the hope of selling them back at a high price to the owners. The move also seeks to prevent other abuses, such as names closely resembling trade marks to capture accidental visitors, and the use of domain names to spread negative information about the copyright owner. These only have limited coverage but do provide a start in further protecting copyright owners over the Internet. The WIPO has developed a clear agenda to extend knowledge of IPR in the digital environment via the Internet but is also seeking to define the liabilities of ISPs and is assisting in the development of electronic systems for the online collection of royalties on digital content.

In developing the appropriate IPR regime, policy makers have to be mindful of three concerns, namely that:

1. the level of protection offered to IPR does not deter further innovation – if the originator of a technology is given too many rights it limits the opportunity for other innovators to develop and improve the product;

2. there exist links between the market power granted by the IPR and sectors that do not fall under the scope of protection – this can be especially detrimental if these links are in new, important product areas;

3. enterprises may develop consortia between themselves mutually to exploit their own and one another's IPR without prosecution resulting in lower innovation and new barriers to entry.

These concerns evidently create an interface and potential conflict between the desire to ensure open markets and efforts to provide incentives for innovation. Typical of these concerns are moves by some enterprises to patent methods and processes rather than innovations with the result that electronic trading is stymied. This is especially true if the result is that the patents result in added costs for online trading. This highlights the concern that if patents are defined too broadly they could limit the development of the information economy through making it more costly to function within it. In the case of music over the Internet, the digital delivery of music involves the use of a number of technologies from compression through to watermarking, many of which are patented. Paying royalties on these technologies adds a large extra cost and could endanger the viability of an enterprise's online business model. The copyrighting of business methods, not just software, represents a serious challenge, and reflects how patent offices are lagging behind the development of the information economy. In terms of this latter point, there is a growing trend by online companies to patent their method of electronic business.

Privacy

This refers to personal privacy and that of organizations, though in practice the former tends to be the majority concern. It is a widely held view that the advent of the information economy, and its accompanying powerful computer and communication networks, will lead to a sharp jump in the concerns of personal data privacy. High-speed networks that connect businesses, governments and individuals across the globe will multiply and improve access to the flow of information (including personal information) making it readily more available, collectable and fluid across national borders. This problem is particularly acute in open networks such as the Internet. Consequently, there is an evident need to balance the privacy needs of users with the desire to aid the flow of information across borders. This is important for personal information is an increasingly important corporate asset in the information economy.

Mansell and Steinmueller (1996) highlight three key issues related to privacy in electronic environments:

1. balancing control of illegal activities over the Internet with ensuring basic rights of privacy;

2. the need for all controls and codes of conduct to be universally applicable;

3. the differences between the perception and reality of privacy.

As they point out, privacy issues are hard to address consistently across these areas, especially where different priorities are placed upon different issues (for example, the relative positions upon the legality of pornography).

Advances in computing are at the core of the privacy issue in the information economy. First, they make information easy to collect and second, they make it easily storable, accessible and retrievable. The fears over privacy have been highlighted by the recent storm when Microsoft and Intel developed chips that had unique personal identification numbers enabling them to track where users were on the Internet. Though both denied any wrongdoing, the fact that the potential for abuse of privacy existed warranted concern enough, indicating a clear flaw in the evolving self-regulatory system. Microsoft produced software to disable the identification number whereas Intel's was removed through the actions of the large PC makers. AOL was also in the firing line when it announced in summer 1997 that it was going to sell the names and addresses of all its users to a direct marketing firm. The resulting public outcry forced a change of strategy. This is symptomatic of a growing number of hardware and software technologies that contain personal identification devices to help them interact with one other.

Electronic commerce poses a threat to privacy in so far as the increasing number of databases of personal information will allow businesses to tailor their marketing strategy to suit the individual and pinpoint the type of person they wish to target. Essentially problems emerge when a company chooses to share its data with someone who has not been chosen by the subject of the data or when this information has been given without the knowledge of the consumer. Increasingly many sites collect information about visitors through the use of cookies. These are tiny pieces of data sent to Web servers, which can be placed on the user's system for later retrieval. These can be used innocently just to indicate if a visitor has used a site before. However, they can be used to reveal other sites the user has visited, allowing marketers to create a picture of the consumer's interests and lifestyle. The point is that many of these cookies operate without the user knowing they are there. Cookies can be disabled but this has implications for the interaction as the user is constantly asked to re-enable the cookie.

In electronic commerce, privacy requirements are shaped by:

- the customers' desire that no record is kept of their activities (irrespective of whether payment is made);

- a desire that no 'electronic trail' is left when payments are made so that no record is kept of transactions;

- a requirement that when a 'trail' is left such information is kept confidential.

This fundamentally means that there has to be a culture of transparency in terms of the collection and use of personal data as well as some element of control over personal data by the user. Failure to secure these rights could undermine confidence in the usage of electronic commerce, thereby retarding the development of the information economy.

The desire for privacy is based around limiting and controlling access to personal information within an environment that perceives trans-border data flows as a social and economic necessity. Additionally privacy has to be balanced against the concerns of national security, law enforcement, security of information systems and the protection of IPR. Thus despite the desirability of privacy, it is a right that cannot always be automatically granted or guaranteed. In the light of such concerns, by the end of 1997 over 30 states had adopted laws determining the handling of personal information. Where there are no laws, a self-regulatory code is frequently applied.

Policy actions on privacy

Privacy is one area where there has been a notable absence of any concrete global or international agreement. There is a tradition of national and increasingly regional legislation to sustain this objective. Attaining privacy on an international basis is likely to prove troublesome; the legal systems reflected in national privacy laws are a reflection of hundreds of years of evolution usually within the context of a single culture. The challenge, over a few short years, is to change this outlook fundamentally.

Generally, privacy and data protection are more prevalent amongst developed states, most of which follow these core principles:

- accountability – the need for actors to be accountable for their own compliance with the relevant laws;

- collection – the means of attainment and processing of data should be fair, lawful and, where applicable, with the consent of the subject;

- data quality – the data should be relevant to the purposes for which it is collected;

- purpose specification – the use of the data should be made known to the subject when collected;

- use – personal data should only be used for the purposes for which it was collected;

- security safeguards – data should be protected against unauthorized access, destruction, misuse, modification or disclosure;

- individual participation – the person should have the right to know data has been collected about him or her and know who has collected it;

- accuracy – the information should reflect the facts;

- trans-border data flow – the flow of personal data should be restricted to states that protect personal privacy through national public law or any other means (such as standards or self-regulation);

- special personal data categories – sensitive personal information should not be collected without the knowledge of the person concerned.

Despite the existence of such principles, not only is global harmonization absent but also most states have no legislation at all. Notwithstanding this, there are three international legal instruments that may establish some gravity for the development of international harmonization and provide a framework for national measures with regard to privacy. Many of these national measures reflect the 1980 OECD Guidelines on the Protection and Trans-Border Flows of Personal Data. This has been enforced lately by efforts of both the EU and the US to develop effective privacy mechanisms. The former has chosen relatively strict regulatory measures, the latter a series of self-regulatory agreements. These clearly have a pivotal role to play, as the development of a global information economy will rely upon the exchange of data between these regions.

Most instruments share common basic principles that personal data should only be processed with the informed consent of the individual or where such processing is allowed by law. All recognize that the individual has the right to be informed that information about them is being processed and a right of access in order to check the accuracy of this data. Legislation and self-regulatory measures requiring government and private sector organizations to maintain systems of name-linked records to observe agreed best practice are now in operation in over 50 states.

There are clearly growing interdependences between different regulatory regimes, but splits between the EU and the US over the degree of privacy required are preventing agreement. The US feels that the EU's data protection directive is too costly upon businesses and could therefore limit the roll-out of electronic commerce. Controls over how companies use data can directly limit their capabilities in developing a presence in the information economy. The US argues that such tight controls are unnecessary, as many responsible companies already offer sufficient protection through voluntary codes. These codes, according to the US, result in the same degree of protection at lower cost. The US basically believes that privacy is a marketable commodity in the information economy and therefore the market will deliver the required level of privacy as a means of securing and pleasing customers. Because of this, there is no need for formal regulation. However, the US government is seeking to develop a plan to bring the US in line with the EU though this is being resisted by businesses until they are more fully aware of the costs.

There are evidently vast differences in the culture of the privacy of data between the US and the EU. In the US, companies can collect, use and share information about consumers with few restrictions. In the EU, consumers are assumed to have a legal interest in how data is used and therefore must be informed by companies about their intentions. For Europeans, privacy is an inalienable right – reflecting the higher social value placed upon information in this region. For Europe more direct regulation is desired over and above the largely self-regulatory approach followed in the US. Failure to agree to this by the US will inhibit the free flow of information, as EU states could cut off exports of data to those states that do not offer similar privacy guarantees. Clearly the EU does not want European data moved to states that have lower levels of protection. To meet these concerns within a self-regulatory framework, sites are moving towards displaying 'seals of approval', which specify through an independent intermediary that the site offers best practice in terms of privacy. Clearly the US needs to prove its self-regulatory system works if it is to cut any ice in negotiations. Increasingly the US is pushing for a system where non-profit organizations (NPOs) set codes, and a Web site's adherence to that code is indicated via the appropriate symbol. This, in theory, creates a commercial incentive to possess the symbol. The NPOs would police the Web, ridding it of fake symbols and revoking violators.

Both sides need to be flexible and recognize that different regimes can breed the same result. However, it seems that many European states have an in-built cynicism to the effectiveness of self-regulation. The cost of privacy is becoming ever more important as enterprises rely more and more upon massive databases to run and control an increasing number of enterprise functions. It is estimated that UK companies will need to spend nearly £1 billion to meet privacy rules, partly owing to the sheer complexity involved in a system where the number of communications to be tracked is rising exponentially. This process has been partly simplified by the use of devices such as standard consent forms. There is, of course, a fear that the cost of obeying privacy could stimulate the relocation of businesses towards those areas with less protection. In addition, it could scare off information-hungry enterprises, thus creating 'data havens'. The problem is not with the EU's rules *per se*, but just with the fact that much of the rest of the world does not agree with them, that they potentially represent a restraint upon international trade – a point that lies at the core of the US's argument – and that they may result in trade disputes if the US feels its enterprises are being unfairly treated.

Despite self-regulation in the US, it is evident that US regulators are also becoming concerned over the use of personal data by enterprises. The Federal Trade Commission (FTC) has warned enterprises that, unless they show clear privacy policies, it will regulate. This concern was driven by the aforementioned consequences of the trails of cookies unknowingly left by users. The FTC wants greater clarity given to users by enterprises specifying how and where information collected can be used. Despite the claim of US business in favour of self-regulation, a recent survey by the Federal Trade Commission found that only 2 per cent of Web sites had an explicit privacy policy.

Developing a holistic framework upon this issue is of paramount importance in preparing the legal basis for the information economy. Indeed there has been considerable debate about setting up an international privacy secretariat. Any agency would be funded by its members and expected to track privacy issues globally. To be successful its membership would have to be extensive. The process is also complicated by the fact that the development of privacy policy is an activity that takes place in anticipation of largely unknown technological developments and dangers. Any laws developed would have to possess sufficient flexibility to be able to embrace such unknowns. Policy makers can only really do this by offering very general principles.

As privacy becomes a more prevalent issue (as electronic commerce expands), so the information industry is developing responses. Software is being developed that allows users to specify how they want their 'volunteered' information to be used. If Web sites contravene these wishes, they are denied access to the information. Other more advanced software allows control of user identification, allowing users to give fake identification if they do not wish to be identified. Other more innovative firms plan to give users copyright over their details, which would allow companies that abused those details to be sued. The most advanced systems being developed encrypt a user's online activities, thus denying even the ISP knowledge of what the user is doing online. However, such privacy software could find itself running up against security concerns of governments.

Security

Security is the totality of safeguards in a computer-based information system, which protects both the system and the information contained therein. The risks associated with technical failure (with resulting lost information) and with access procedures are the basis for the security requirements demanded by the development of the information economy, especially with regard to the maturity of electronic commerce. Such requirements need to be based upon the principles of:

- confidentiality – where information is unavailable to unauthorized parties and, where required, subject to authentication or verification by users;

- integrity – the data is free from the possibility of unauthorized alteration or destruction;

- availability – the information is readily available to authorized parties, and technical problems will not result in lost information.

Recent history has shown how global networks are prone to attack from viruses (and other computer-malicious codes), security breaches and misconduct. Such violations have been most notable in the plethora of hacking incidents over the Internet. A consequence has been the development of encryption technology by major software companies. Like privacy, security is becoming a marketable commodity in its own right though it is more closely controlled by states, which wish to ensure that the technology developed for security is not used to cover illegal or treacherous activities. This raises the possibility of friction between the concerns of the state on the one hand and the right of the individual to security and privacy on the other.

Generally security tools have been based upon access controls and monitoring, user authentication and/or trusted systems and operational controls. These methods are seen as vulnerable to security breaches (for example, passwords being leaked). The result has been the development of new forms of security systems, notably cryptography. A cryptographic system is a software-based set of functions that are paramatized by keys and used for the purpose of data security. A derivative of this is the encryption system, which scrambles (or encrypts) data, thereby concealing it from anyone not knowing the key for decryption. Traditionally, this technology has been mainly used by governments. It is only over the last decade or so that it has started to have more widespread applicability as more commercial activity takes place over electronic networks. There are two general types of cryptography: 1) single key – where there is a single key for the encryption and decryption of information (and each party shares the secret key in advance); and 2) public key – where there are two keys, a public key for wide circulation and a private key, which is not. When a message is encrypted with the former it can only be decrypted by the latter. Thus other users use the recipient's public key to send messages that can be decrypted only by the private key known to the final recipient.

Public key cryptography, through its association with digital signatures, is proving especially important to the development of the information economy. Digital signatures can be used to verify the integrity of the data and/or the authenticity of the user as well as offering protection for IPR. When a signature is provided by the appropriate key, it generates certainty over the source, recipient and credibility of the transaction – a key facilitator in increasing consumer confidence in electronic commerce. Central to this and many other aspects of the security system are 'trusted third parties'. These provide security services to clients. These third parties are useful in bilateral relationships in so far as they provide the means by which users can identify and authenticate one another. They usually do this through the issuance of a certificate identifying the party and assuring the others that the party is trustworthy. The use of digital signatures is being heavily promoted by the finance sector through the Secure Electronic Transactions (SET) standard. With the SET system the merchant carries the risk, therefore inspiring a greater degree of consumer confidence whilst the merchant is still assured of the validity of any transaction under the system.

The widespread use of cryptography raises a number of issues for governments, as a number of their activities are directly implicated by its expansion. The privacy rights of citizens, facilitating security, stimulating electronic commerce, ensuring public safety, raising revenues and law enforcement are just a few of the areas affected by the wider application and usage of this technology. The problem is that, whilst the technology is essential for the spread of electronic commerce, it also challenges the ability of governments to manage the information economy effectively in both a commercial and a legal sense.

Electronic money: an introduction

Many of the security issues surrounding the development of electronic commerce are related to the fuller development of online forms of payment. There is widely seen to be a strong positive link between confidence in the use of electronic forms of payment and the take-up of electronic commerce. Inevitably in a section of this length, many of the major issues can only be addressed in limited depth.

Electronic money is made possible through public key cryptography and digital signatures. Currently there are three main types of payment method available for use over the Internet:

1. credit-card-based systems – where the card number is encrypted and transmitted over the open network or verified off-network;

2. digital checking systems – whereby electronic cheques are sent over the Internet and cleared off-network;

3. digital money – which is transmitted and cleared on-network at the time of the transaction (includes smart cards, store value cards and downloaded electronic wallets).

The schemes noted above, with the exception of digital cash, are online equivalents of their physical counterparts. To many, digital money is seen as the real innovation, replacing notes and coins with digital bits contained on cards, and has the perceived advantage of allowing anonymity in online transactions. In the case of digital cash, the monetary value is stored upon the chosen format (such as the smart card). There are two major levels at which digital cash systems operate. The first is to replace credit and debit card transactions, and the second is to replace cash for the payment of 'everyday transactions' (such as purchasing a newspaper). These systems require not only the elimination of payment risk and the necessary degree of security but also the instant clearing of funds. It is estimated that, by 2006, electronic cash worth some $9 billion will be circulating globally, generating sales of over $150 billion per annum.

Payment systems have developed along with the Internet, and in 1995 there were seven competing schemes from firms such as DigiCash and Cybercash. These emerged before there was really a need for them, and many believe they committed a fundamental error – the belief that an expansion in electronic commerce would bring a boom in micro-trans-actions. For example, an individual could pay for an individual article from a magazine. If there is a rise in micro-transactions where the use of the credit or debit card is uneconomic, then digital cash makes a lot of sense. This has yet to become especially evident. The growth has been limited by the fact that commission would need to be paid on every micro-transaction. Such usage-based charging has proved unpopular (in trials), especially when most users had the perception that existing methods tended to work very well. Consumers also hated to be reminded of the cost of every transaction. Pay-as-you-go systems – which are among the core micro-payment systems – have proved notoriously unpopular. Thus electronic commerce could flourish with credit cards and did not need these new payment methods.

Consumers still have evident concerns about the twin issues of privacy and security in the use of electronic cash for online purchasing. Traditional payment schemes allow them privacy and security, and consequently many remain to be convinced about the new forms of payment. Electronic cash needs to be user-led, and the hesitancy of consumers towards it reflects the concerns many have about electronic commerce in general. Business could clearly benefit from electronic money if it facilitated another method of receiving payment from consumers. For if it is to realize the benefits, the new forms of cash need to be easier to use than existing forms and must also provide an added value not available from the traditional payment formats. Thus to be successful new forms of cash have to reflect consumer concerns over areas such as fraud, security and cost. This could be achieved through software development. As electronic cash is essentially software, it could be programmed to do things that paper money could never do. For example, electronic money could be programmed so that it could only be used for special purposes.

In the development of these systems, governments have to ensure that:

- the financial stability of the system is secured;

- there is adequate legal protection for consumers;

- there is little interference in the ability of central banks to manage the monetary system;

- there is no hindering of the process of law enforcement;

- the system is both low-cost and low-risk.

With the development of electronic cash, there is sound reason to believe that a separation between state and economy could occur. It will become that much more difficult for the state to monitor and tax transactions. It also makes it that much more difficult to manage the currency. This is reinforced by the potential of the advent of electronic cash effectively to disintermediate banks.

It is evident that there is a mixed case for electronic cash. On the plus side, it is more convenient and flexible than traditional payment, it offers efficiencies for banks and it offers a potentially greater degree of privacy than credit card transactions. On the minus side, the development of electronic cash could undermine state control of the monetary system, money could be lost due to technical problems and electronic cash could foster a have and have-not society. There are also broader legal concerns based upon the extent to which the advent of electronic cash could aid money laundering and tax evasion, create a new market for counterfeiters and increase the potential damage that hackers could do on Internet accounts. In response to these accusations, the developers of electronic cash argue that the low cash value on smart cards means that they are unsuitable for money laundering and other illegal activities involving vast sums and that the state through wire-tapping technologies can easily monitor flows.

Many are putting their faith in smart cards as the driver of electronic cash. In their latest form, these cards could not only act as credit and debit cards but also act as a forum for electronic cash. These products, which could be inserted into mobile phones or televisions, are ideal drivers to stimulate the rise of electronic commerce payment systems, though the cost of this system – to both banks and retailers – is proving an evident deterrent. A New York-based US experiment proved a failure, as neither customers nor retailers found the cards especially valuable. The take-up of the smart card as a device to stimulate and aid the development of electronic commerce needs to be aided by the ability of manufacturers to increase the capabilities of the card, lower costs in the manufacturing process and enhance security. In the wide range of applications available on a smart card, the electronic purse is proving to be the 'killer application' that could drive these products into commercial reality. The electronic purse is based upon embedded cash, and can be reloaded at cash points, etc. This should see smart cards used for low-value transactions. However, as smart cards move to multi-functionality, so security moves further up the agenda.

International cryptology and security

Most states and enterprises involved in the development of the information economy recognize that the following basic principles of security need to be achieved by the system for it to mature commercially:

- *Accountability principle.* The responsibilities and accountability of owners, providers and users (and other parties) of information systems should be explicit.

- *Awareness principle.* All interested parties need to be aware of the existence and methods of security.

- *Ethics principle.* Security should be managed in a manner that does not infringe the rights of others.

- *Multi-disciplinary principle.* Practices need to take account of a spectrum of relevant concerns from administration through to education.

- *Proportionality principle.* The level of security should be proportionate to the sensitivity of information.

- *Integration principle.* Security mechanisms should be coherent across an organization.

- *Timeliness principle.* Actions upon security need to be swift to ensure breaches are curtailed.

- *Reassessment principle.* Security systems need to be reassessed periodically.

- *Democracy principle.* Any security system needs to be compatible with the broader democratic interests of society.

The principles are designed to promote cryptography, develop electronic commerce and boost user confidence as well as addressing the core concerns of data security and privacy protection. They need to ensure that free choice of security methods remains, that markets drive secure solutions, that technologies are standardized, that government regulation is applied in a consistent and coherent manner, and that liability over security breaches is established. These issues need to be secured through international agreement – failure to co-ordinate national security policies at the international level is likely to introduce more obstacles to the evolution of the information economy.

Establishing agreement between states on the use of security measures has led to serious reservations by some states, notably with regard to the use of cryptography. These concerns are driven by the aforementioned fear that national security may be undermined by more readily available cryptography technology. The result is that many of the leading industrial states (notably the US) choose to regulate closely both the import and export of encryption technology. International business is increasingly challenging such controls in the light of political changes, new and improving technology, and the need to facilitate global flows of information.

In the US, industry is proving capable in some areas of developing the necessary security measures (for example, the SET system) to promote enhanced security within electronic transactions. These, in conjunction with state-sponsored agreements under organizations such as the OECD, are leading the development of secure information systems. This is complemented by the increasing need to develop a common framework for digital signatures, ensuring that they provide users with all the necessary information. However, some of the solutions have been dogged by teething problems such as the length of time to make a secure transaction. This is derived from the sheer complexity of encryption required.

Effective data security has to start with the adoption of the right management practices at the corporate, organizational and governmental levels. These must start with a recognition of the danger in lack of security, which implies active engagement in employee and customer education, physical protection of assets, access limitations and the application of robust cryptographic techniques. This underscores the further point that ultimately security is up to the enterprise itself. It is needed not only to protect the information systems of enterprises but also to secure consumer confidence in their ability to purchase an enterprise's products through the electronic medium. Enterprises need to adopt a basic security policy as a starting-point for secure communications using Internet technology. Despite this, there is growing evidence suggesting that firms are still not following through this concern with increased expenditure upon building secure networks. The advent of electronic commerce has to change this, for no longer will the organization end at the enterprise's boundaries. This change places the emphasis upon the enterprise to create a framework of trust between itself and its partners in the changing value chain.

Security needs to rise up the international policy agenda given the growing evidence that Internet fraud is on the increase. Visa, the international payments card group, estimates that despite Internet trade making up only 1 per cent of total sales volume, it represents nearly half of all fraud and disputed transactions. Visa is recommending the swift introduction of the SET system as a necessity to ensure confidence in electronic commerce is not nipped in the bud by the uncertainty generated by these levels of fraud. This is clearly needed, with even the US government threatening legislation unless industries agree a common framework soon. There is a feeling that the transaction is often treated too informally with a corresponding lack of concern given to consumer interests. With the development of new products such as Microsoft's Passport (which effectively acts as an electronic wallet), the whole process of balancing security with the need to stimulate electronic commerce is reaching commercial maturity. This reflects the fact that in the information economy security is not only a legal right and necessity but also a marketable commodity in its own right.

Content control

As highlighted in the previous chapter, content in all its forms is the vital raw material of the information economy. The globalization of information flows, associated with the development of the information economy, implies that as national, regional and international markets start to integrate so the content delivered will increasingly start to circumvent the traditional controls placed upon it by state authorities. These concerns are ultimately derived from the following phenomena associated with the development of the information economy:

- the likely massive expansion of the television programming market with a resultant globalization of content provision;

- scarcity of capacity – this is less of an issue, and hundreds of channels are likely to be offered due to the deployment of digital and compression technologies;

- the emergence of new services and applications;

- the development of technology that does not acknowledge borders, such as digital satellite broadcasting;

- the globalization of media companies.

These themes stress how the emerging global information market is going to alter the type and form of content accessible to all users irrespective of their geographical location. The result has been increased concern by the state to regulate and control content delivered based upon the desire to: 1) sustain global cultural and linguistic diversity, and ensure that markets do not result in unfair competition between cultures with resulting harmonization with or domination by a single culture; and 2) control content that is considered either illegal or potentially harmful (for example, fraud and pornography).

Over the short to medium term, these concerns have expressed themselves about the growing emergence of the Internet and the content that is available over this medium. The emergence of new media poses new challenges to existing rules and regulations that have traditionally sought to control access to harmful and illegal content over broadcast and other media. Policy makers are seeking to ensure that such challenges are curtailed and their effects minimized.

Despite the general promotion of self-regulation, regulators are stressing to Internet service providers the need to control the content they deliver to users. Thus there are moves to:

- establish a code of conduct for ISPs;

- initiate hotlines for the public to complain about content;

- develop self-regulatory bodies to advise on breaches of codes of conduct.

This does not imply liability for the service provider unless it is the content provider itself or has failed to take action where a code has been breached. Consequently most states are establishing a light regulatory framework to support the process of self-regulation. These moves are supported by the use of the relevant technology (such as software filters), ratings systems and codes of conduct (which, despite being voluntary, are incorporated into the licence of the operator to ensure compliance).

Control of content is a careful balancing act between allowing markets in information services and applications to flourish and protecting the 'national' interest. In some cases, the desire for state restriction over content can easily be interpreted as a protectionist measure. This problem is not aided by social, economic and political systems within the global economy that are incredibly diverse and lead to differing definitions of what is and what is not desirable content. A notable issue is balancing the desire for free speech with the desire to sustain social order. Despite these concerns, most (if not all) states are involved in some form of content determination.

Issues of cultural diversity

Global information flows will provide the focus for cultures to interact with one another. The impact of such changes is a matter for debate. Some believe that the new technologies associated with the information economy will provide more opportunities for the expression of cultural and linguistic diversity. Others see the importing of other states' cultural products as a threat. The latter point results in many states seeking to control content to sustain national or regional cultures. To many the main threat comes from the delivery of much more US-based English-language content, which may emerge at the expense of locally determined production. Some states perceive this trend to be nothing short of 'cultural imperialism'. Indeed leading Francophones (such as the French and French Canadians) raised the spectre of quotas over the audio-visual sector to ensure that dominance by English-language-based content (which is sourced largely from the US) was resisted. They have subsequently backed away from the prospect of controls, having attained US reassurance about domination of cultural production. The leading industrialized states agreed a framework that allows states to possess sufficient flexibility to promote diversity of content. The issue of flexibility revolves around opening doors to other cultures while ensuring that local creators have access to both their own and global markets.

The constraints states have placed upon the media have often expressed themselves in restrictions upon the foreign ownership of newspapers, radio and TV broadcast channels. These measures are established in the belief that indigenous owners will be more sympathetic to the representation of national and regional cultures. Such restrictions are likely to come under pressure within emerging global information markets. Foreign ownership restrictions, given the increasingly global nature of investment, will be more difficult to justify.

In preserving cultural and linguistic diversity, states have backed away from explicitly protectionist measures. Despite this, the market-led development of the information economy implies that the content delivered will be exactly what users demand of it. Thus efforts to preserve linguistic and cultural diversity may be solely token measures if the content demanded reflects something other than indigenous culture. In this context, the issue of state funding for linguistic and cultural products emerges. This then raises issues of the extent to which the state should fund content and the extent to which it should penalize mass-market content providers to finance indigenous content.

Illegal and harmful content

The problems of content control have been further highlighted by the explosive growth of content deemed illegal or harmful by the authorities – a problem compounded by the ease with which this content can be distributed, copied or accessed through the Internet. There are especial concerns over information that contravenes the following:

- national security (for example, information on drugs or other illegal substances);

- protection of minors;

- protection of human dignity (for example, racist literature);

- economic security (prevention of fraud);

- information security;

- protection of privacy;

- protection of reputation;

- intellectual property rights protection.

It is necessary to differentiate between illegal and harmful content. These different categories pose different problems for regulators. With illegal content, regulation needs to focus on the source of the content. Harmful content regulation focuses upon measures aimed at raising user awareness and empowerment. Governments have traditionally attempted to regulate illegal and harmful content by broadcasting restrictions, whilst the individual consumption of 'offensive' material has been deemed a private right. This distinction is being challenged by digital means of production and distribution. Digital technology allows the targeted and closed delivery of content that can be defined neither as broadcasting nor as individual private consumption.

The desire to control illegal and harmful content requires a level of regulation that balances the need for control with the desire for broad access to the Internet. This has led to understandable concern from the information industry. IBM suggests that the control of the use of the Internet should be guided by the five core principles below:

1. Only material that is illegal within society should be deemed as illegal when offered over the Internet.

2. Content rules should be no stricter than those exerted for other forms of media.

3. International co-ordination is needed over the principles of what is considered illegal and harmful content.

4. Technology (such as software filters) is more likely to offer controlled content than any regulation based upon traditional forms of regulation in political spheres of influence.

5. Regulation can only be based upon an in-depth knowledge of the way the Internet works.

In practice, in the absence of an agreed international framework, governments are having to work with industry to define and classify content likely to offend or be harmful. There is little agreement between states on the method by which access to illegal and harmful content can be controlled. Broadly the options are:

■ a software system that allows users to identify content;

■ a user-led approach where individuals are able to define their own form of censoring devices or practices;

■ government definitions of what is suitable material.

Most regulatory authorities have taken an approach that centres upon industry and user self-regulation as the most desirable method for the control of harmful content. This is perhaps the only realistic solution given the global nature of information sources. To facilitate self-regulation, industry and users have combined to develop assorted methods of content control such as content rating systems, software filters and labelling of site contents.

Taxation issues in the information economy

The emergence of the information economy represents challenges for tax authorities through:

■ the lack of any readily identifiable location for a transaction – this makes it more difficult to determine where an activity takes place;

■ problems in identifying users (for example, it may be difficult to identify Web site ownership);

■ the increased complexity of jurisdiction – most tax authorities rely upon physical evidence of a transaction to determine which tax authority has jurisdiction over it, something which is often lacking in electronic commerce;

- the increased accessibility of tax havens – these will generally become more accessible to a broader range of taxpayers than would otherwise be the case;

- the elimination of the need for intermediating institutions to operate as taxing points where liabilities can be identified.

The Internet not only eliminates national borders but also offers new opportunities to exploit differences in tax rates and even avoid such commitments. Existing taxation strategies and measures are also going to be challenged on certain issues. The first is identifying the tax authority that should have the right to claim tax sourced from a network-enabled transaction and the resulting income stream. The second is determining how the income earned from electronic transactions is classified when products are delivered electronically. These transactions and whether they are classified as the sale of a good, licence of copyright or provision of a service will determine how and if they are taxed. The third is the extent to which ISPs should be made liable for tax collection. These challenges when combined with the process of globalization necessitate increased co-ordination between national tax authorities not only to remove regulatory uncertainty for legitimate business but also to ensure domestic revenue bases are not severely undermined. These legal concerns need to be balanced against a desire not to stymie the growth of electronic commerce.

In theory, online enterprises are subject to the same tax laws as other businesses, but the advent of the Internet has, as mentioned, complicated the task of application. This is especially true where products can be downloaded direct from the Internet, avoiding the traditional retailing forums where activities are easy to measure and tax. For example, a UK consumer buying a US enterprise's software through a shop clearly entails tax being paid in the former state. If the software is purchased over the Internet, US rates apply (US sales taxes tend to be lower), and this deprives the UK exchequer of revenues. If electronic commerce grows as expected, then such trends are likely to have a profound impact upon the sales tax revenue generated by states – in some states sales taxes represent up to 30 per cent of total revenue.

Policing products downloaded from the Internet is remarkably troublesome. For example, small companies cannot be expected to collect sales taxes from customers and then distribute them right across the globe – this is simply impractical. Similarly, if it is left to consumers it is hard to believe that all will be honest. Catching those who seek to avoid tax by downloading from the Internet is made more difficult by the fact that the marginal cost of downloading and providing an extra unit is next to nothing, making evidence based on comparing inputs with declared outputs difficult to verify. If the price of the intangible good is also close to zero, then there will evidently be little opportunity to tax the commodity in question. In addition, the Internet will reduce the role of intermediaries (such as banks) that report actions to the tax authorities. Tax authorities can compare interest income declared with that paid out by the bank. The problems are likely to be compounded by the more widespread use of electronic money, which will aid tax evasion through increasing the potential for anonymous transactions, as increasingly there will be no paper trail left for the tax inspector to pick up. This is coupled (as mentioned above) with easier access by more people to offshore tax havens. Furthermore, there is growing uncertainty as to how to deal with the taxation of services derived from the convergence of technologies and how the differing tax regimes of the respective sectors should be altered.

Resolving Internet taxation issues on an international level will be troublesome, partly due to the fact states differ markedly in terms of tax regimes and underlying philosophies. The US is concerned about over-taxing the new innovative services whereas the EU is concerned more about how revenue bases are undermined. Many EU states are also concerned that different taxation regimes could undermine competitiveness, as footloose enterprises and consumers register transactions in those states with lower tax rates. These concerns related to electronic commerce are greater in the EU where sales taxes have traditionally represented a greater proportion of overall tax revenues. The challenge for different states is further underlined by the idiosyncrasies of the different tax regimes. In the US, mail order sales are not exempt from tax in the place where the enterprise maintains a place of business. If they are made out of state, then an exemption applies. In the EU, electronic commerce raises the possibility of undermining the destination-based principle of value added tax (ie the tax is paid where the commodity is consumed). Removing such inconsist-encies is going to be important – lack of certainty over taxes will inevitably impede the spread of electronic commerce as well as leading to the establishment of Internet tax havens.

International actions in Internet taxation

Unsurprisingly since it is the major arena for electronic commerce, it is the US that has tended to lead actions on the taxation of the Internet. It believes that, where possible, existing tax laws should be applied to Internet transactions, that companies should be protected from being taxed in two jurisdictions for the same transaction and that new tariffs upon down-loadable goods and services should be resisted. The core agenda was shaped by the concern that being too heavy-handed in terms of tax could severely retard the spread of electronic commerce. The result was the Internet Tax Freedom Act, which blocks individual US states from imposing new taxes on Internet access and new types of electronic transactions – though the act does allow for US states to apply the same taxes to the same goods whether they are sold over the Internet or not. Thus states can continue to tax electronic transactions but only using existing methods. The act bans many new Internet taxes but would permit a few new ones, which, it is contended, would be uniform and simple. The ban on new Internet taxes is tabled to last until the formative years of the new millennium. Policy makers are seeking to use the moratorium to come to an agreement about how to tax the Internet. Initial evidence seems to suggest that there is a desire for Internet retailers to pay the same taxes as their physical equivalents though they are disputing how to do it (ie in a traditional manner via a simplifying of sales taxes or through developing relevant software). It is felt, however, that the cost of collecting local taxes may be prohibitive and limit the potential of electronic commerce.

These actions have been resisted by those states that want to overcome any shortfall in revenues derived from the expansion of electronic commerce. Already some US states are planning new taxes upon Internet access and electronic commerce. The problem for authorities is that, for goods bought over the Internet, the purchaser is responsible for the declaration to the tax body. Many are simply failing to do this with the result that many states are losing vast revenues due to the rules being almost impossible to enforce. The US government and some individual states are reticent about new taxes, believing that if sales taxes are levied upon the Internet, domestically produced goods and services will be less attractive to foreign customers. This is an advantage that these states currently have over EU states, where such purchases are subject to VAT. The logic is that if Internet purchases are offered as a tax-free environment more activity will take place over this medium, increasing company profits and therefore leading to increased revenue through corporate taxation. This is complicated by the fact that not all US states have corporate tax.

Consequently, the US is pushing for the Internet to be established as a duty-free zone where it is used to deliver, electronically, goods and services, with taxation dealt with by the conventional taxation systems. Broadly under the umbrella of the OECD, the major industrial states have agreed with this position. None of these states plans new taxes for the Internet, agreeing that existing tax structures should apply where possible. The US has been forthright in its opposition to the EU's discussion about the possible introduction of a 'bit tax' (see the box below). The US position of a totally VAT-free Net is resisted by many states that need the revenue from these taxes. The OECD stance reflects the perspective that ultimately electronic commerce is not very different from its conventional counterpart. The OECD states are keen to ensure the neutrality of the tax system, ensuring that no form of transaction medium is either implicitly or explicitly favoured. There is also a plan to establish rules within the context of the WTO to cover trade-related aspects of Internet commerce – though members have already agreed amongst themselves that no tariffs be imposed upon Internet transmissions.

The EU with its discussion of 'bit taxes' has shown that it is prepared to be more interventionist on the matter than the US. Clearly the EU cannot act unilaterally, for any decision to impose new taxes upon the Internet will simply drive electronic business out of the EU. Thus in some contexts, Europe finds its hands tied by the first-mover advances made by the US. The EU believes that electronic commerce transactions should be taxed as services and that, consequently, consumers should pay VAT upon them. This fails to address the core issue of how it would actually collect the revenue owed from such taxes. It also proposes tax-free breaks for the electronic purchase of European 'services' by non-EU individuals, though this still leaves the prospect of EU shoppers going online and purchasing from outside the European continent and thereby distorting the emerging market for online shopping.

Internet taxation: the issue of 'bit taxes'

A more direct solution to the problems of taxing electronic commerce is the introduction of a 'bit tax'. This amounts to little more than a direct tax upon electronic commerce falling upon the transmission of information. The tax would be in effect a turnover tax upon interactivity digital traffic levied upon each digital bit of information. That the digital traffic is interactive is important, for this makes the transaction valuable. This solution was mooted by the EU's High Level group on the information society as a solution to developing a fairer distribution of the benefits of electronic commerce. The concern is that the new wealth generated by the new economy through tax avoidance would fail to permeate all levels of the socio-economic spectrum. The arguments surrounding the feasibility of such a tax are reflected in Table 5.1. It has been suggested that the tax would be levied at approximately 0.000001 cent per bit and be collected by telecommunications companies, and satellite and cable networks, and then passed on to the respective treasury authorities.

There is perhaps an intuitive logic in the 'bit tax' as the economy shifts from tangibles to intangibles. However, industry also puts a compelling case against it, arguing that the embryonic information economy needs space and light regulatory control to reach maturity. This can be countered by the argument that the application of a petrol tax did little to slow down the growth of the automotive industry. The European Commission, which raised the discussion of the 'bit tax', rejected it as inappropriate since VAT already applied to these transactions and it feared any new direct tax

Table 5.1 *The pros and cons of a 'bit tax'*

Advantages	Disadvantages
Adjusts the tax base to reflect new forms of wealth creation.	The tax is not related to the value of the good.
Replaces lost revenues from new forms of commercial transactions.	Could be viewed as a tax on the freedom of speech.
Tax on information is not new: people already pay tax on telecommunications.	Discourages use of the Internet. Difficult to implement.
Could reduce congestion on the Internet.	If not implemented on a world-wide basis, it could distort international competitiveness.
Could promote more efficient use of information.	
Does not contravene privacy concerns.	

would trigger double taxation. It was also felt that a 'bit tax' would not really solve the tax problems of electronic commerce and would only further hinder the development of the Internet in the EU – an area where it already lags behind the US. Many feel that it is too premature to conclude that existing taxes are unable to deal with the new forms of transaction and that the problem lies in technology and not in implementing new taxes.

Despite such disputes, potential solutions to the challenges of Internet taxation are emerging. Germany, for example, is promoting the use of embedded software within products as a means of tracking sales over the Internet. This could ensure taxes are automatically withheld and transferred to the state where the purchase was made. However, this does raise privacy issues and is unlikely to be well received by software developers. Another method is for international parcel delivery companies to add VAT for all products ordered online, but as these make up only a small percentage of electronic commerce transactions other methods will clearly be needed. Other potential solutions advocated include the use of ISPs as tax intermediaries, as they can monitor all transactions their customers make (something to which they are opposed), or the use of financial institutions (which would tax according to the amount of electronic transactions their clients perform). Inevitably as tax bases are eroded so policy makers will need to seek solutions. If the problem is technological then there need to be incentives offered by IT enterprises to develop the necessary software. Other solutions are possible but the problem at the moment is that the issue of online tax avoidance is still small when compared to other forms of tax evasion. One feels that only when electronic commerce takes off will tax authorities be sufficiently motivated to put into place the necessary solutions. At the moment many of the problems exist only in theory. Indeed initial evidence from Ernst and Young (www.ey.com) seems to suggest that, over the short term, the tax issue is not a great one, as there is little evidence to suggest electronic commerce is having any great effect upon tax revenues with less than 0.1 per cent being lost in this manner. Only when this changes will concrete efforts to solve the problem ever really be made. Under the umbrella of the OECD, the leading industrialized states have agreed to find co-operative solutions to the problem. To this end, agreement stresses neutrality and the need to avoid double taxation. This effectively rules out the development of a bit tax, and states have agreed that taxes should be levied on place of consumption. How the place of consumption is defined is still legally uncertain.

Conclusion

This chapter has sought to outline the major regulatory and legal challenges posed by the development of the information economy. It is clear that in a process that is largely commercially driven, the government will play a passive role with any activism being limited to the initial stages of the evolution of the information economy. Government does have an important role to perform in establishing the necessary and complementary legal environment to address the needs of both users and producers within the information economy. In many instances, the state may decide that pushing industry towards self-regulation (for example, in the case of security or privacy) is sufficient to secure the needed safeguards. In other areas, more direct regulation is needed (such as in IPR or in securing competition). Whatever form of action is taken and no matter who implements it, it is clear that these issues need to be addressed if the information economy as a commercial phenomenon is to be realized.

6 The information economy – a concluding perspective

Throughout the preceding chapters, it has been argued that the evolution of the information economy is going to have a profound impact upon the performance of business. This impact is evident on both the demand and supply sides of the emerging information market. It has also been argued that the development of the information economy is likely to streamline and transform business processes through the application of ICTs to support activities such as teleworking and electronic commerce. It is at this point that I wish to draw together the issues raised within the previous chapters to offer a concluding perspective on the themes addressed within the text. This perspective seeks to stress how each of the themes addressed within the text is key to understanding the development of the information economy.

The competitive challenge of the information economy

Throughout the text it has been stressed that the adoption of ICTs and the evolution of the information economy is driving the changing competitive environment of business. The interlinked processes of technological change and globalization are key drivers behind the pressures upon business to adopt new technologies and change processes to reflect these changes. The shift to the information economy also alters the competitive paradigm of the economy as information and knowledge assets become increasingly central to an enterprise's commercial success. The importance of these assets is underlined by the fact that in the information economy speed to the market and flexibility are proving key to competitive success. These, in turn, will depend upon the interface between information or knowledge and human resources. This interface is essentially twofold depending as it does upon the quality of knowledge or information embedded within the work-force and the ability of the labour force to utilize the information or knowledge resources to enhance the enterprise's competitive positioning.

Importantly, if ICTs are to work to competitive advantage then their application has to be about more than simply inducing increased operational efficiency within the business. If it wants to be successful, the business needs to recognize the following:

- The emergence of information as a salient resource changes both products generated by, and processes within, the enterprise.

- The utilization of information has to be based upon the cross-sharing of information resources between the different functions of the enterprise to ensure it works to the benefit of the entire business.

- Outsourcing is a credible alternative for a number of functions where the organization does not possess the necessary in-house expertise to maximize the value from a particular information capability.

- The right infrastructure has to be in place to support the efficient and effective use of knowledge and information as core enterprise resources.

The Internet as the leading technology of the evolving information economy has the potential to change all aspects of the commercial environment. What is more, it is ushering in such changes at a pace that is proving more rapid than previous logistical revolutions such as electricity or the car. Despite the evident potential, we are still in a commercial environment where the majority of economic agents (especially consumers and small business) are not connected to the Internet or at the very least are not using it for substantial economic activity. This situation could clearly lead to a vicious cycle of immaturity within the information market leading to a situation where many of the benefits of the information economy go unrealized. It is for this (and other reasons) that governments are active in the initial stages of the development of the information economy (see below).

Despite general lack of maturity, the development of the Internet is already having a tangible impact upon business (especially large businesses) in terms of increasing the flow of information coming into the enterprise from both suppliers and customers. Consequently, enterprises are using Internet technologies to develop closer and direct links to both their customers and suppliers. Such developments deliver advantages to the enterprise in a number of areas such as lower costs of production and the generation of a greater degree of consumer loyalty. Many enterprises are in the process of adapting business models to realize the competitive advantage from these developments. This acceptance of the need to change the business is key to the development and commercial maturity of the information economy. This will be compounded by so-called 'network effects', which basically means that the more businesses engage in electronic business the more it encourages others to do likewise. The advent of electronic commerce and the increased salience of information as a commercial tool are fundamentally altering the value chain. This is not merely in terms of the demand and supply chains noted above but also in terms of the creation of a virtual value chain. This highlights how the utilization of information at each stage of the value chain can provide added competitive advantage to enterprises.

The expansion of electronic commerce

As has been consistently highlighted, electronic commerce is seen as the key driver behind the development of the information economy with the vast majority of its growth generated through business-to-business as opposed to business-to-consumer transactions. The potential of electronic commerce has been spotted by many and is one of the key factors behind the so-called 'Internet bubble' currently being exhibited within global stock markets. Despite this, over the short term, electronic commerce (that is, sales generated either directly or indirectly through online communications) is more likely to be seen as a complement rather than a rival to the more traditional forms of commercial activity.

Despite this current lack of maturity, many enterprises are developing electronic commerce strategies, as indicated in the growing importance of ICTs within corporate strategy. This very much reflects the aforementioned point regarding the increased salience of information and knowledge as commercial resources. Evidently electronic commerce will become more of a commercial issue as the virtual value chain becomes more evident and as enterprises start to realize how it can alter both their product offerings and their business processes. This is already evident in sectors as diverse as banking and travel. The development of an electronic commerce strategy is increasingly driven by competitive necessity. Either an enterprise acts quickly or it risks losing competitive positioning.

Accompanying the emergence of electronic commerce has been the development of new business models to reflect the commercial challenges posed by the development of the information economy. Currently, few of these business models are commercially viable. Over the short term, dedicated online businesses are likely to remain rare. Those dedicated online businesses that do exist and are successful seem to have achieved commercial success through a careful targeting of their customers (notably those that are cash-rich, time-poor and/or well educated). Others have achieved a modicum of success through exploiting the key characteristics of the Internet, allowing thinly spread demand to be aggregated. This latter point has been particularly salient in facilitating the success of business models such as electronic auctions. The businesses most likely to be successful (at least in the formative stages of electronic commerce) are the infomediaries – effectively online middlemen – that allow online markets to function. They enable users to make sense of something that, in many cases, can appear chaotic, are difficult to dislodge and improve the efficiency and effectiveness of existing operators.

Ultimately the maturity of electronic commerce depends upon its take-up by large business. This should enable the information market to achieve the desired degree of commercial maturity. This is likely to happen when the large businesses spread their use of electronic commerce throughout their supply chains, notably to include SMEs. This has been typified by the shift of both Ford and General Motors to utilizing the Internet for the purposes of procurement. Ford has an extended supply chain worth over $300 billion with over 30,000 separate suppliers. This evidently has the potential to stimulate a great deal of electronic commerce. Indeed such developments highlight the coming of age for electronic commerce and will effectively create electronic business ecosystems that will change the form and manner of business. Dedicated online business may be novel but the big change will come when the high-street enterprises (such as Wal-Mart) with strong brands and a high degree of consumer loyalty develop online strategies *en masse*. Coupled with falling call charges, this should facilitate electronic commerce within lower income groups.

Overall, if electronic commerce is to aid an enterprise's competitive advantage then the system has to support complex series of inter-relationships for both business-to-business and business-to-consumer activities. In addition, the system has to support EDI and ERP (enterprise resource planning), and achieve the desired degree of supply chain integration. Such expectations underline why so many managers are as yet uncertain as to the exact impact or potential of electronic commerce upon their current business model.

The key role of the information industry

The development of an information industry is based around the convergence of the previously separate telecommunications, IT and content sectors. This convergence is driven both by technology and markets, and has its most visible expression in the development of the Internet. The state of the information industry is key to understanding how enterprises are able to gain and sustain competitive advantage from the development of the information economy. The information industry is the supply side of the information economy, and its ability to respond effectively and efficiently to the demands of users is central to enabling enterprises to realize competitive advantage from its development.

Central to the evolving information industry's ability to meet these needs is how enterprises respond to the challenges of the emerging integrated value chain within the sector. This trend is leading enterprises to alter radically their perspective upon what their role will be in the information economy. The challenge to telecommunication operators is especially noticeable as the core source of value shifts from their key asset of the network to content delivered. Right across the industry a process of consolidation is under way (both within and across sectors) as enterprises seek to offer integrated services on a global level. Already many large players (such as Microsoft and AT&T) are altering product portfolios – via both alliances and acquisitions – to meet this challenge head on. Enterprises are looking at their place within the integrating value chain and assessing how services and product offerings must change if they are to succeed in the emerging integrated environment. This trend has had its most visible expression in the high-profile merger between Time Warner (a leading content producer and broadcaster) and America On-line (the leading Internet service provider).

The full implications of this process of convergence have yet to be fully worked out. How the industry will eventually restructure and where enterprises will finally position themselves in a converged environment are yet to be fully understood. It is evident that, as the process matures, so enterprise strategy will adjust to ensure enterprises offer the necessary service coverage to secure their competitive position. The lessons of businesses such as IBM is that enterprises need a constant reappraisal of their service offerings if they are not to lose out to smaller, nimbler rivals that are more adept at utilizing the latest technological advances. Over the short term, the major challenge facing enterprises is responding to the development of the Internet and its impact upon both current and future product offerings.

Towards the necessary policy solutions

The development of the information economy – notably in terms of the evolution of electronic commerce – requires a number of policy and regulatory actions. Both sides of the emerging information market need certain legal and regulatory rights and guarantees to be in place if the information economy is to mature. Failure to secure these rights will evidently lead to a situation where users are reluctant to engage in electronic transactions for fear that they may become subject to fraud or another unethical activity that contravenes their preferences. Overall policy and regulatory activity needs to:

- establish the trust of users and consumers;
- establish the ground rules for competition in the digital market-place;
- enhance the supporting information infrastructure for electronic commerce;
- maximize the benefits from the information economy.

On the demand side of the information economy, information users need to be certain of security and privacy over online transactions, and that access to such advanced services and applications is both cheap and standardized. On the supply side, there need to be guarantees related to the necessity to sustain competition and secure IPR, and to the ability to generate the necessary standards for the technology so as to support the proper commercial evolution of the information economy.

Many of these issues are made especially salient by the fact that the information is transnational in nature and therefore needs global solutions. In many cases, global agreement upon these topics has proved elusive, a feature that will evidently impede the development of the information economy as a global phenomenon. Despite a recognition by all states that there needs to be global agreement on these issues, there has been at best only intermittent progress in this area. The rules to develop the information economy are developing in an inconsistent manner with states differing on the means of control and the pace at which they need to be implemented. In some cases failure is due to patchy implementation (as in the case of telecommunications and IPR) and in others to disputes upon the very nature of control required (as in the case of privacy and security).

The differences between states over the form and type of regulation, and the general absence of a globally agreed framework to manage the emergence of the information economy are compounded by further problems related to legal jurisdiction in an era where business is borderless but the law is not. Given the nature of the information economy (ie transnational and technologically fluid), there is the evident potential for growing conflict between differing legal regimes in deciding exactly whose rules will apply to which electronic transactions. This is an issue that is especially important in areas such as contract and consumer protection law, and has an evident ability to limit the growth of electronic commerce.

At the time of writing, the regulatory framework to secure the development of the information economy is uncertain. Reconciling the different approaches of the core players is proving difficult. Policy evidently needs to harmonize the different regulatory traditions of the key players in the evolution of the information economy. In this scenario, business needs to take a proactive approach either to convince policy makers that it can (where possible) credibly regulate the system for itself or to sustain pressure upon the relevant bodies to secure coherent and consistent policies between states. Consistency is evidently key; without it the information economy will fail to mature and deliver the benefits expected of it.

Conclusion

Whether the information economy will be revolutionary in the true sense of the word is as yet uncertain. It may just turn out to be more complementary to existing systems than currently envisaged. However, the Internet goes more to the core of business process and transformation than other comparable technologies such as the telephone. Whilst the source of competitive advantage is changing – with information becoming a key resource and electronic commerce a key facilitator – there are still a number of unknowable issues. Such unknowable factors seem to revolve around how the development of the information economy will affect how economic actors work with one another. This is especially critical when the development of technologies allows businesses to collaborate more completely than they ever did before. How far this collaboration will reach outside firms – to suppliers, rivals and customers – is uncertain. The development of the information economy is as much about strategy as it is about technology. It is important to stress that the information economy will only come of age when the main actors within the established environment start to turn to electronic business. These enterprises and their customers will define the information economy and exactly how profound its impact will be.

Glossary

application   Technology that has a specific usage (such as the growing use of ICT within healthcare).

Asymmetrical Digital Subscriber Line   A compression technology that allows broadband services to be offered on traditional narrowband (mainly copper) infrastructure.

Asynchronous Transfer Mode   A set of internationally agreed standards that define a new method for sending large quantities of data, voice and video simultaneously over the network.

bricks and mortar   A term used to describe the traditional physical format of retailing.

clicks and mortar   A term given to denote the emerging retail model that stresses both online and traditional retailing formats.

Electronic Data Interchange   Computer-to-computer communication involving the interchange of data between trading partners – it is seen very much as the precursor of business-to-business electronic commerce.

interactivity   The capability of the user and information system to inter-work so as to select and transform information to meet specific needs.

MP3   A computer file that enables the downloading of music from the Internet.

multimedia   Communications services that combine the use of different media (such as video-on-demand).

operating system The software that enables specific applications to be run upon the necessary hardware.

platform independence The offering of content independently of a specific form of medium (for example, music can be offered on the Internet, CDs, etc).

public switched telecommunications network The traditional analogue communications network.

services Uses of a technology with generic appeal across an array of user groups.

Synchronous Digital Hierarchy A set of standards defining rates and formats for optical networks.

World Wide Web A networked system for organizing information upon the Internet, using hypertext links.

References

Analysys (1998) Adapting the EU telecoms regulatory framework to the developing multimedia market, www.analysys.com/products/internet/ecreport

Andersen Consulting (1998) *eEurope 98/99*, London

Berryman, K *et al* (1998) Electronic commerce: three emerging strategies, *The McKinsey Quarterly*, (1), pp 152–59

Boch, M, Pigneur, Y and Segev, A (1996) On the road to electronic commerce, www.nyu.edu/~bloch/docs/

BT (1998) *World Communication Report 1998*, London

Chappell, C and Feindt, S (1999) *Analysis of E-Commerce Practice in SMEs*, KITE Project, Brussels, January

Chattell, A (1998) *Creating Value in the Digital Era*, Macmillan, London

Department of Trade and Industry (UK) (1999) Measuring the information economy: an international comparison, Spectrum analysis – research undertaken for the DTI, www.isi.gov.uk

Earl, M (1999) *FT Information Management Review* (1)

Economist (1997) A survey of electronic commerce, 14 September

Economist (1999a) Advertising that clicks, 9 October

Economist (1999b) The net imperative: a survey of business and the Internet, 26 June

Eurescom (1995) Shaping the information society, Working paper, January

European Commission (1997) The future of content, Info 2000 online

European Commission (1999) Proceedings of the EU workshop upon the industrial aspects of electronic commerce, Brussels, 8 April

Financial Times (1998) Review of the telecommunications industry, 10 June

Financial Times (1999a) *Guide to Digital Business*, Supplement, Autumn

Financial Times (1999b) Telecommunications: a survey, 18 March

Financial Times (1999c) Review of information technology, 2 June

Financial Times (1999d) Review of information technology, 7 April

Financial Times (1999e) New organisational forms, *Mastering Information Management*, Supplement, (5), 1 March

Harrington, L and Reed, G (1996) Electronic commerce (finally) comes of age, *The McKinsey Quarterly*, (2), pp 68–77

Information Strategy (1998) The global Internet 100: a survey, November

ITU (1997) The regulatory impact of telecommunications convergence, *Regulatory Colloquia*, (6), Berne

Kittinger, W and Hackbarth, G (1999) Electronic commerce, *Financial Times*, Information Management Supplement (7), pp 13–14

KPMG (1998a) Managing transformation in the new economy, http://www.kpmg.ca

KPMG (1998b) *Knowledge Management: Research report 1998*, London

Mansell, R and Steinmueller, E (1996) Security in electronic networks, FAIR working paper (7)

Merrill Lynch (1999) e-Commerce: virtually here, Working paper, Global Securities Research and Economic Working Group, www.ml.com

Negroponte, N (1995) *Being Digital*, Hodder & Stoughton, London

OECD (1995) *The Changing Role of Telecommunications in the Economy*, Paris

OECD (1998a) *Industrial Performance and Competitiveness in an Era of Globalisation and Technological Change*, DSTI/IND(97)23/Final

OECD (1998b) *The Economic and Social Impact of Electronic Commerce*, October, DSTI/ICCP(98)15/REV, Paris

OECD (1998c) *Electronic Commerce: Process and Consumer Issues for Three Products: Books, Compact Discs and Software*, DSTI/ICCP/IE(98)4/Final, Paris

Paranov, S and Yakovleva, T (1998) *Internet Based Economy of the 21st Century*, Working paper, Institute of Economics and Industrial Engineering, Russian Academy of Sciences, Moscow

Phillips, R (1994) The management information value chain, *Perspectives*, Spring

PhoCusWright (1999) *eMarketer*, 22 June, www.emarketer.com

Porter, M (1985) *Competitive Advantage*, The Free Press, New York

Porter, M and Millar, V (1985) How information gives you competitive advantage, *Harvard Business Review*, **65**, pp 149–60

PriceWaterhouseCoopers (1999) Electronic business outlook, www.pwcglobal.com

Samuelson, R (1998) The five business models of e-commerce, eVine online, 23 December, www.searchz.com/articles/1223983.shtml

Shelly Taylor Associates (1999) Report, 3 August, www.emarkteer.com

Sheth, J and Wallace, W (1994) Convergence: driving the information industry, *Transformation* magazine

Tapscott, D (1995) *The Digital Economy*, McGraw-Hill, New York

Timmins, P (1998) Business models for electronic commerce, *Electronic Markets*, **8** (2), pp 3–8

US Department of Commerce (1997) *Framework for Digital Global Electronic Commerce*, Washington, DC

US Department of Commerce (1999) *The Emerging Digital Economy II*, Washington, DC

Further reading and information

Aguirre, P (1999) The success of emerging telecom carriers, *Telecommunications* magazine online, January

Attan, M (1998) Fixed-mobile convergence: fusion or confusion, *Telecommunications* magazine online, March

Berendt, A (1998) The meaning of convergence, *Telecommunications* magazine online, June

Brynjolfsson, E and Hitt, L (1998) *Information Technology and Organisational Design*, Working paper, Massachusetts Institute of Technology

Bytheway, A (1995) *Electronic Markets: A framework for the analysis of trade and its potential for development*, Conference paper, MCB University Press

Cairncross, F (1998) *The Death of Distance*, Orion, London

Caruso, D (1999) A new model for the Internet, *New York Times* online, www.nytimes.com, 19 July

Cawkell, AE, ed (1987) *Evolution of an Information Society*, Aslib, London

Cortese, A (1997) A way out of the web, *Business Week* online resources, 24 February

Coyle, D (1997) *The Weightless World*, Capstone, London

Demetriou, S (1999) Creating a foreign policy, *Telecommunications* magazine online, January

Dordick, HS and Wang, G (1993) *The Information Society: A Retrospective View*, Sage, London

Dowling, H, Lechner, C and Thielmann, B (1998) Convergence – innovation and change of market structures between television and on-line services, *Electronic Markets On-line*, **8** (4), pp 31–35

Economist (1996) The hitchhiker's guide to cybernomics: survey of the world economy, 28 September

Economist (1997) The disappearing taxpayer, 31 May

Economist (1999) The new economy, 24 July

Economist (1999) The real Internet revolution, 21 August

Ernst, H and Jaeger, C, ed (1989) *Information Society and Spatial Structure*, Belhaven, Aldershot

European Telecommunications Standards Institute (1995) *European Information Infrastructure*, Report of sixth strategic review committee

Evans, P and Wurster, T (1997) Strategy and the new economics of information, *Harvard Business Review*, September–October, pp 71–82

Financial Times (1991) World telecommunications, 7 October

Financial Times (1992) International telecommunications: a survey, 10 October

Financial Times (1993) Information and communications technology: a survey, 10 March

Financial Times (1993) International telecommunications: a survey, 18 October

Financial Times (1994) Information and communications technology: a survey, 16 March

Financial Times (1994) International telecommunications: a survey, 17 October

Financial Times (1995) International telecommunications: a survey, 3 October

Financial Times (1996) International telecommunications: a survey, 19 September

Financial Times (1996) Review of information technology, 6 November

Financial Times (1996) Review of information technology, 4 December

Financial Times (1997) Review of information technology, 8 January

Financial Times (1997) Review of the telecommunications industry, 17 March

Financial Times (1997) Review of the telecommunications industry, 4 June

Financial Times (1997) Review of information technology, 7 October

Financial Times (1997) Review of the telecommunications industry, 5 November

Financial Times (1997) Review of the telecommunications industry, 19 November

Financial Times (1998) Review of information technology, 3 June

Financial Times (1998) Review of the telecommunications industry, 2 September

Financial Times (1998) Telecommunications: a survey, Sections I and II, 18 November

Financial Times (1999) Review of information technology, 13 January

Financial Times (1999) Improving company performance, *Mastering Information Management*, Supplement, (1), 1 February

Financial Times (1999) Competing with knowledge, *Mastering Information Management*, Supplement, (2), 8 February

Financial Times (1999) Managing IT in the business, *Mastering Information Management*, Supplement, (3), 15 February

Financial Times (1999) The smarter supply chain, *Mastering Information Management*, Supplement, (4), 22 February

Financial Times (1999) Knowledge management, *Mastering Knowledge Management*, (6), 8 March

Financial Times (1999) Electronic commerce, *Mastering Information Management*, Supplement, (9), 15 March

Financial Times (1999) Strategic use of IT, *Mastering Information Management*, Supplement, (9), 29 March

Financial Times (1999) Knowledge management: a survey, 28 April

Girishanker, S (1998) Virtual markets create new roles for distributors, *Internet Week*, Electronic commerce supplement, 6 April

Hale, R and Whitlam, P (1997) *Towards a Virtual Organisation*, McGraw-Hill, London

Hawkins, R, Mansell, R and Steinmueller, E (1998) Towards digital intermediation in the European information society, Electronic working paper, (25), Science Policy Research Unit

Henry, B and Rosen, D (1998) Formulating the new business model, *Telecommunications* magazine online, January

Hepworth, M and Ryan, J (1997) *Small Firms in Europe's Developing Information Society*, Report for European Commission, April, Brussels

IBM (1997) Living in the information society, Discussion paper series online, www.IBM.com

Information Market Observatory (1995) *The Role of the Content Sector in the Emerging Information Society*, Working paper 95/5, Luxembourg

Janowiak, R, Sheth, J and Saghafi, M (1997) Communications in the next millennium, *Telecommunications* magazine online, March

Jarillo, JC (1993) *Strategic Networks: Creating the borderless organisation*, Butterworth-Heinemann, Oxford

Kemerer, CF, ed (1997) *Information Technology and Industrial Competitiveness*, Kluwer, Dordrecht

Lakelin, P (1998) IP telephony: opportunity or threat, *Telecommunications* magazine online, November

Lesley, E, Hof, R and Elstrom, P (1997) Is digital convergence for real?, *Business Week On-line*, 23 June

Long, T (1999) Telecom enterprises forge links to broaden services, *Techweb On-line*, 10 May

Maamria, K (1997) The challenge of Internet telephony, *Telecommunications* magazine online, March

Martin, W (1995) *The Global Information Society*, Aslib/Gower, Aldershot

Masud, S (1998) Telecom merger mania, *Telecommunications* magazine online, October

May, M (1998) In short supply, *Information Strategy*, 3 (9), p 44

McClure, C (1998) *Taxation of Electronic Commerce*, Stanford University

Mole, C (1999) Winning in a converging world, PriceWaterhouseCoopers online resources, www.pwcglobal.com

Moules, J (1998) Small is profitable, *Information Strategy*, September, **3** (7), p 48

Noam, E (1995) Towards the third revolution of television, Paper presented at symposium on productive regulation in the TV market, 1 December, Gutersloh, Germany

OECD (1995) *Workshops on the Economics of the Information Society No 1*, June, OECD/GD(95)116, Toronto

OECD (1996) *Workshops on the Economics of the Information Society No 4*, June, OECD/GAD(96)158, Helsinki, Finland

OECD (1996) *Workshop on the Economics of the Information Society No 5*, October, OECD/GAD(97)42, Seoul, Korea

OECD (1996) *Content as a New Growth Industry*, Working Party on the Information Economy, DSTI/ICCP/IE(96)6/Final

OECD (1997) *Electronic Commerce: The Challenges for Tax Authorities and Tax Payers*, Turku

OECD (1997) *Measuring Electronic Commerce*, OECD/GP(97)185, Paris

OECD (1998) *A Borderless World: Realising the Potential of Global Electronic Commerce*, October, SG/EC(98)11/REV2

OECD (1998) *Cross-Ownership and Convergence: Policy Issues*, Working Party on Telecommunications and Information Services Policies, DSTI/ICCP/TISP(98)3/Final

OECD (1998) *Implementing the OECD Privacy Guidelines in the Electronic Environment: Focus on the Internet*, DSTI/ICCP/REG(96)6

Ovenden, F (1999) Taming the Internet, *Telecommunications* magazine online, January

Pearce, F (1997) The convergence of broadcasting and telecommunications services, *Telecommunications* magazine online, June

Porter, M (1990) *The Competitive Advantage of Nations*, Macmillan, New York

Robson, W (1997) *Strategic Management and Information Systems*, Financial Times/Pitman Publishing, London

Sahlin, JP (1999) *Outsourcing Electronic Commerce*, Usi Business Case White Paper

Shapiro, C and Varian, H (1998) *Information Rules: A strategic guide to the network economy*, Harvard Business School Press, Boston

Sheth, J (1999) Convergence: during the information industry revolution, *Transformation* magazine online

Soete, L and Kamp, K (1998) Fiscal issues in the growth of electronic commerce, FAIR working paper (33)

Soete, L and Ter Weel (1998) Globalisation, taxation and the Internet, MERIT working paper, Maastricht University, Netherlands

Swindells, C and Henderson, K (1998) Legal regulation of electronic commerce, *The Journal of Law, Information and Technology*, **3**

Thrasher, BH and McNamara, R (1996) How merger mania has re-defined the communications landscape, *Telecommunications* magazine online, October

US Department of Treasury (1996) *Selected Tax Policy Implications of Global Electronic Commerce*, Washington, DC

Webster, F (1995) *Theories of the Information Society*, Routledge, London

Wigand, R and Benjamen, R (1994) Electronic commerce: effects on electronic markets, *JCMC*, **1** (3), www.ascusc.org/jcmc/vol1/

Young, L (1998) Following the market lead, *Telecommunications* magazine online, January

Zabarsky, M (1997) Computer telephony: calling the future of communications, *Boston Business Journal*, 27 October

Web resources

The list is by no means exhaustive but is indicative of the Web resources used during the writing of this book and is a useful starting-point for others undertaking research in this domain.

http://www.ac.com – Andersen Consulting: an excellent selection of research material on electronic business.

http://www.activemedia.com – Activemedia is a leading online strategy consultant.

http://www.allec.com – An excellent resource for up-to-date electronic commerce news.

http://www.analysys.co.uk/vlib – A library of resources upon this topic; the logical starting-point for anyone wishing to undertake research upon this topic.

http://www.brint.com – An excellent selection covering the interface between technology and business.

http://www.bsa.com – The Business Software Alliance home page.

http://china.si.umich.edu.edu/telecom/telecom-info.html – A site linking a long list of Web resources on the information economy.

http://www.commercenet.com – An excellent resource for electronic business information.

http://www.dataquest.com – The home site of a leading research and consultancy business specializing in information economy work.

http://www.ey.com – Ernst and Young's site has a good array of electronic commerce research.

http://www.emarketer.com – A useful research resource relating to latest developments in electronic commerce.

http://www.forrester.com – Forrester Research is a leading consultancy house specializing in cutting-edge research dedicated to tracking the development of the information economy.

http://www.ft.com – The *Financial Times* has good up-to-date coverage of all the issues covered within this text.

http://www.ispo.cec.be – The European Commission's core resource upon the development of the information economy; especially good on policy issues.

http://www.internetindicators.com – A first-rate resource for statistics on the development of the information economy.

http://www.nua.ie – A site containing a vast array of studies and statistics relating to the growth of the information economy.

http://www.oecd.org – The Organization for Economic Co-operation and Development is especially good on addressing the policy issues related to the development of the information economy.

http://www.regulate.org – An excellent resource that brings together the various regulatory programmes linked to the development of the information economy.

http://www.totaltele.com – Offers good reviews of developments in the communications sector.

http://www.wilsonweb.com – An excellent selection of resources covering electronic commerce, especially its interface with marketing.

Index